WORCESTERSHIRE
THROUGH TIME

Jacqueline Cameron

AMBERLEY PUBLISHING

Dedicated to my sister Gill, who celebrates her seventieth birthday in October this year

First published 2013

Amberley Publishing
The Hill, Stroud, Gloucestershire, GL5 4EP
www.amberley-books.com

ISBN 978 1 4456 0997 3

British Library Cataloguing in Publication Data.
A catalogue record for this book is available from the British Library.

Typesetting by Amberley Publishing.
Printed in Great Britain.

Appointed GPSR EU Representative: Easy Access System Europe Oü, 16879218
Address: Mustamäe tee 50, 10621, Tallinn, Estonia
Contact Details: gpsr.requests@easproject.com, +358 40 500 3575

Introduction

The beauty of living in central England is its close proximity to some of the most picturesque shires in the country. One such shire is Worcestershire, a favourite haunt for Sunday school outings; as a young girl growing up in the Midlands, I went on many such trips to enjoy the freedom of the Malvern Hills and to visit Worcester Cathedral in all its glory.

Dominating the city of Worcester, the cathedral was founded by St Oswald in 983 as a Saxon monastery and stands on high ground on the eastern bank of the River Severn. Worcester Cathedral is the burial place of King John, who died in 1216. In the eighteenth century, the tomb was opened and the King's remains were found wrapped in an embroidered robe and a monk's cowl. Above his tomb, in the choir, is the oldest royal effigy in England, made of Purbeck marble. Every three years, Worcester Cathedral is also the setting for Europe's oldest music festival, the Three Choirs Festival. This accolade has been shared with Gloucester and Hereford since 1719.

In 1751, a group of local businessmen led by Dr John Wall established the first Worcester Porcelain manufactory. They were to produce Chinese blue-printed and richly ornamented ware. In 1825, two local men, John Wheeley Lea and William Henry Perrins, created the famous Worcestershire Sauce; they began bottling their celebrated sauce just five years later in Broad Street.

Berrow's Worcester Journal, founded in 1690, claims to be the world's oldest surviving newspaper. The city is also home to one of the oldest racecourses in the country, and in the summer months county cricket is played across the river from the cathedral. In 1670, the River Severn broke its banks and the subsequent flood was the worst ever seen in Worcester. Despite frequent flooding, nothing has come close to the flood of 1670; the nearest contender took place in July 2007, when the river flooded in torrential rains.

Worcestershire is the home of Sir Edward Elgar, who was born at the Firs in Upper Broadheath in 1857 and attended school in Worcester. I remember coming home from school to find my mother sitting in the house next door watching Queen Mary's funeral on the television set to the haunting sounds of *Nimrod*, which, even at that young age, impressed me and left me with a love for this piece of music throughout my life. This was at a time when televisions were a luxury, and to find a neighbour who could afford one was a godsend, as everyone would converge in their lounge to watch the screen on state occasions.

For many years, Elgar lived in Great Malvern, where he was much inspired by his walks across Worcestershire's hilltops and water meadows. It was while walking on the high beacons on the Malvern range that he got the inspiration for those beautiful *Enigma Variations*. Elgar had a lot to thank his father for, as he had a small music shop in Worcester where he tuned pianos. It is a well-known fact that Elgar was a self-taught composer, having studied the music available in his father's shop, and he was able to play a variety of instruments. Elgar would often sit in the church porch at Longdon Marsh. It was here, during a violent thunderstorm, that the music for *The Apostles* first entered his thoughts.

Immortalised in the works of the poet A. E. Housman, Bredon Hill in the Vale of Evesham was instrumental in the work of this great man. Who could not be impressed by his much-acclaimed poem, 'A Shropshire Lad'? It certainly left an impression on me when we studied it at school. If you were to take a walk over Bredon Hill and the nearby villages today, you would still capture the rural idyll that is portrayed in his work.

Worcestershire has a number of impressive towns, one of which is Evesham, in the Vale of Evesham. 'Ham' was a Saxon name for a piece of land in the loop of a river, and the defensive position provided by this ham meant that Evesham became a strategic town through the ages.

Harry Workman built the famous Evesham Bridge over the River Avon in 1856, which was funded by public subscription. Near the Workman Bridge on the eastern bank is the recently restored public quay, which for centuries was the landing stage for goods brought up the river from the sea. From the Workman Gardens, you can look across the river and see the Abbey Park, the nineteenth-century bell tower and twelfth-century churches. One of Britain's finest abbeys once stood on these grassy slopes, but it would meet its demise in 1539, at the hands of Henry VIII's commissioners.

Six miles west of Evesham is the market town of Pershore, which, like Evesham, lies on the banks of the River Avon. Pershore is in the Wychavon district, and is part of the West Worcestershire parliamentary constituency. The town is best known for Pershore Abbey. Part of the abbey stands in an expanse of public grassland, close to the centre of the town, and dates from the eleventh century. The current structure is far smaller than the original buildings, which also met their demise during the Dissolution of the Monasteries.

Upton-upon-Severn used to be a port, and was the only nearby river crossing. To this day, Upton's bridge is the only Severn crossing for miles!

Another claim to fame in Worcestershire is Kidderminster and its association with the manufacture of carpets. Flemish weavers arrived in the town in the thirteenth century, and Kidderminster was to become one of the leading cloth producing centres in Europe. Sir Rowland Hill, creator of the Penny Post, was also born there in 1795. Kidderminster is approximately 15 miles north of Worcester city centre and is twinned with Husum in Germany.

South of the industrial Midlands is the town of Redditch, famous for the manufacture of needles, fish hooks and bicycles. The Forge Mill Needle in Redditch represents a fine example of water-powered needle scouring and is the only remaining mill of its kind in the world. It last worked commercially in 1958 and is now a museum.

Malvern owes its existence to the priory, which was built in the 1080s by Uldwyn, a Benedictine monk, and was closely linked to the mother house of Westminster Abbey. Little Malvern also had a priory, which was founded by two brothers from Worcester, Jocelin and Edred, who were to become the first two priors of the house from 1131.

Harvington Hall, once home of the Pakingtons, a Roman Catholic family, is another place worthy of mention. In an age when being of Catholic faith could see you killed, the family blessed the house with seven priest holes. This charming old Elizabethan house is gabled and mullioned.

Droitwich, in contrast, was renowned for its salt and brine springs; as such, it was to be become a Spa town from the 1800s. John Corbett, a local industrialist, obviously saw an opportunity for financial gain from the waters and built St Andrews Brine Baths in the 1830s. He also built several palatial hotels and refaced the medieval Raven Hotel to accommodate guests seeking the health benefits his baths had to offer. By far his most impressive achievement, however, was the charismatic Chateau Impney, an imposing nineteenth-century house. Built in the style of a chateau in the time of Louis XIII, it took two years to build, commencing in 1873 and completed in 1875. Although it was built for Corbett's wife, Hannah Eliza O'Meara, whose parents were of French and Irish descent, she actually never lived there.

Tenbury Wells became famous in the 1830s with the discovery of the Saline Springs, where treatment could be given for glandular troubles, congestion and scurvy. This is the beautiful countryside where Worcestershire and Herefordshire meet.

No account of Worcestershire would be complete without mentioning the Lenches, five beautiful villages that stand on the eastern border of Worcestershire, with stunning views of the Malvern Hills. Rous Lench is the largest, the main house being Rous Lench Court, a black-and-white, sixteenth-century building. While Church Lench has a rather interesting Victorian church, the one at Rous Lench is even more intriguing. Sherrifs Lench is home of The Poplars, which was the marital home of Joseph Comely Bomford and Mary Hughes from 1834 to 1861.

Castle Hartlebury was known for housing the bishops of Worcester and was referred to as the 'Palace of the Bishops'. The palace was handsome and imposing, with its medieval stone structure and moat. However, it was damaged in the 1640s and 1650s, resulting in considerable reconstruction in the 1660s. Croome D'Abitot owes its existence to the 6th Earl, who employed Lancelot 'Capability' Brown to landscape and plan the great house, Croome Court, in the 1750s.

I cannot finish the introduction without a mention of Bromsgrove. Like its neighbour Redditch, Bromsgrove was famed for the manufacture of nails. It is an old market town with some famous monuments in the church; Sir Humphrey Stafford of Grafton's tomb is a fine example. In 1651, Charles Stuart, disguised as a servant, fled to Bromsgrove after his defeat at the Battle of Worcester.

When I think of Worcestershire, I remember the days when we first had a motor car and went on the Blossom Trail, where the fruit trees were in flower in and around Evesham. There were long queues to cross the old Severn Bridge in Worcester on our way to the seaside in the days before the motorways, and we would catch a glimpse of the cricket match opposite the cathedral as we travelled on our journey.

I have thoroughly enjoyed writing this book for you, as Worcestershire has been a firm favourite of mine since the days of those Sunday school outings. It's just so sad that with the cessation of Sunday schools, today's children have not been given the opportunity to amass these beautiful memories.

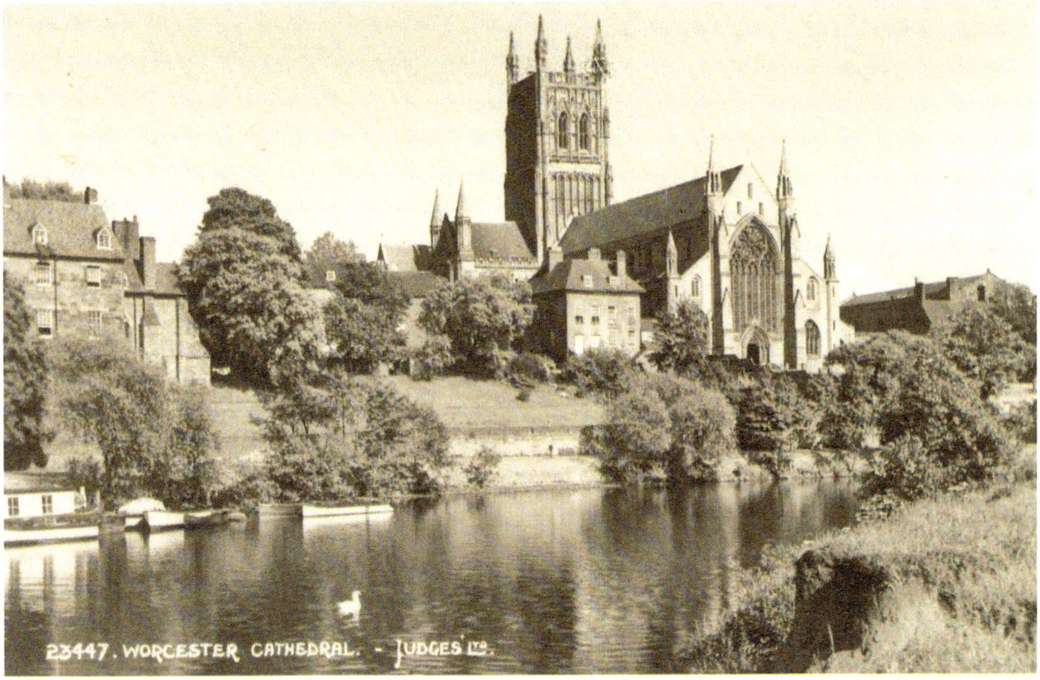

Worcester Cathedral

Standing on the eastern bank of the River Severn is Worcester's majestic cathedral, founded as a Saxon monastery by St Oswald in 983. The bulk of the cathedral was built between the eleventh and fourteenth centuries. The Norman crypt was constructed by St Wulfstan, the only Saxon bishop to keep his office after the invasion of 1066.

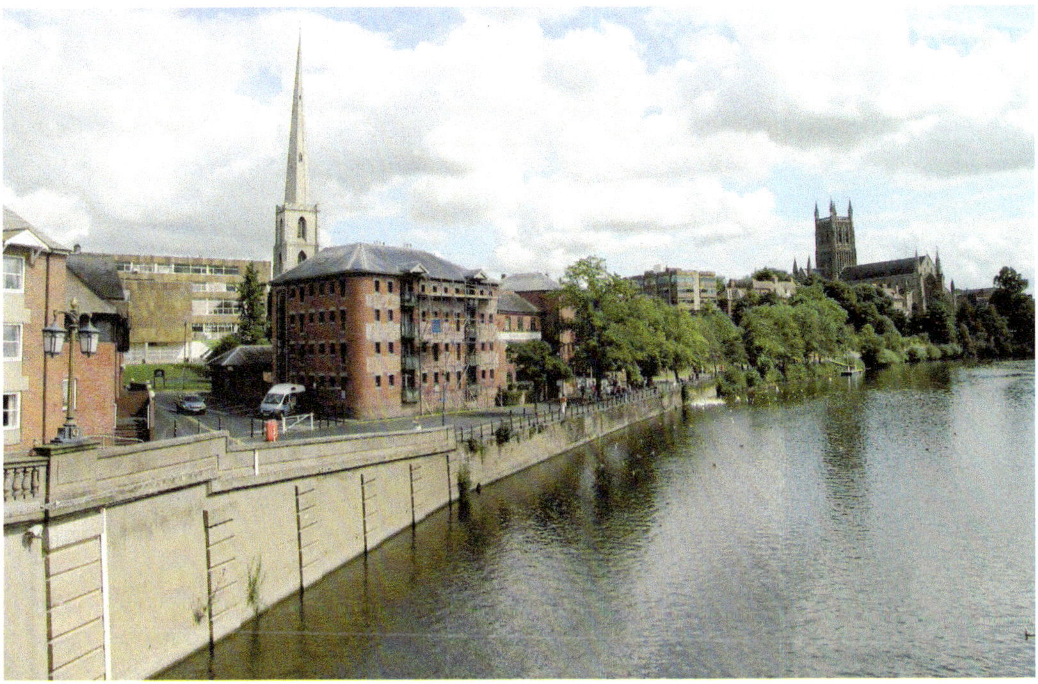

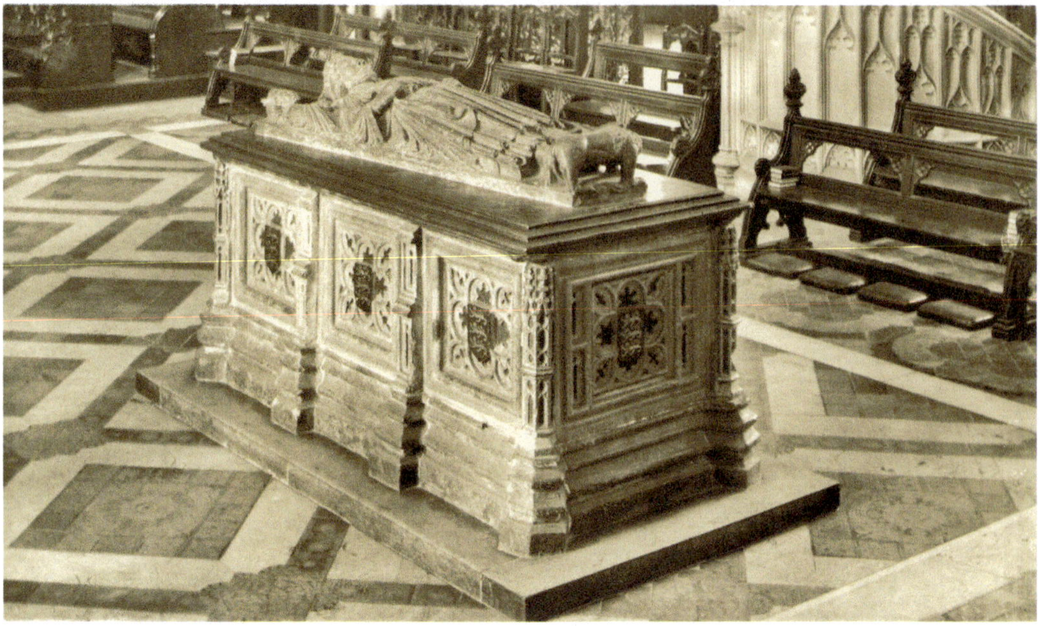

King John's Tomb and the Crypt, Worcester Cathedral

King John, born on Christmas Eve 1167, began his reign in 1199. He was famous for the signing of the Magna Carta. When he died in October 1216, he had lost most of his French land and was in the midst of a civil war against many of his barons. The delightful and mysterious crypt in Worcester Cathedral (*below*) was built by St Wulfstan in 1084, and was used for the preservation of the relics of saints. For well over 900 years, the crypt has been used as the location for an annual service. It is the largest Norman crypt in Britain.

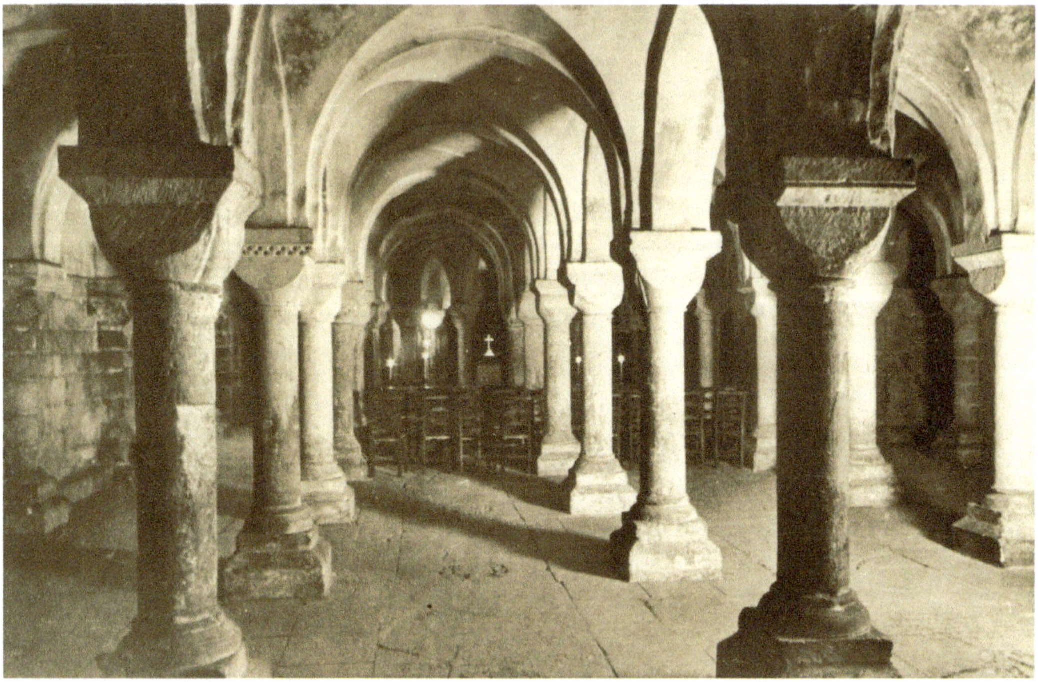

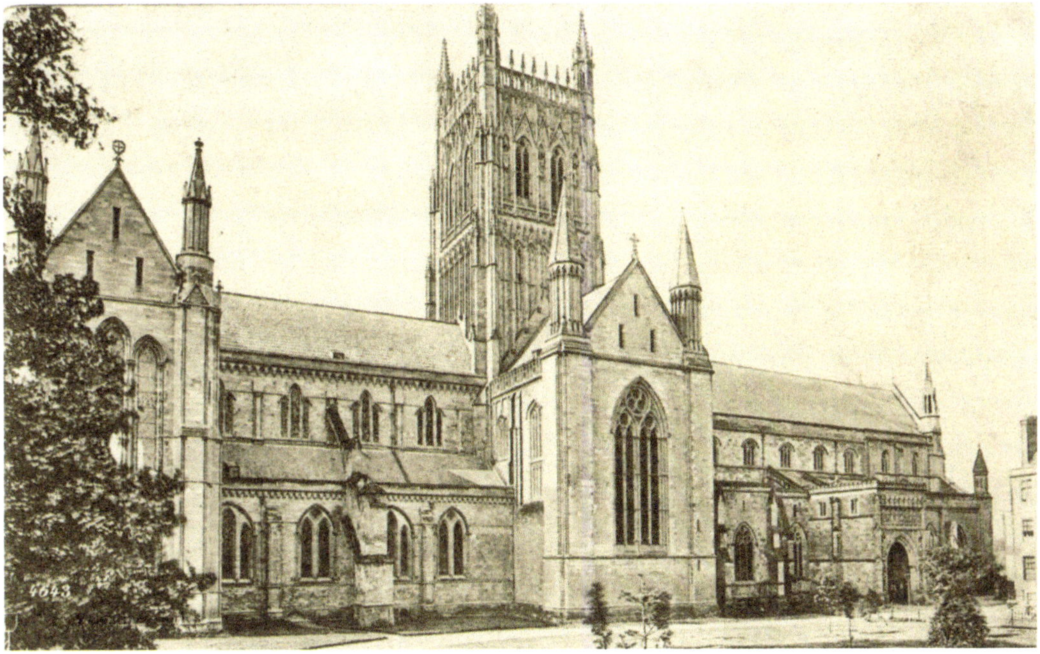

Worcester Cathedral

The majestic cathedral stands in the centre of the city on the eastern bank of the River Severn. Situated between the shrines of St Oswald and St Wulfstan in the chancel just before the High Altar is the tomb of King John, which bears the first sculptured royal effigy in England. It is claimed to be a good likeness of the King.

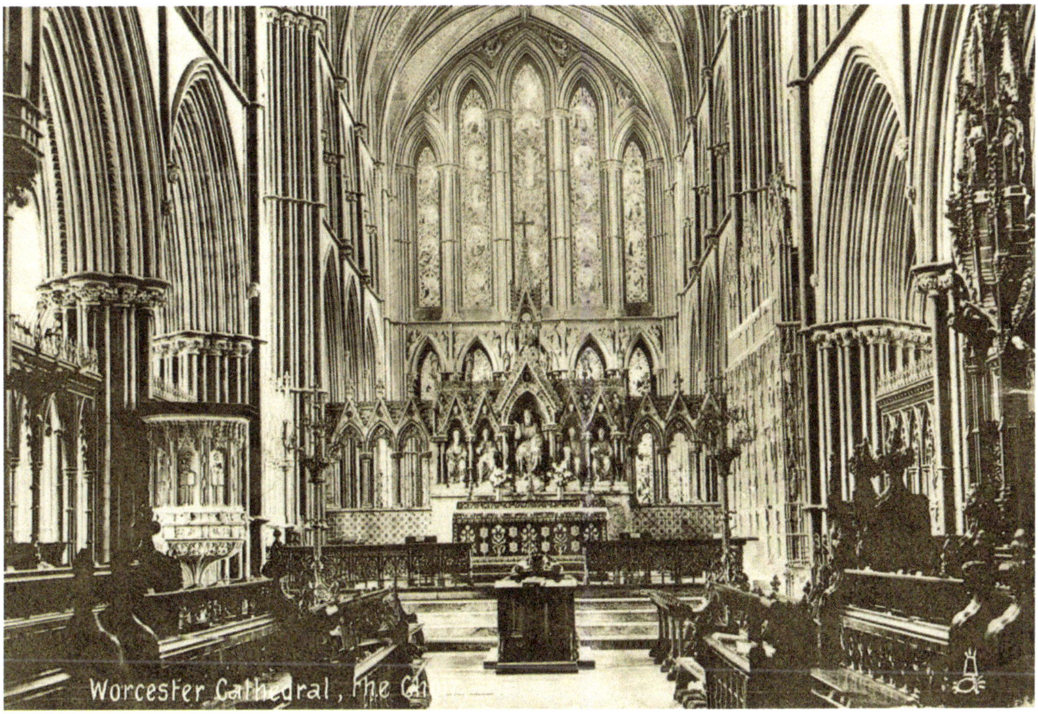

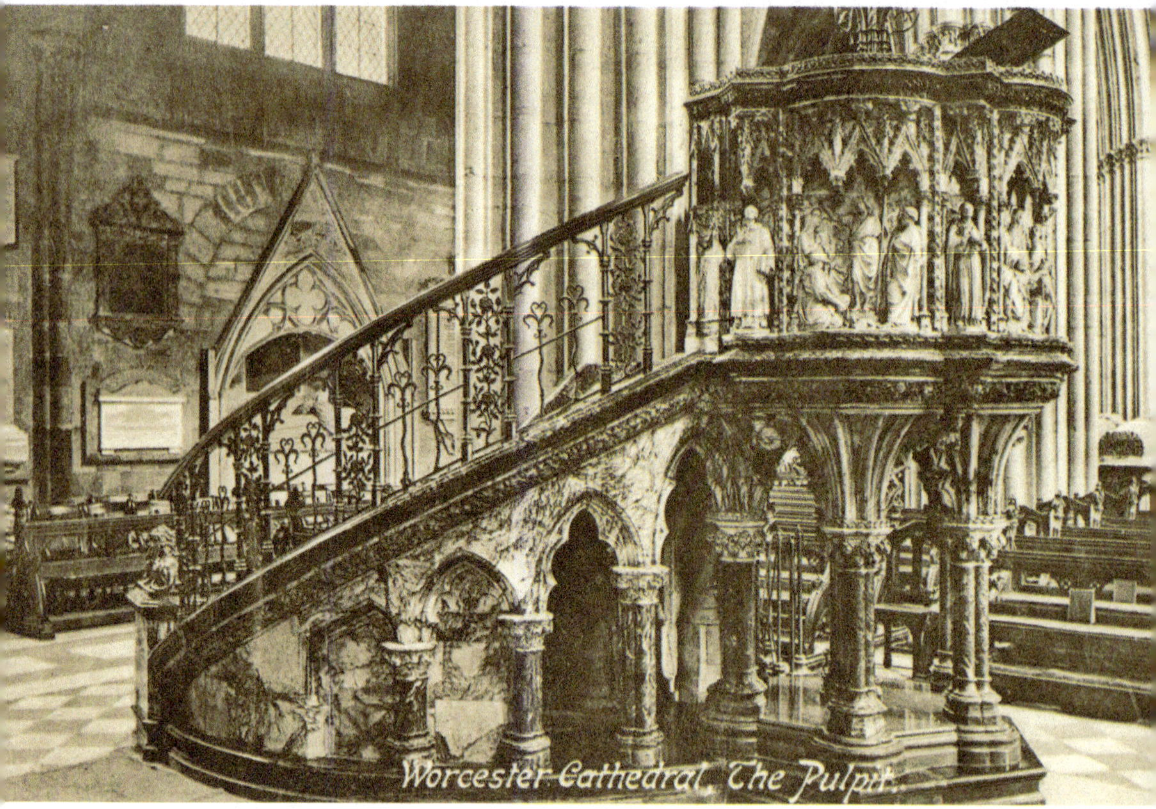

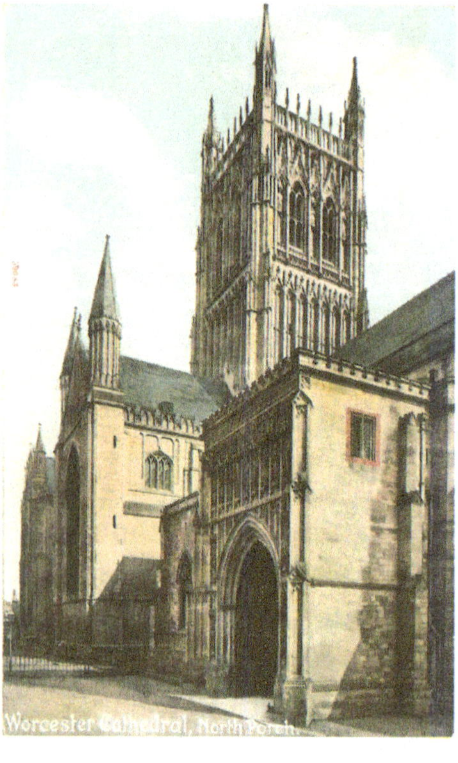

Worcester Cathedral

Above is a postcard showing the pulpit at Worcester Cathedral. It is a beautiful example, with a lovely wrought-iron handrail and impressive effigies. To the left is a further external view.

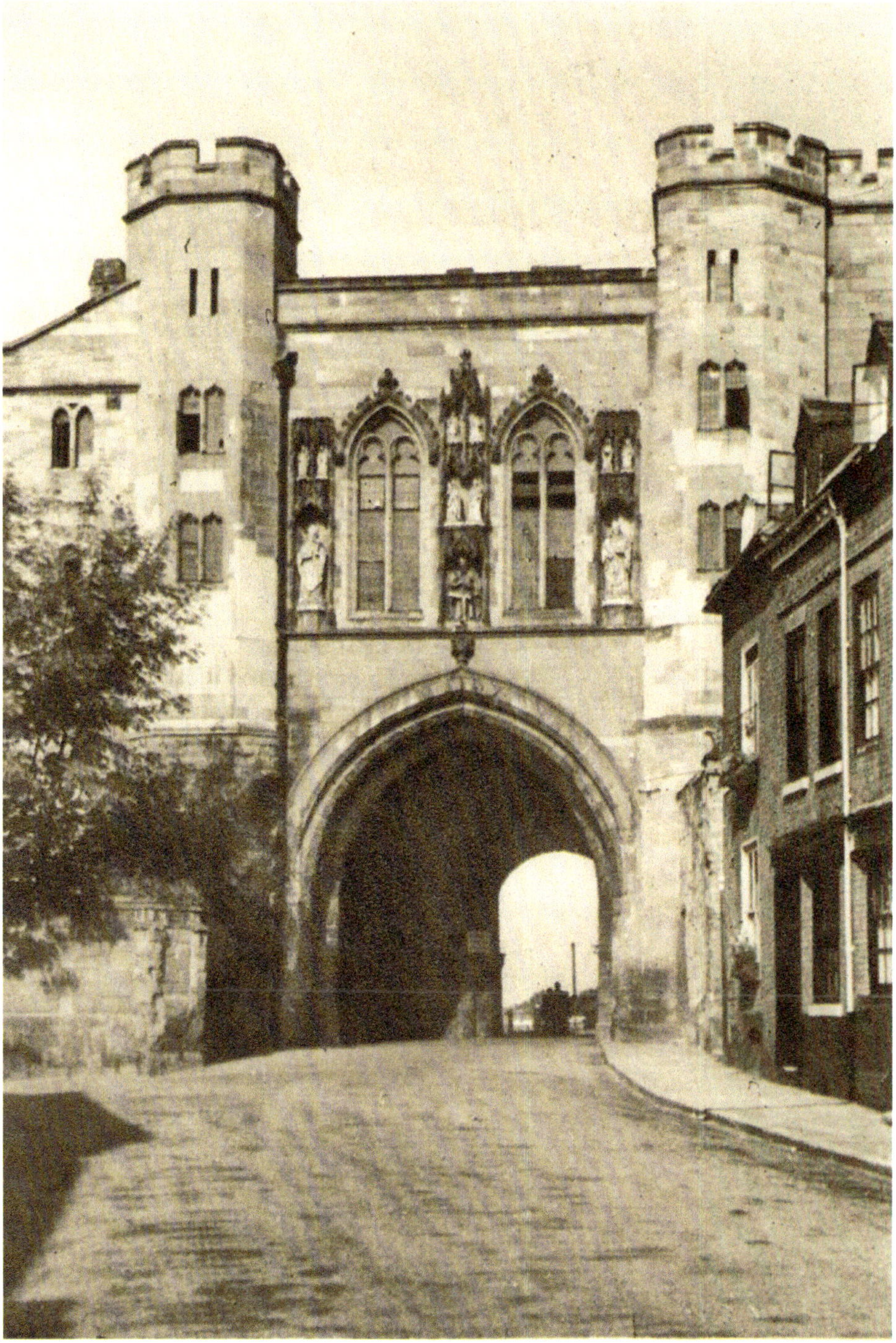

Edgar Tower, Worcester

Edgar Tower, built in the mid-fourteenth century, was formerly known as St Mary's Gate. In the eighteenth century, it was believed to have first been built during the reign of King Edgar in the tenth century, and thus became known as Edgar Tower. The fortified gateway formed the entrance to the monastic precinct.

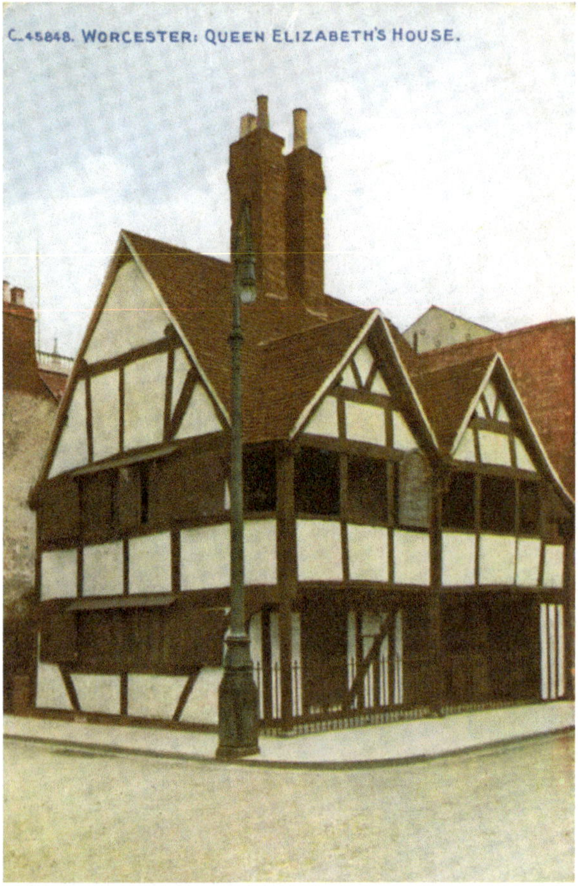

Queen Elizabeth's House and Guildhall, Worcester

The cathedral city of Worcester developed as a settlement in Saxon times, though it did not achieve any importance until after the Norman Conquest. Here we see Queen Elizabeth's House in Worcester. Below, the impressive Guildhall in Worcester stands on the west side of High Street.

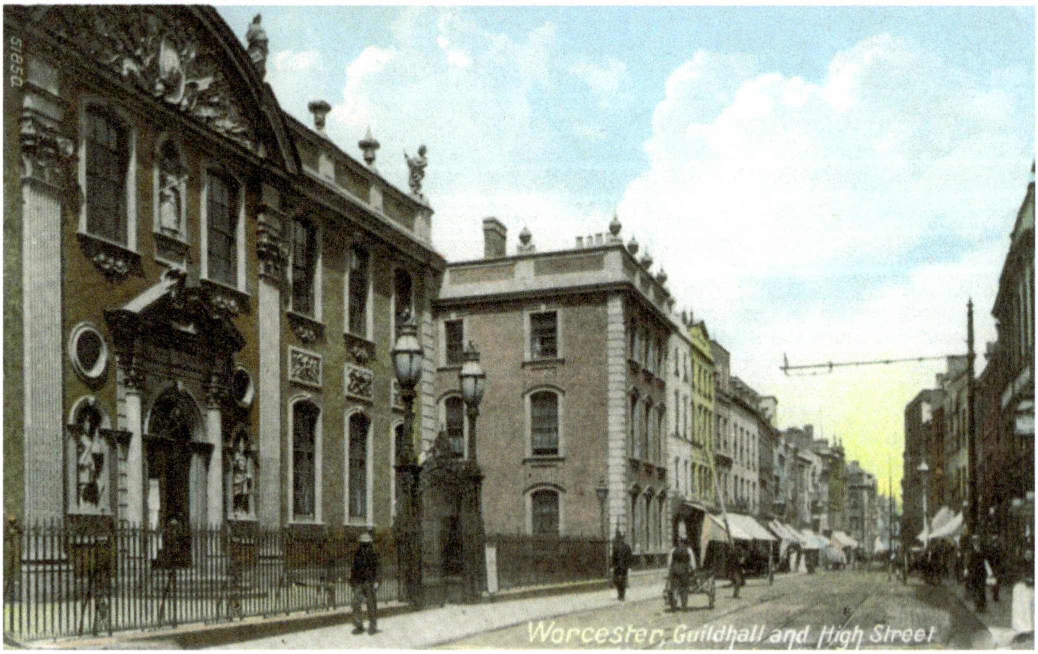

The Guildhall, Worcester

This imposing building was designed by Thomas White, a local man, thought to be a student of Sir Christopher Wren. The Guildhall is home to the statues of Charles I and II, while above the doorway is a statue of Queen Anne. An inscription reads 'May the faithful city flourish'.

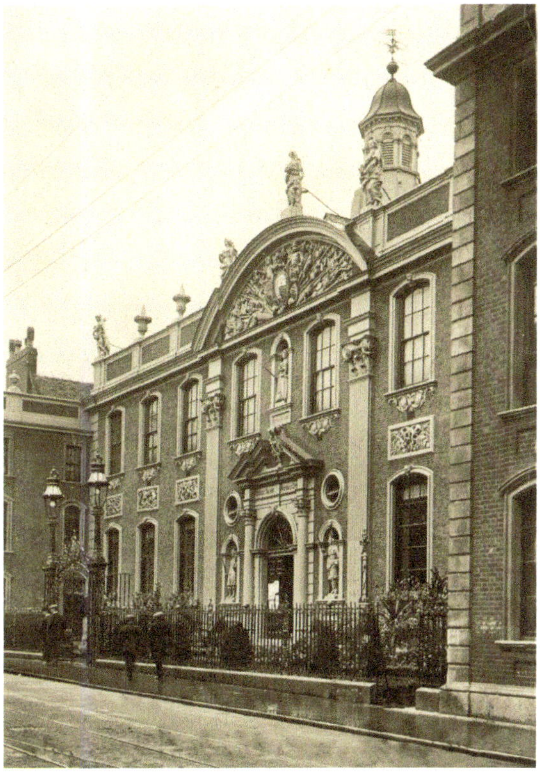

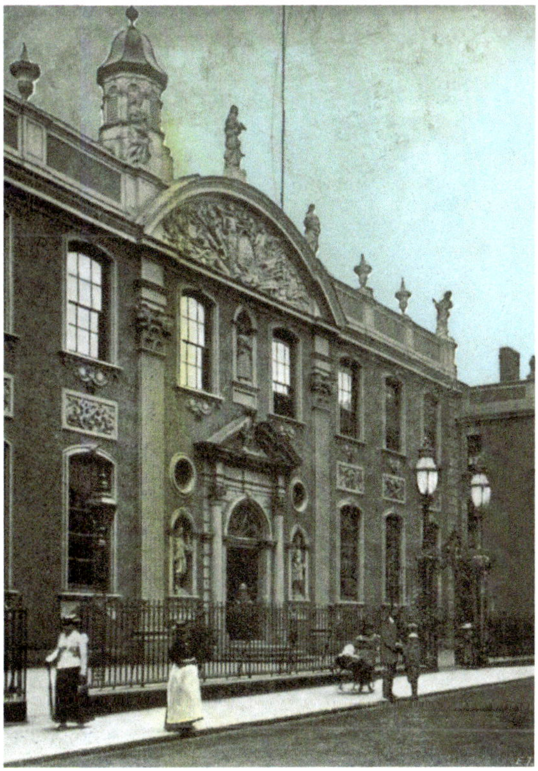

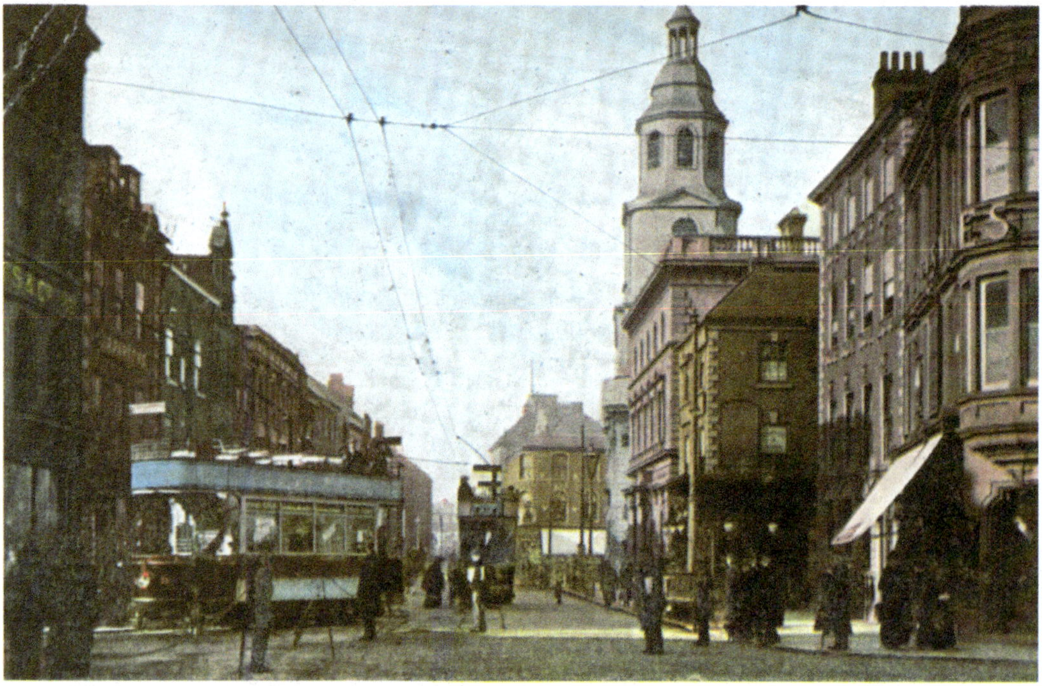

The Cross, Worcester

Continuing from Worcester High Street is the Cross. It was here that Elizabeth I was greeted as she arrived in the city in 1574.

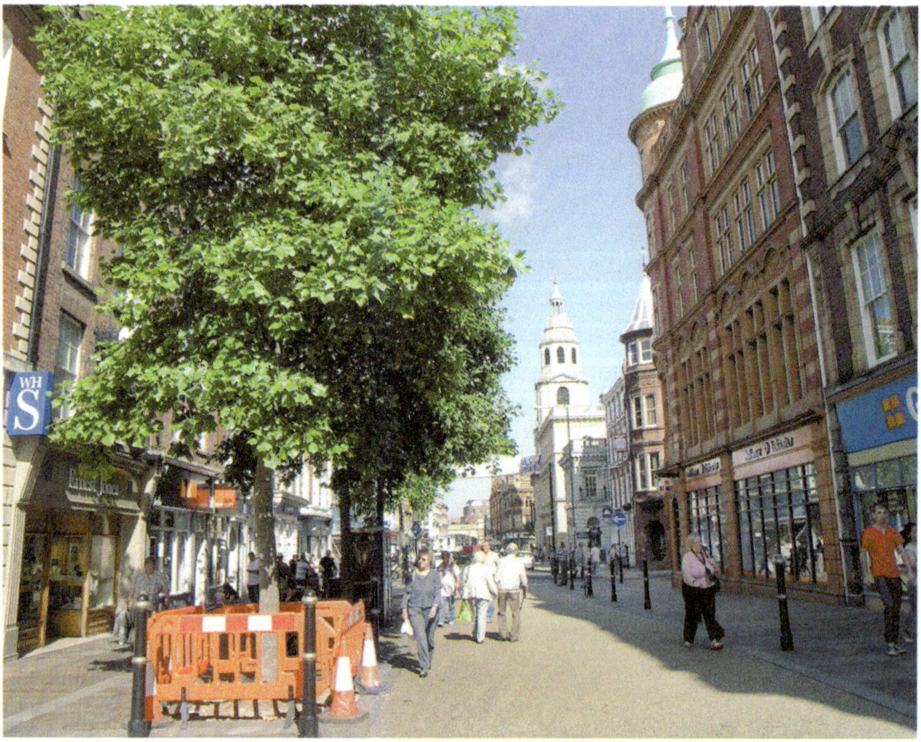

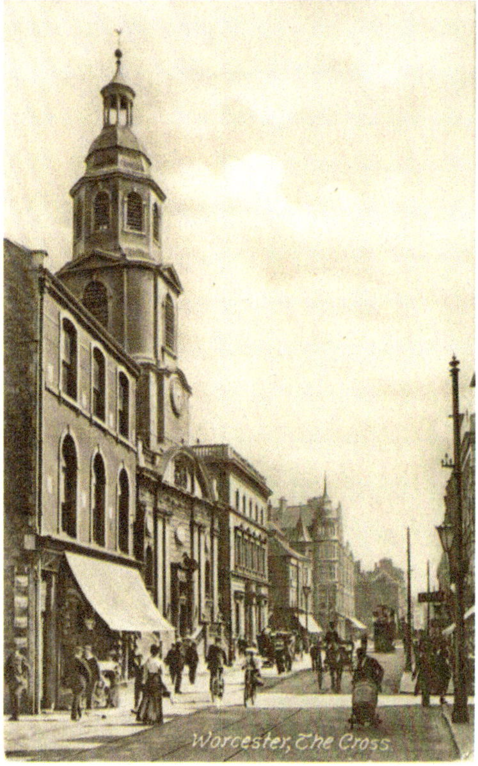

The Cross, Worcester
The street known as the Cross is dominated by the tower of St Nicholas church, which was said to have been originally designed as the church of St Martin-in-the-Fields, London.

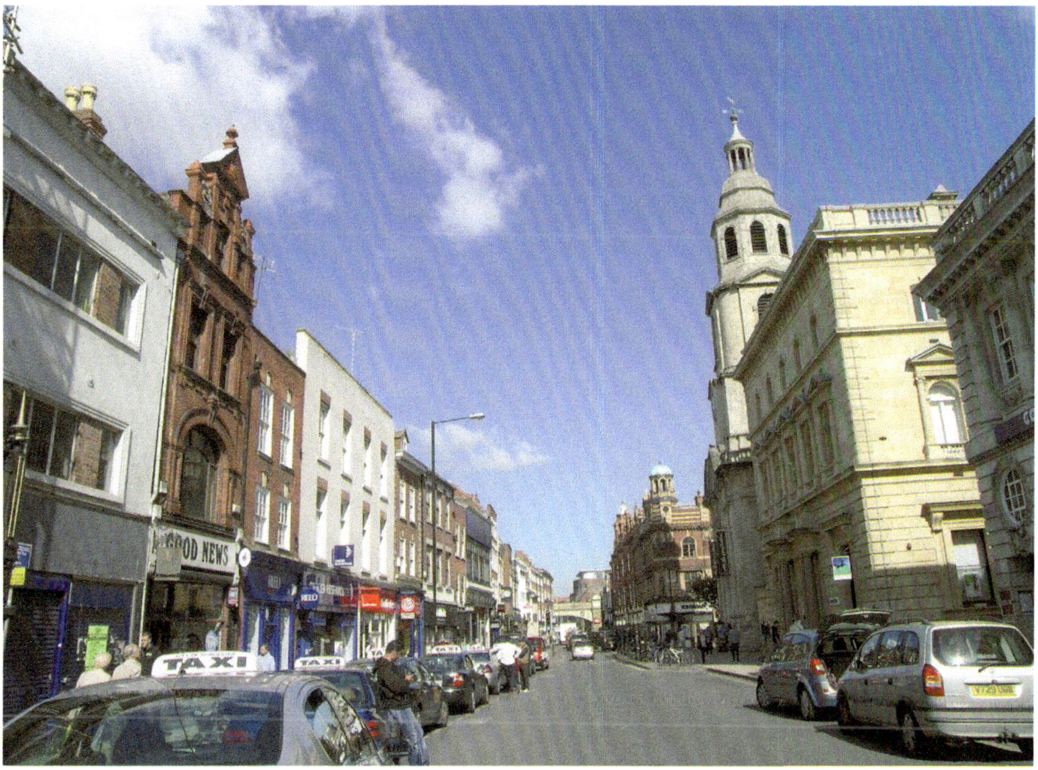

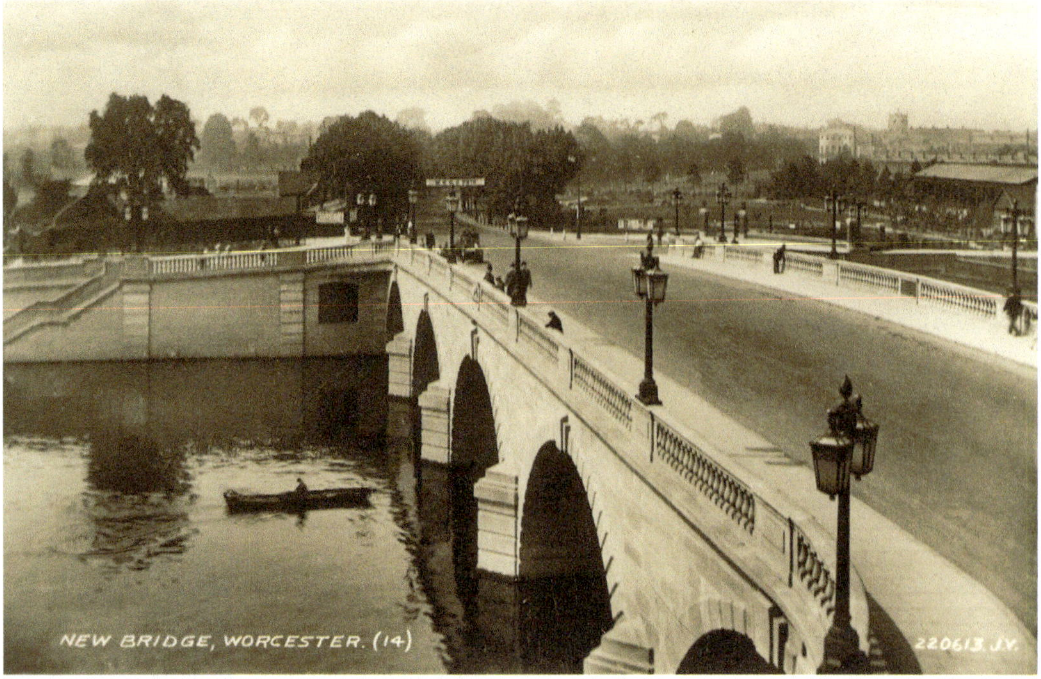

The Bridge, Worcester

Worcester Bridge was constructed in 1781 and is the only road bridge crossing the river in the city centre. As such, it is prone to congestion at busy periods. The bridge forms the middle section of a one-way gyratory system. The River Severn floods frequently at this point.

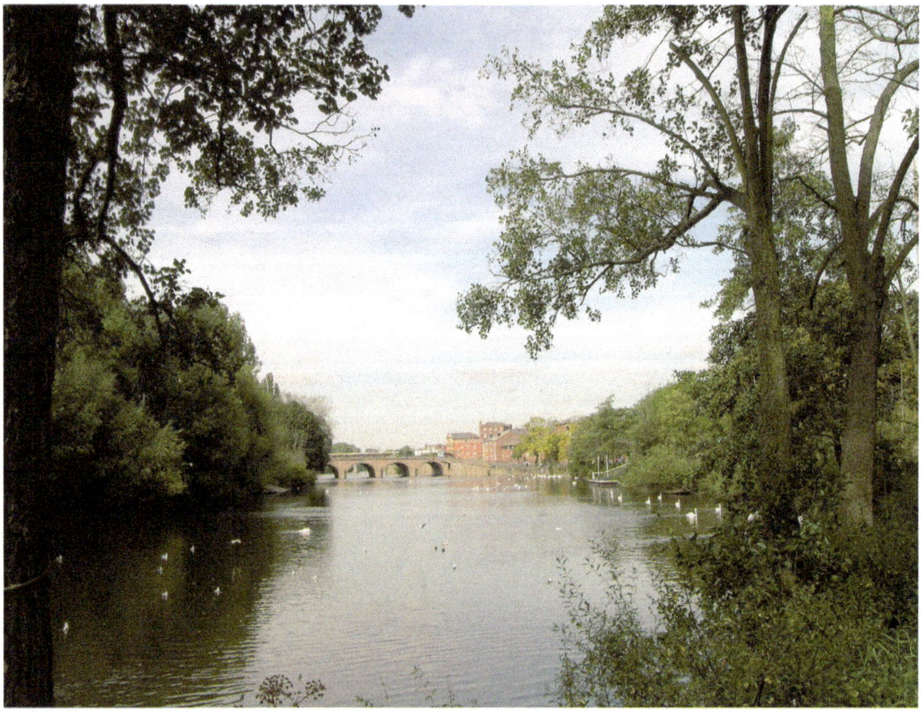

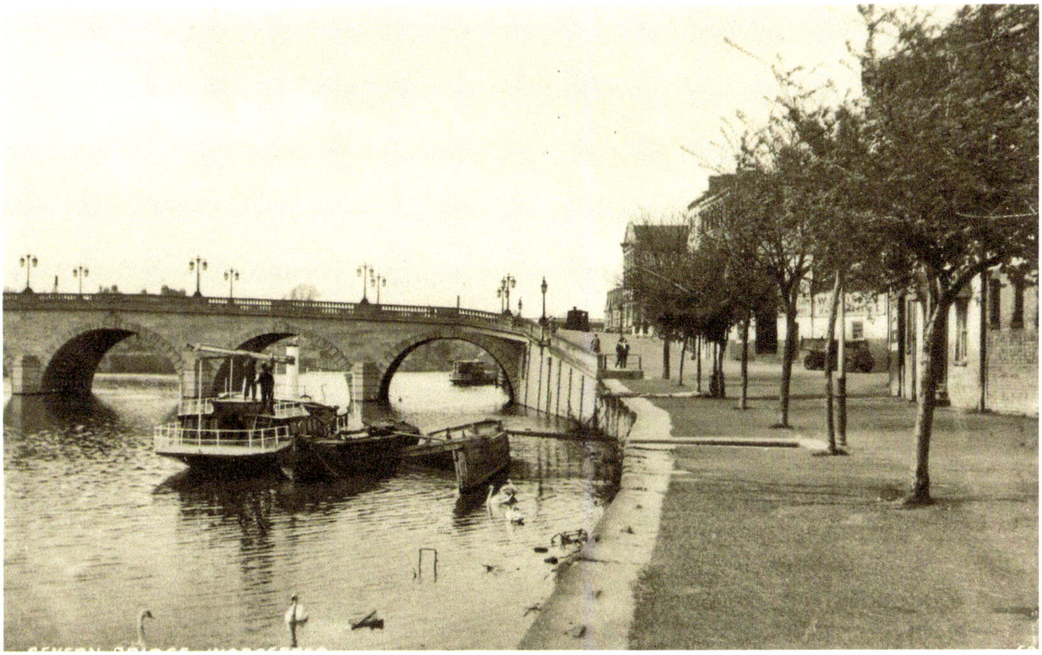

Bridge and Old Rectifying House, Worcester

Worcester grew up around an ancient ford and has always enjoyed a close relationship with the River Severn. There are delightful walks and boat trips from the banks, and one of the best ways to explore Worcester is along its rivers. Here we see the bridge constructed in 1781, the only road crossing within the city centre. Below, the Old Rectifying House is very close to the bridge and appears frequently in pictures of the River Severn in flood here.

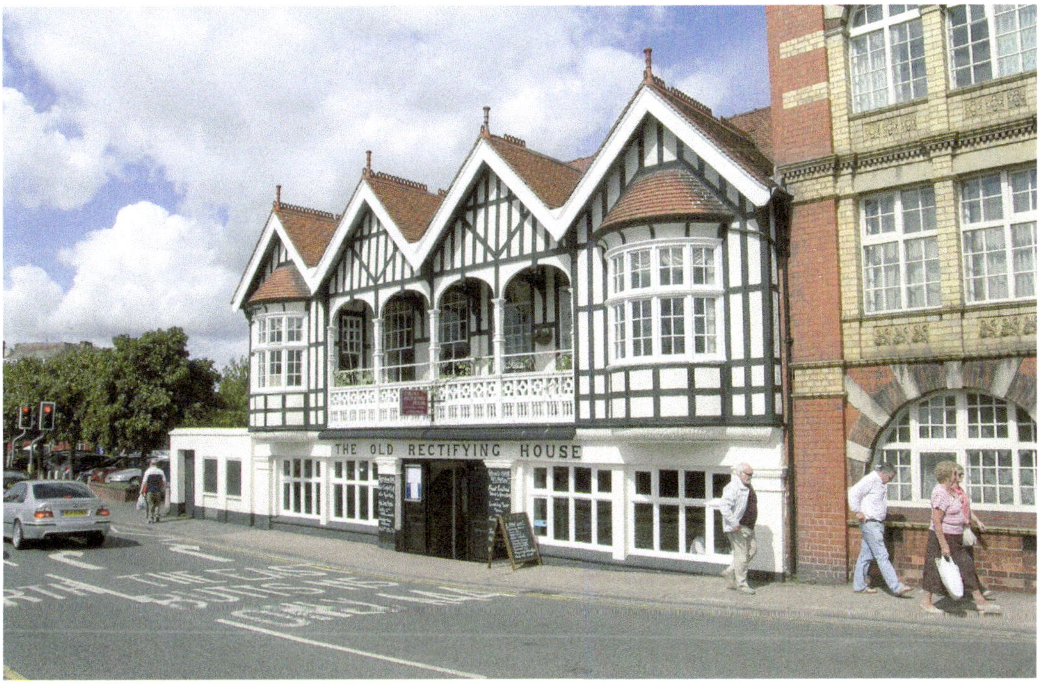

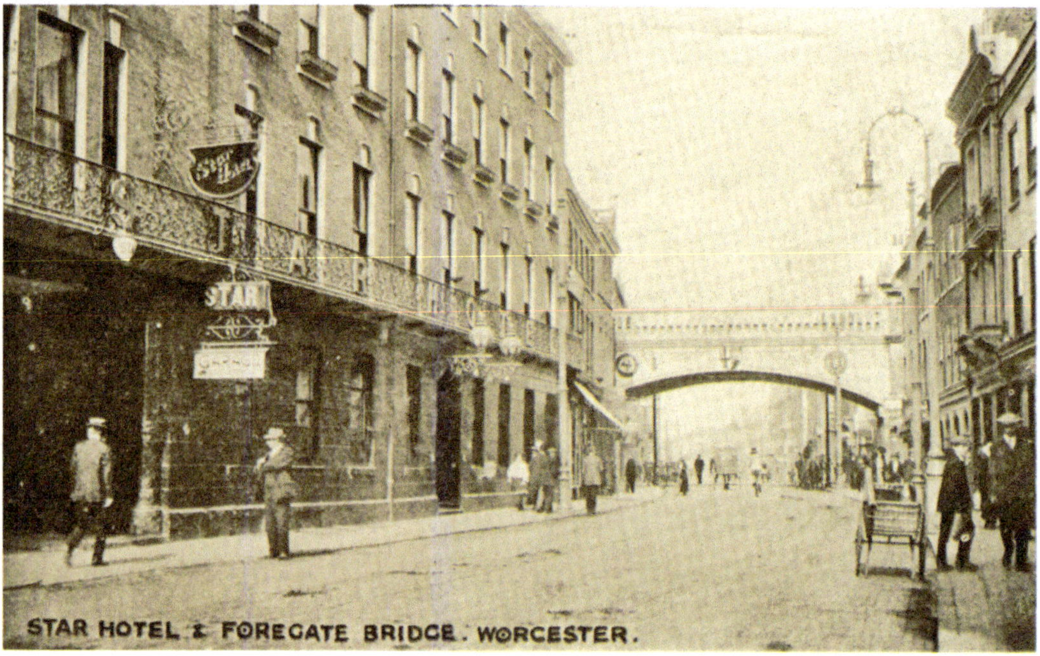

Foregate Bridge, Worcester

Foregate Bridge is a Grade II listed building, dating from 1860. Recently restored to its former glory to the tune of £1.1 million, there are plans afoot to spend a further £785,000 to revamp the adjoining Foregate railway station.

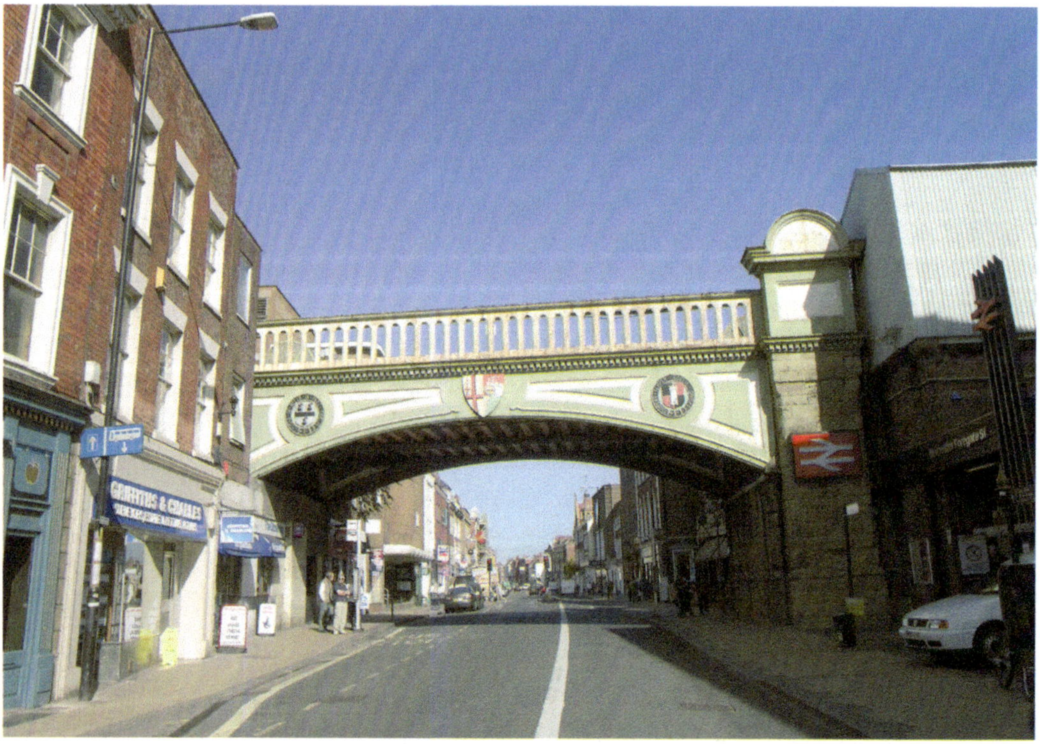

St Peter's Street and Friar Street, Worcester

Worcester is a city with numerous old buildings. Although a number were lost in the twentieth century, many others were renovated and preserved. St Peter's Street and church are a fine example of Old Worcester. Below, another of the wonderful old streets in Worcester; in this case it is Friar Street.

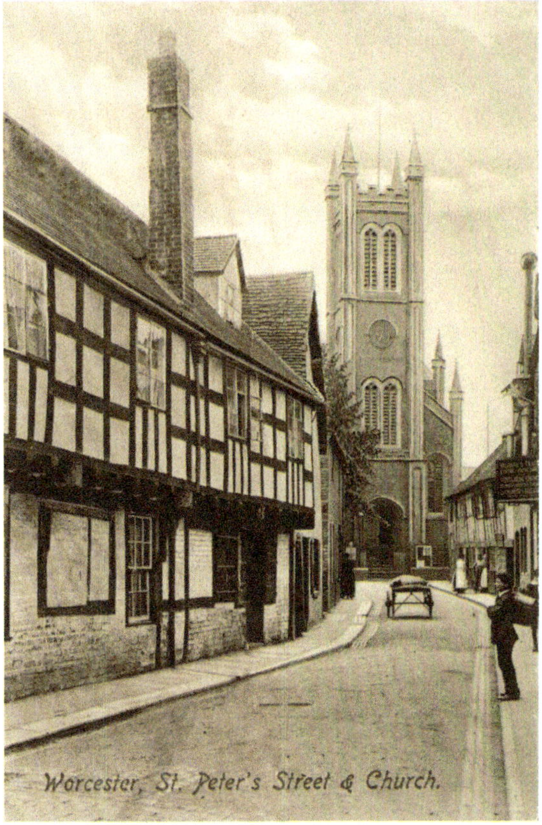

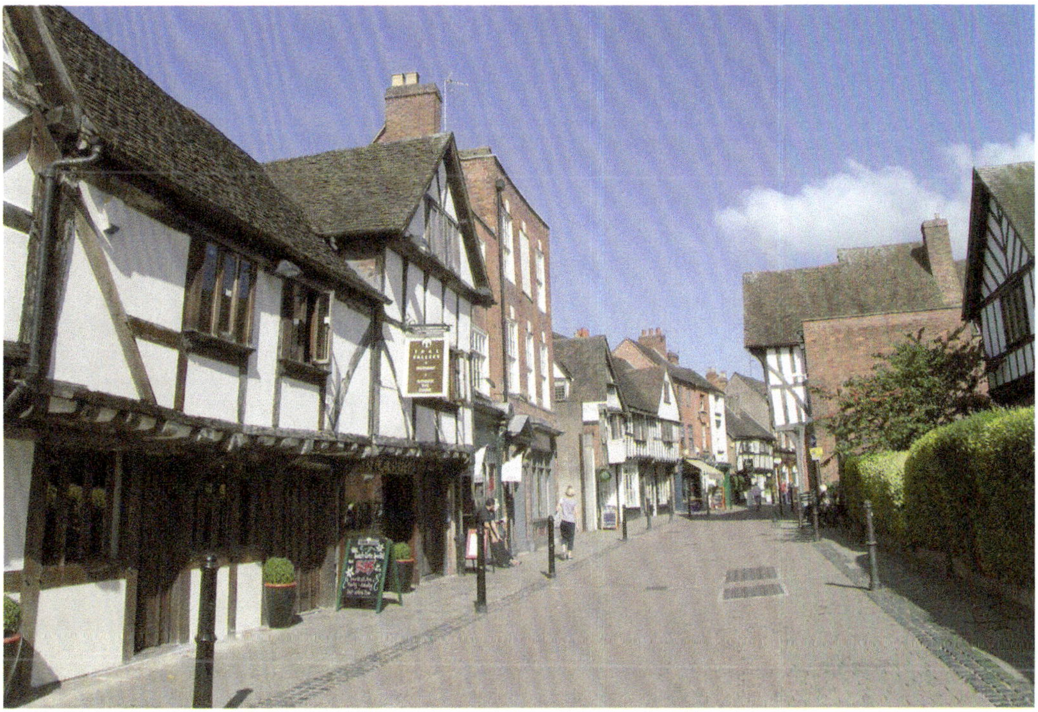

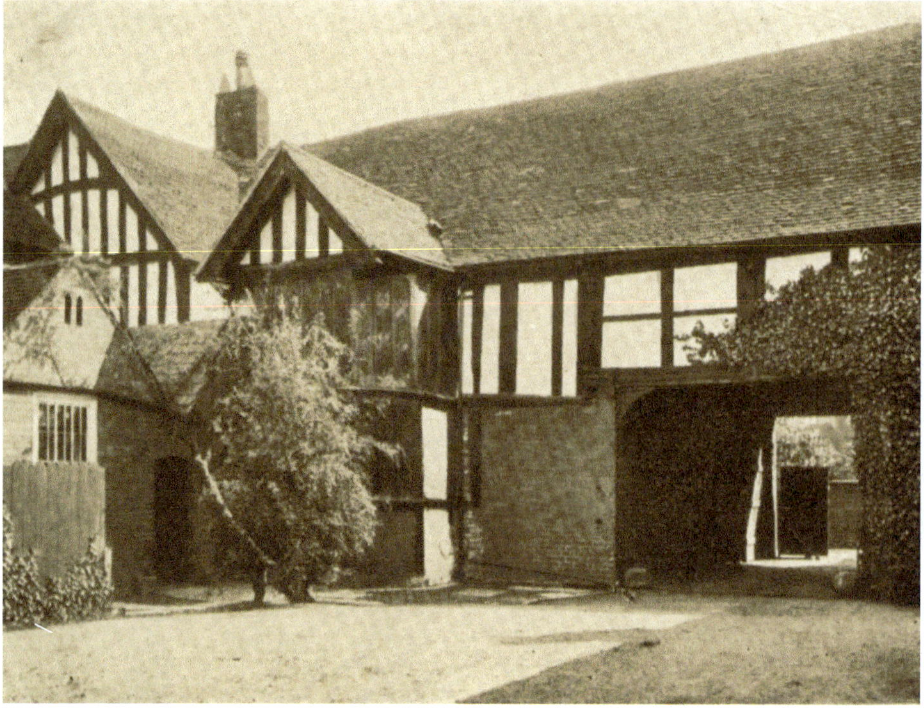

Commandery, Worcester

Although a number of buildings were lost in the twentieth century, Worcester is still a city of elegant buildings. Some were restored to their former glory and preserved for posterity. Here we see the ancient Commandary in a photograph taken from the courtyard.

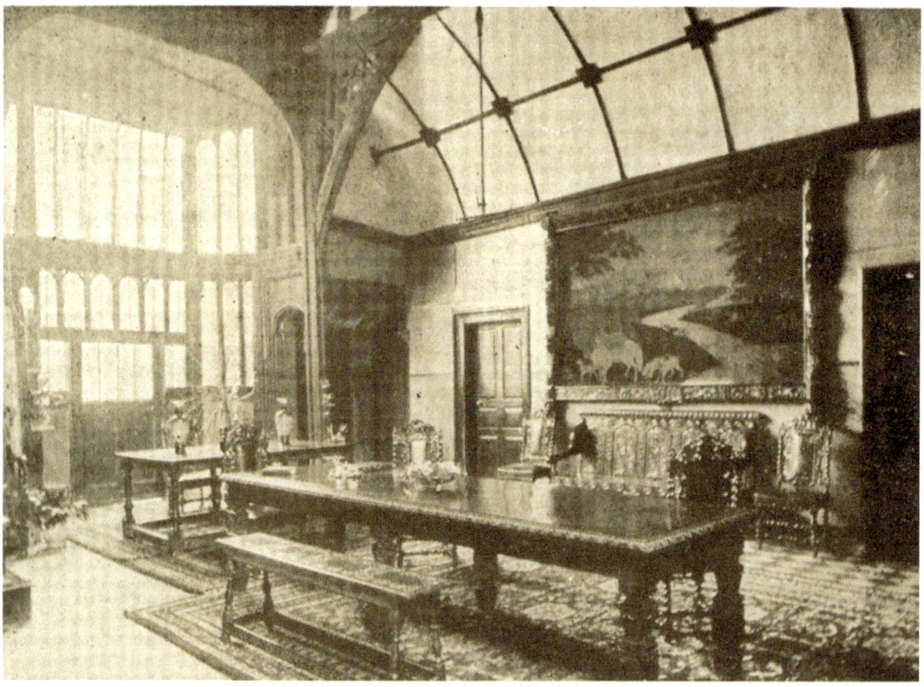

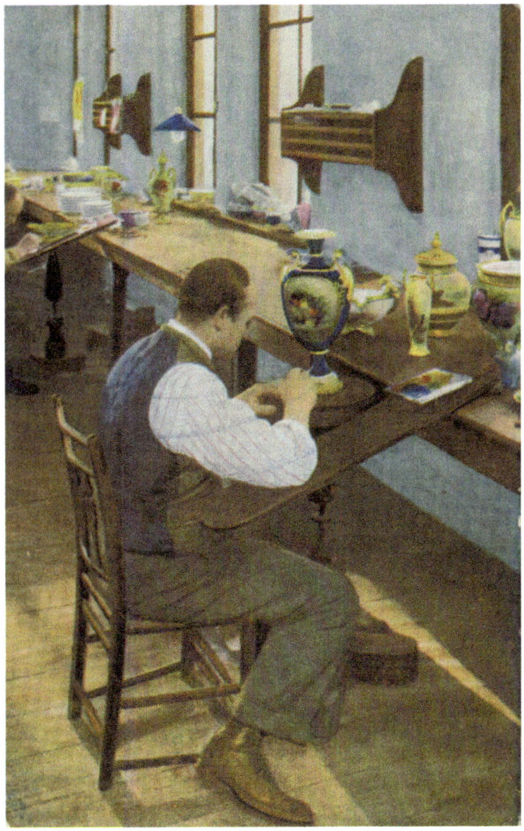

Royal Porcelain Works, Worcester

Synonymous with Royal Worcester china, no account of Worcestershire's history would be complete without mentioning this noble art. Here we see a beautiful china vase being worked on at the work bench. Royal Worcester china is decorated with pure gold and the process for applying this is extremely skilled, requiring many years of apprenticeship.

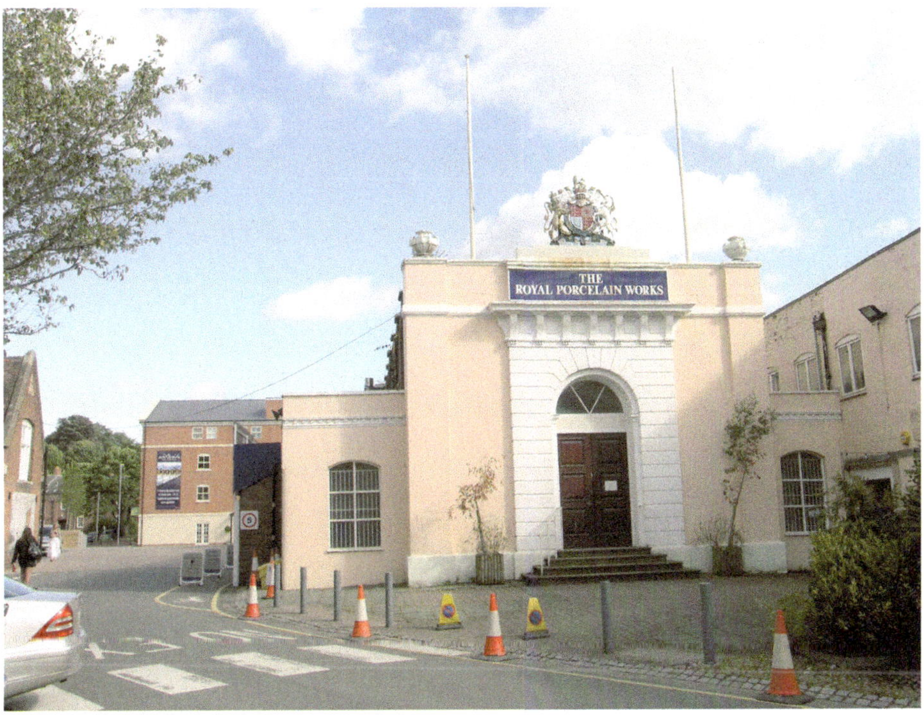

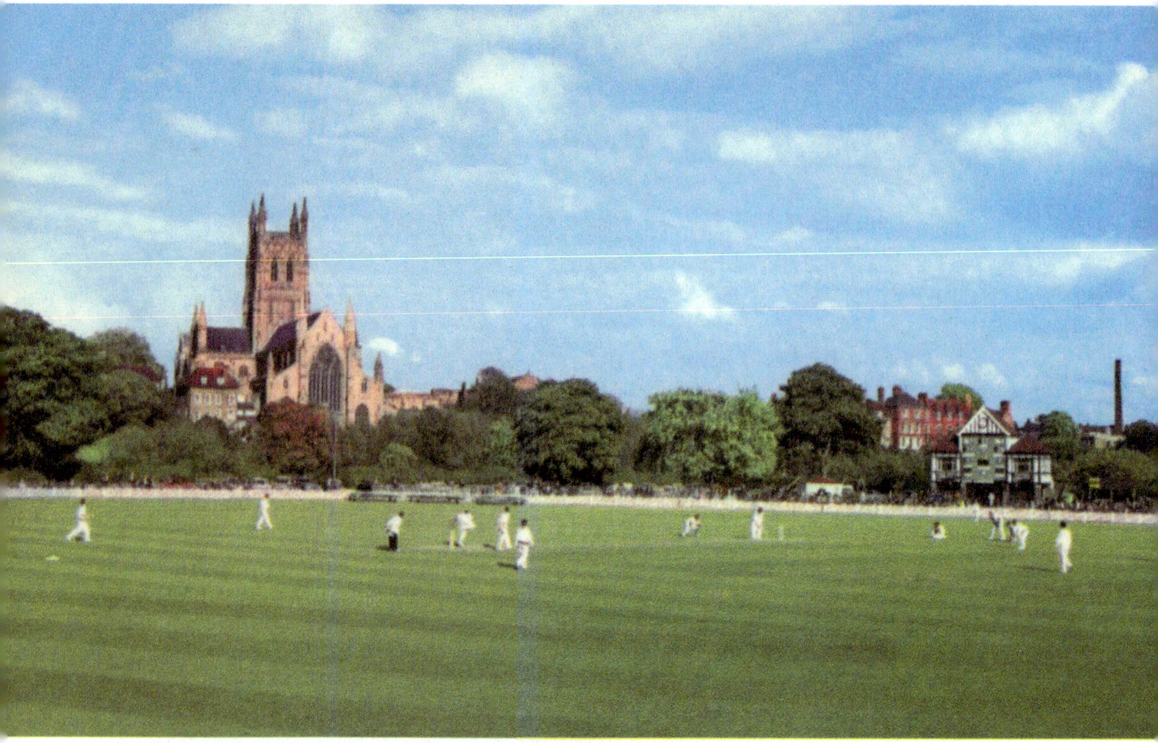

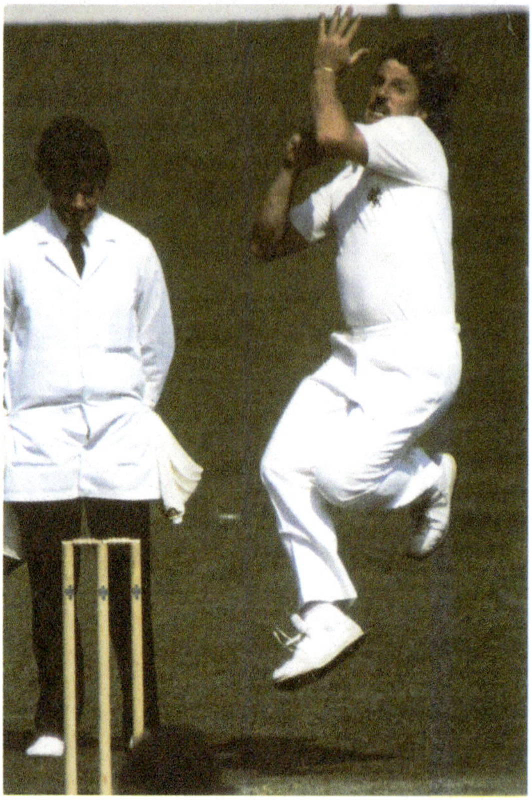

Worcester Cricket Ground

It is also important to mention the famous Worcester cricket ground, which lies on the opposite side of the River Severn to the cathedral. Due to its close proximity to the river, the cricket ground is prone to flooding when heavy rain takes place. One of its famous cricket players, seen in action in the picture to the left, is Ian Botham, who played cricket for Worcester and England.

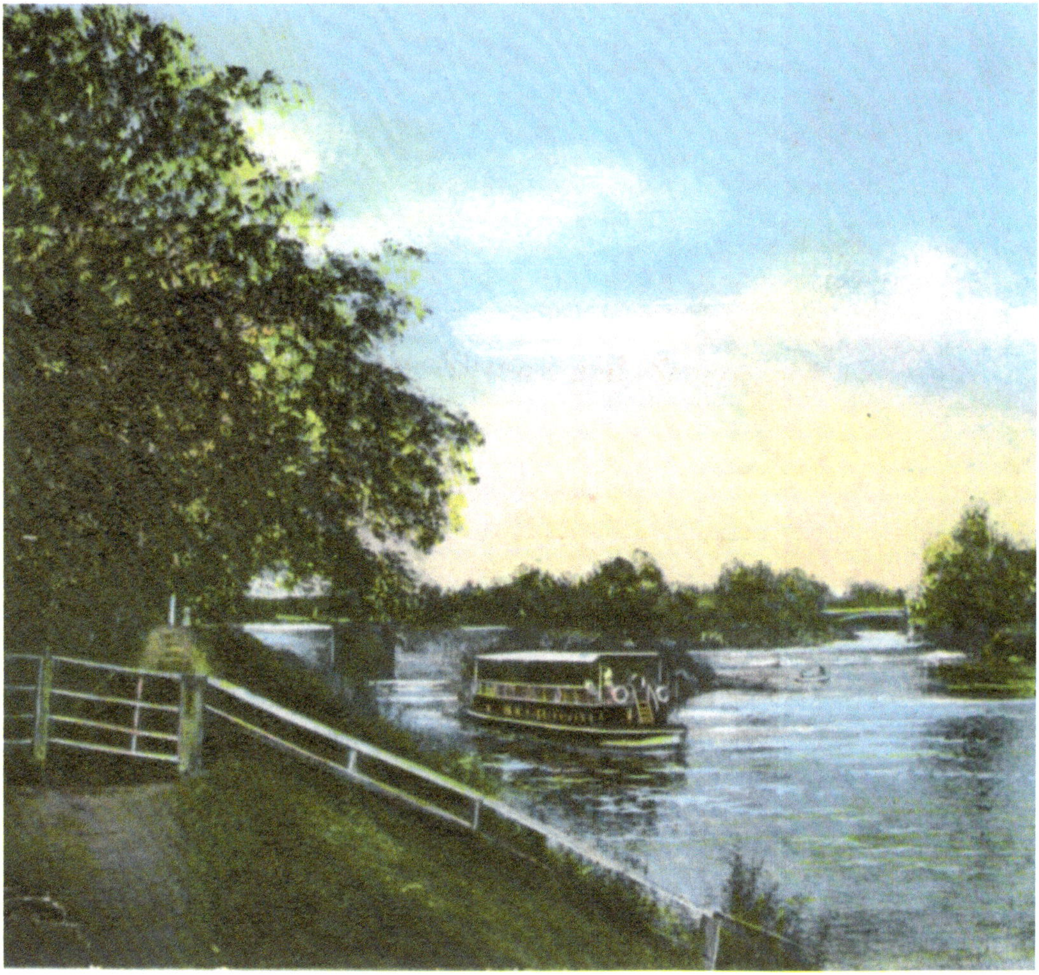

Camp Locks, Worcester

Camp Locks near Worcester is another fine example of the town's very close relationship with the River Severn. There are some lovely walks along the river around Worcester and, for those who are not quite so energetic, lots of opportunities to take a boat ride.

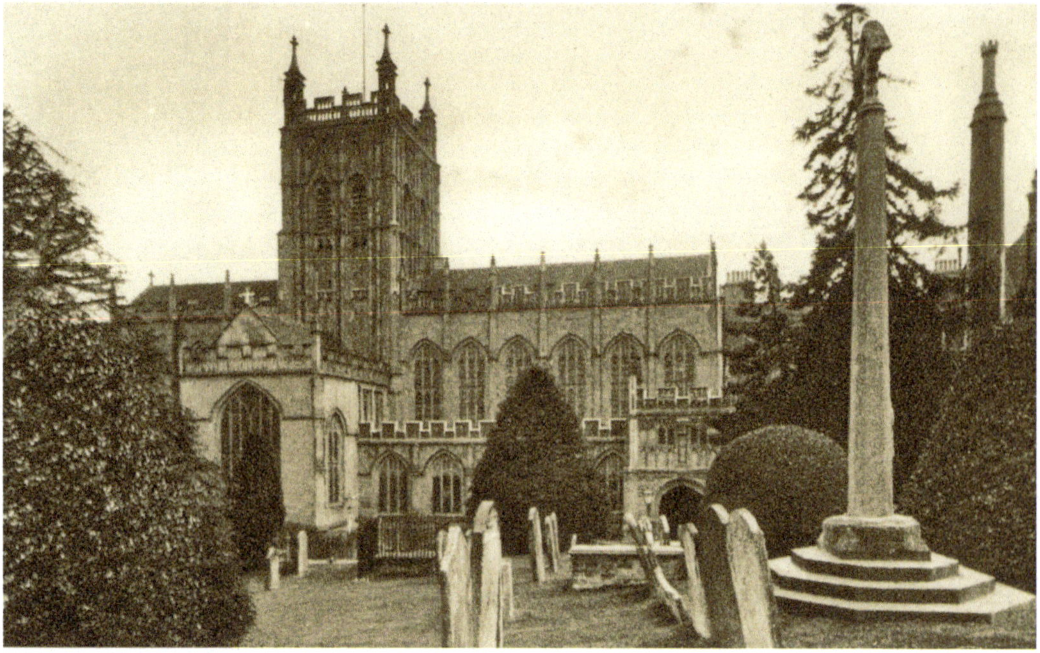

Great Malvern Priory, Malvern
The arrival of the railway in Malvern in the 1840s brought wealth and prosperity to the area, with visitors coming from far and wide. Here we see a postcard view of the priory at Malvern, a minor religious house.

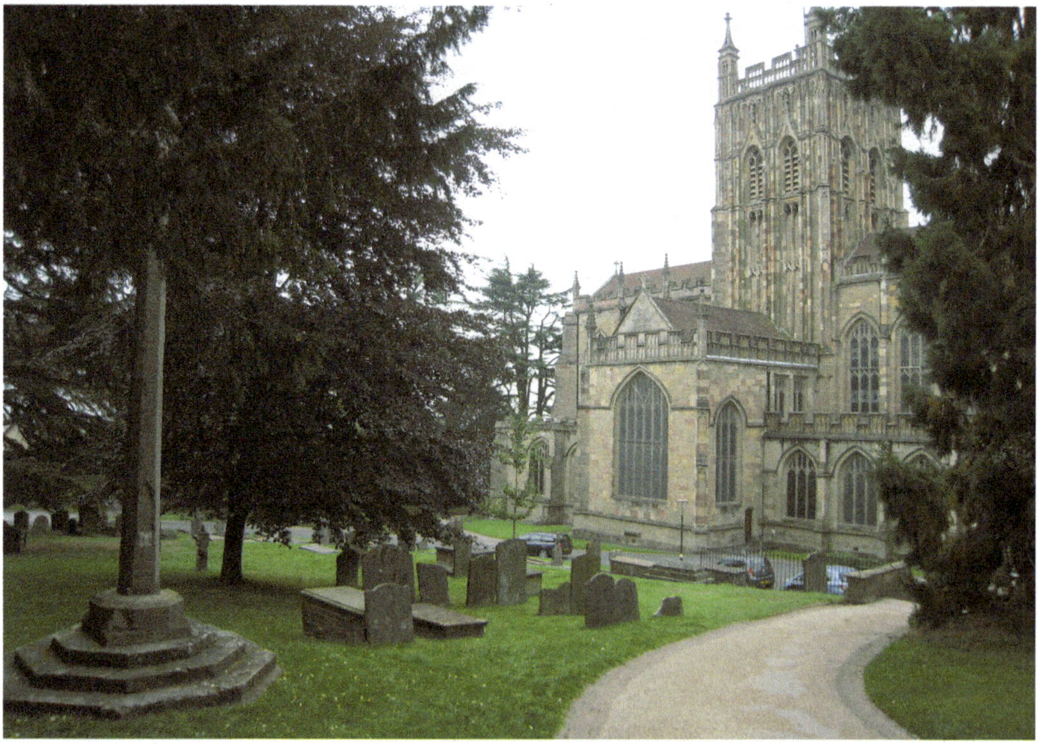

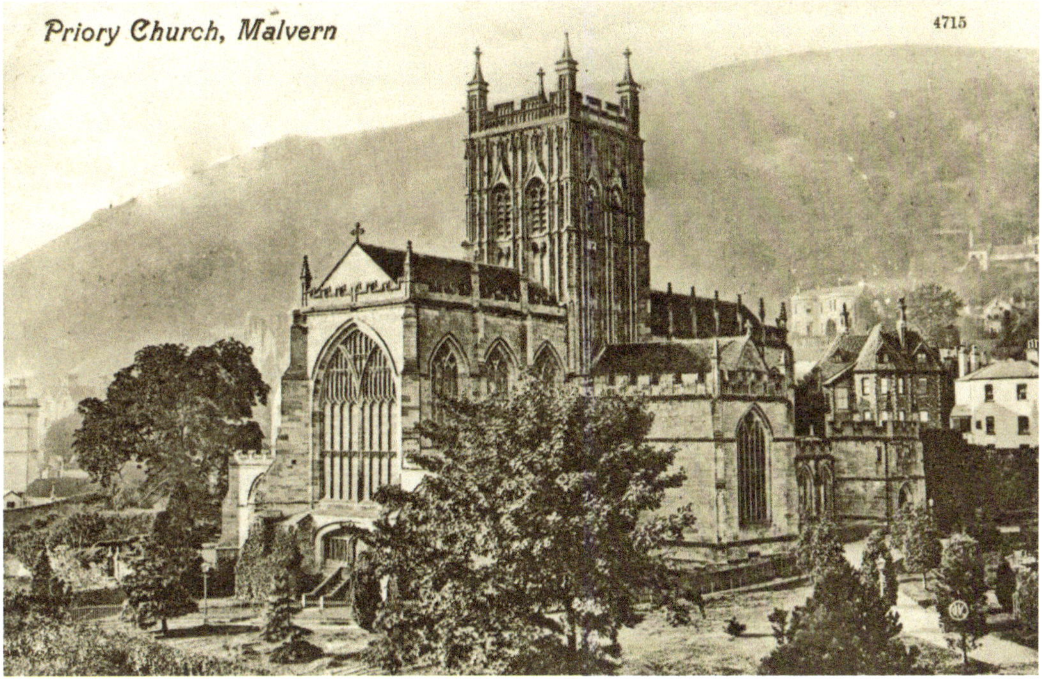

Great Malvern Priory, Malvern

Although Malvern began life around a Benedictine priory, only the church and gatehouse remain, thanks to the events of the Dissolution, when the rest of the buildings were taken down. Here we see the majestic priory church. The wonderful doorway hidden by the tree in the lower photograph can be seen in the inset.

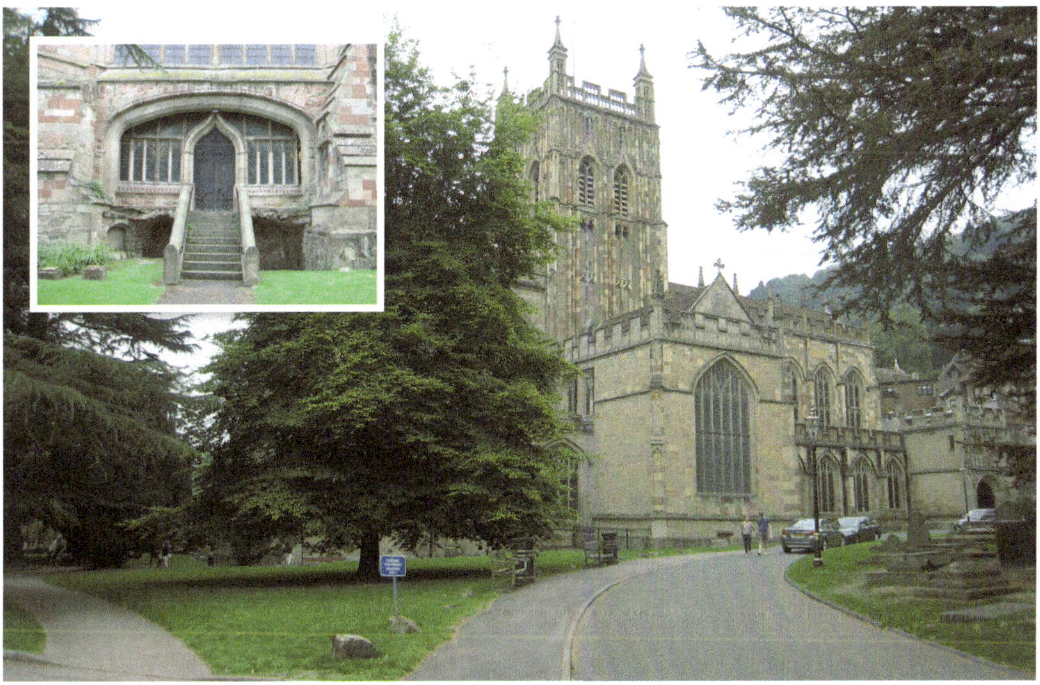

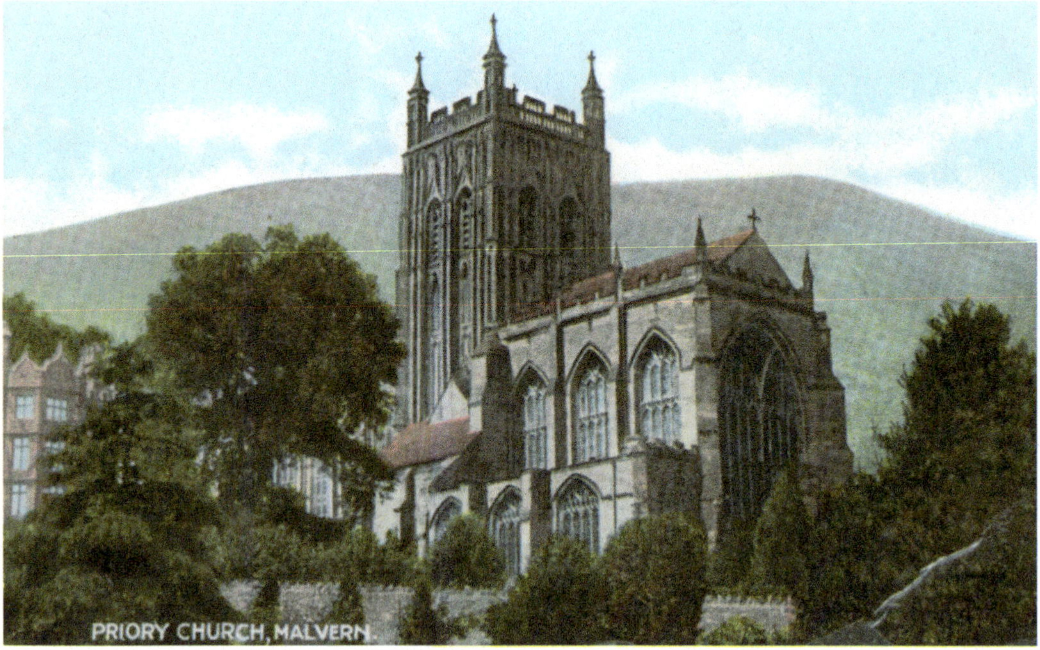

Great Malvern Priory, Malvern

William Longland, born in 1332 at Ledbury, was a monk at the Great Malvern Priory. Inspired by the Malvern Hills, he wrote *The Vision of William Concerning Piers the Plowman*, which remains one of the most important early works of English literature. Great Malvern Priory is divided between Norman and fifteenth-century Perpendicular work. The medieval glass in the windows is likened to that at York Minster in terms of importance.

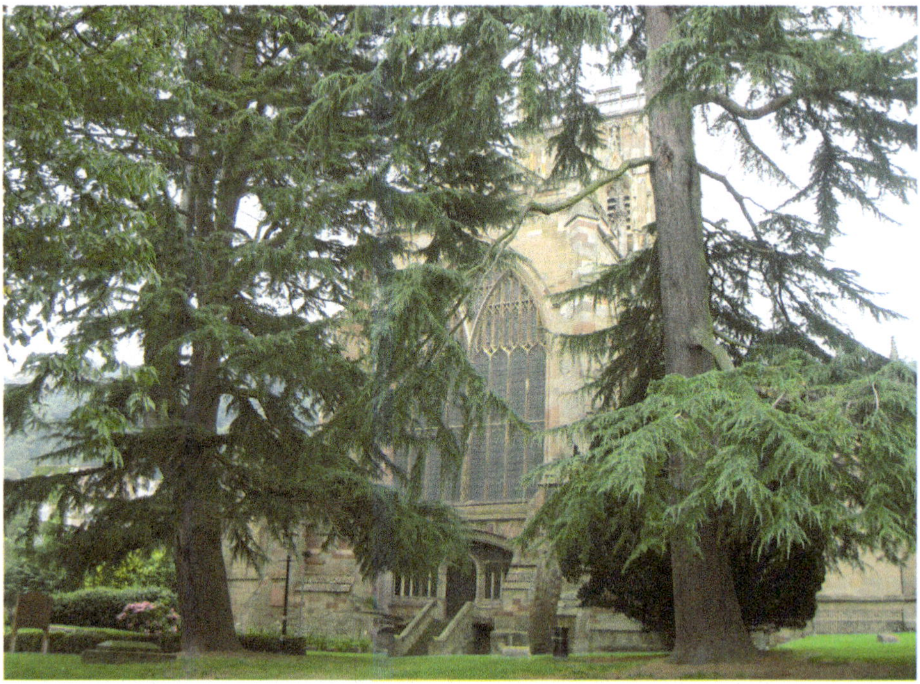

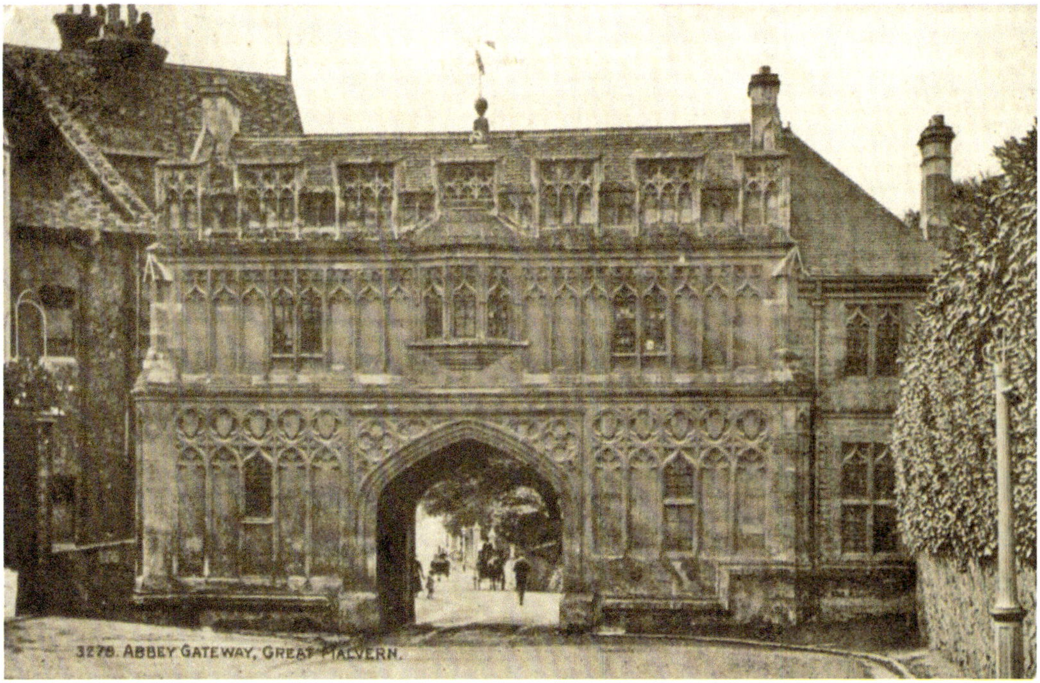

Abbey Gateway, Great Malvern

Written on the back of this delightful postcard view of the Abbey Gateway, Great Malvern, is: 'This is a view of the Abbey. It is a wonderful old building, but the best of all is inside it is simply glorious'. The postcard was sent in 1923.

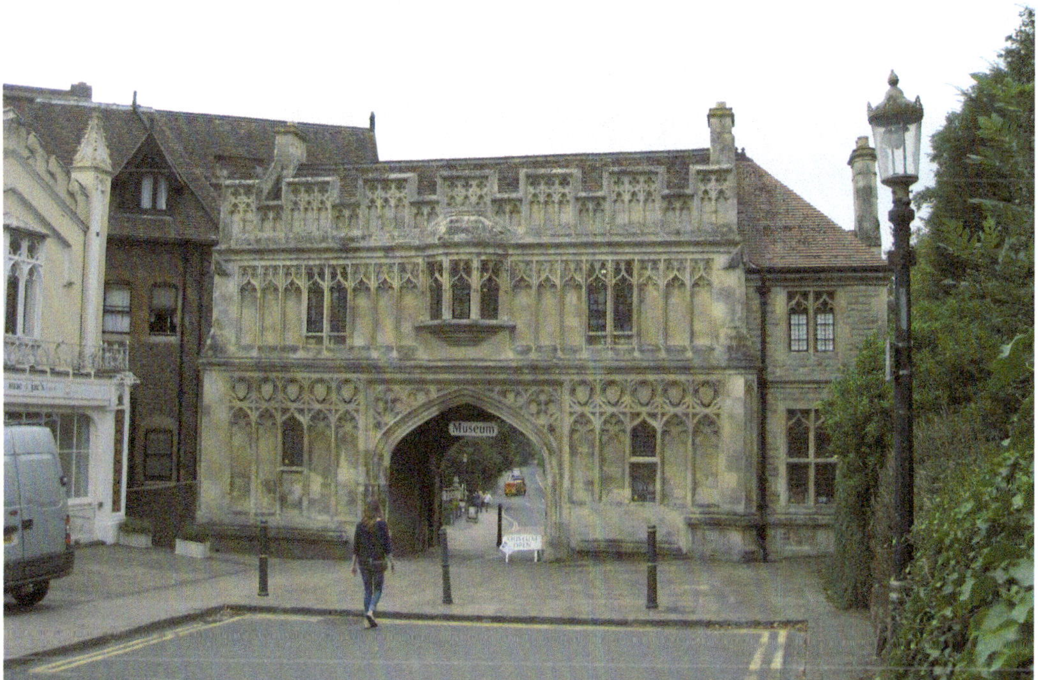

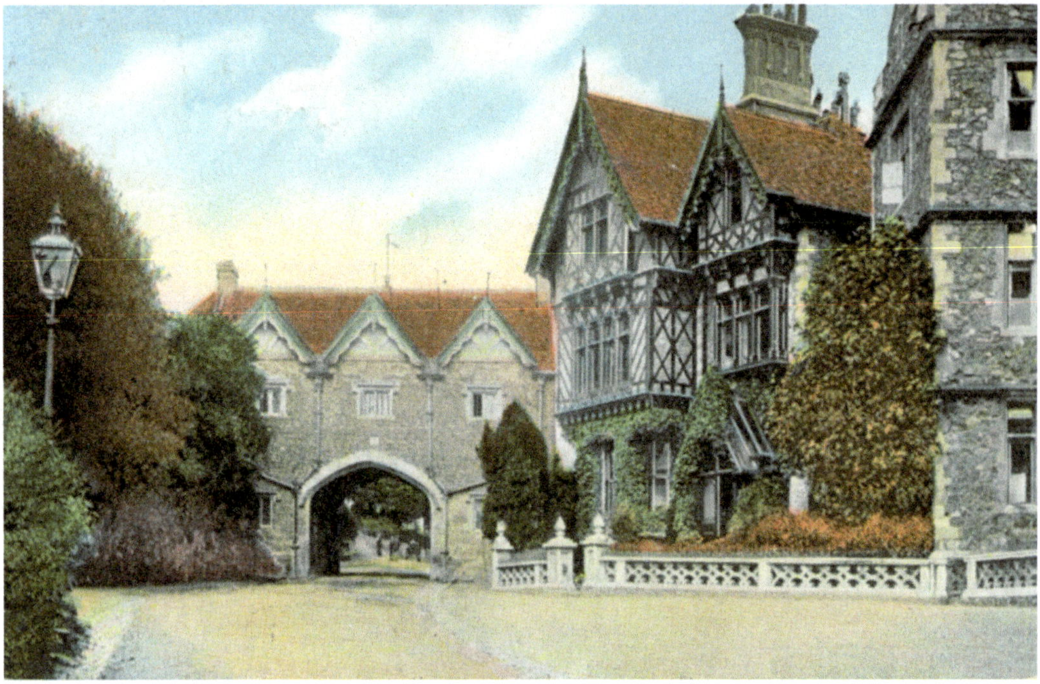

Abbey Gateway, Malvern

The view from the other side of the Abbey Gateway. It is a building that continues to inspire to this day, as the young man drawing highlights. The Gateway houses a museum.

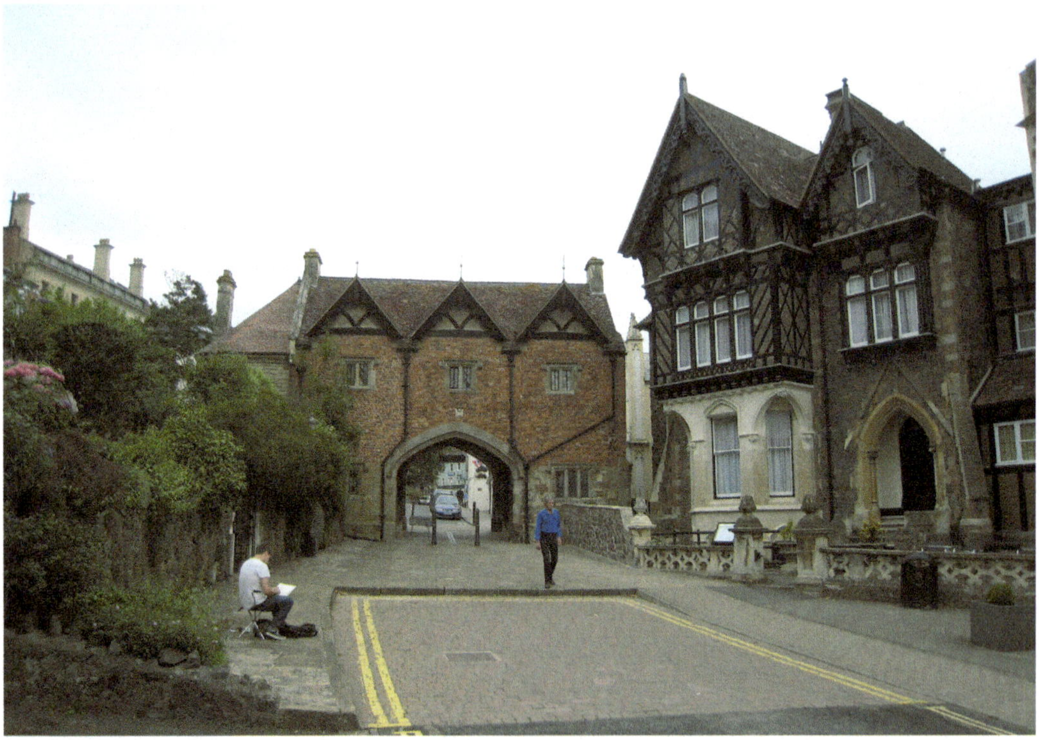

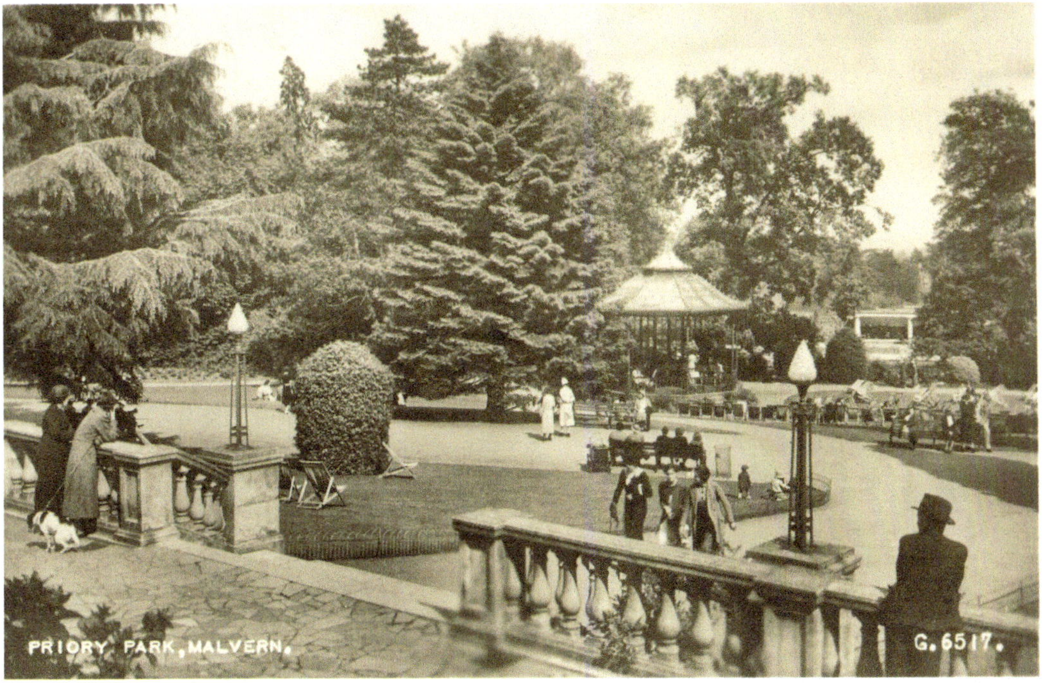

Priory Park, Malvern

Only the church and gatehouse remain of the priory, and here we see the lovely Priory Park. The demise of the priory came about as a result of Henry VIII's Dissolution of the Monasteries. Thanks to the generosity of Thomas Cromwell, the architect of the destruction of the building, the occupants, the prior and eleven monks were given pensions. The park remains a place to sit, walk and feed the ducks.

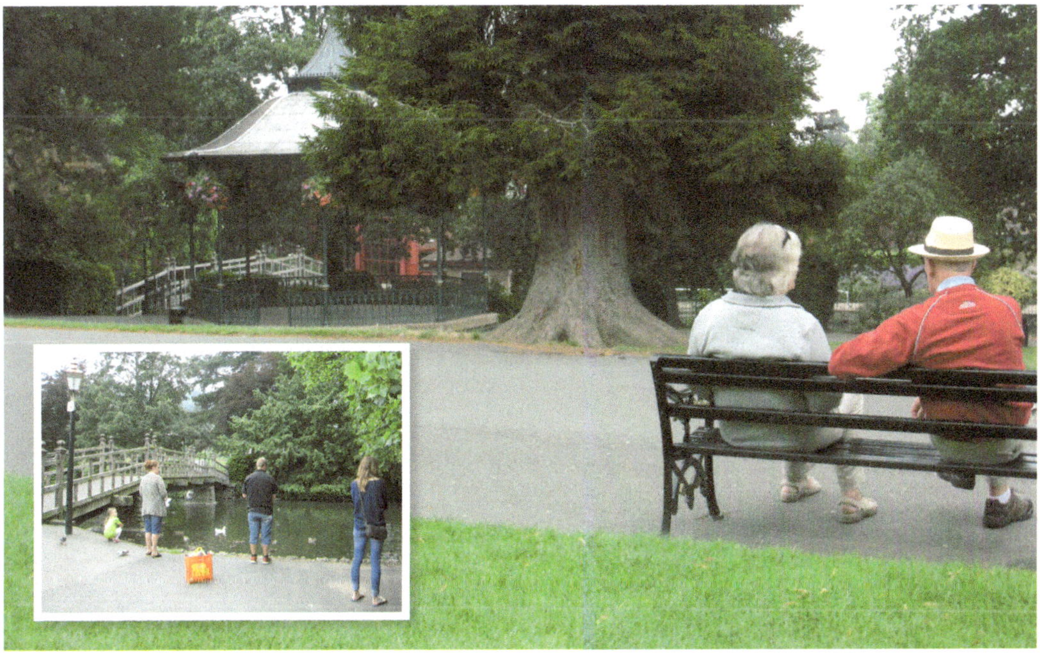

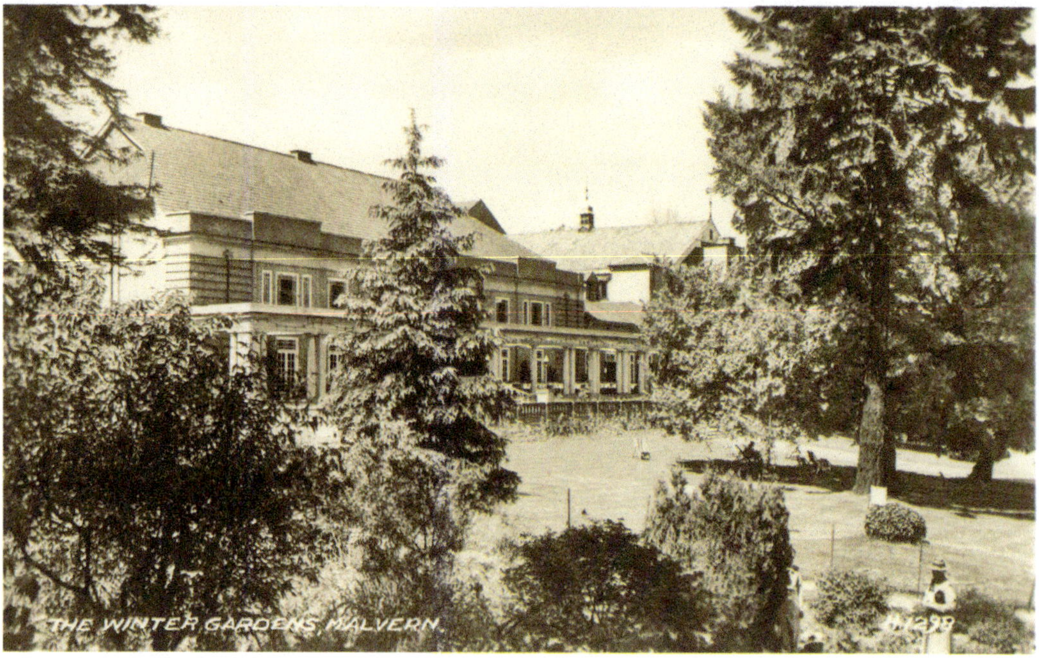

Winter Gardens, Malvern

Here we see the Malvern Winter Gardens, also known as Priory Park, with their flowerbeds and delightful buildings. At the time that the Domesday Book was compiled, this part of Worcestershire was described as a 'wilderness' because of its numerous and vast thickets.

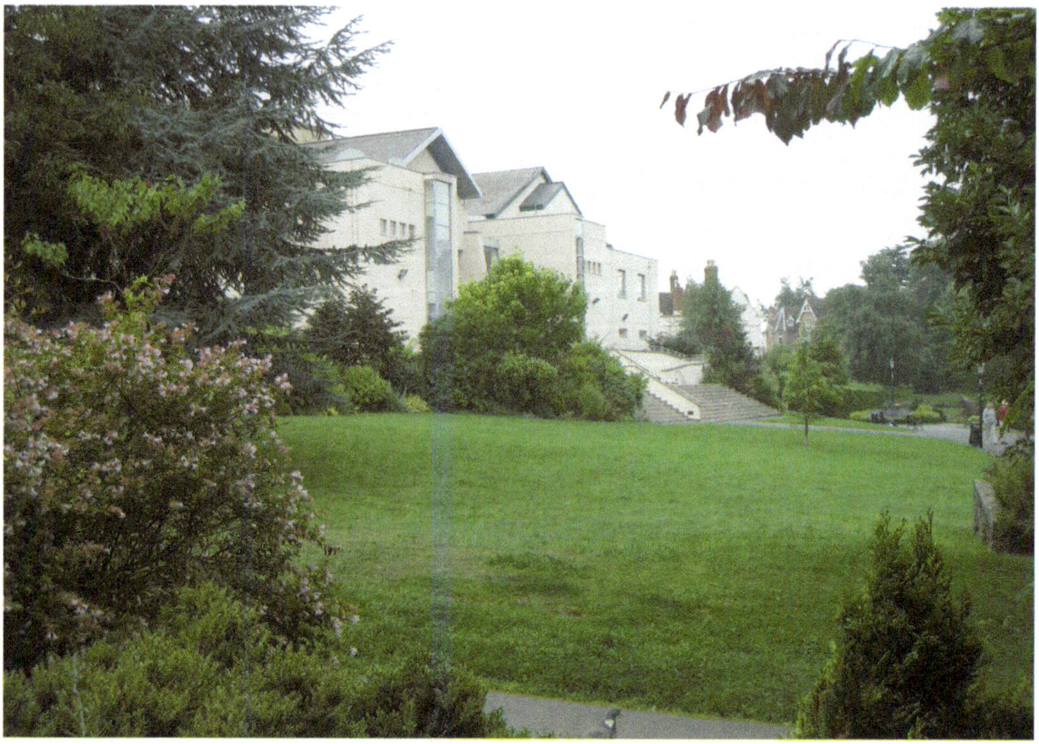

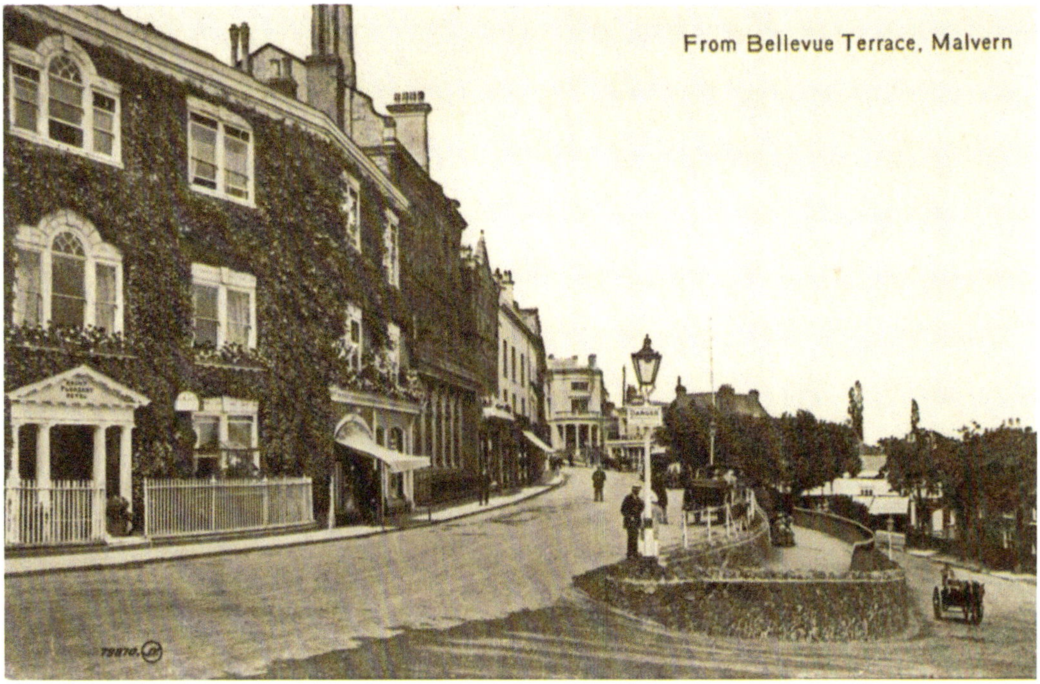

Bellevue Terrace, Malvern

Malvern, taken from Bellevue Terrace, has many claims to fame: it is the burial place of Sir Edward Elgar in Little Malvern and the medical values of the waters were renowned for the treatment of eye problems. Such well-known individuals as Charles Dickens, Carlyle, Gladstone and Florence Nightingale all came to Malvern to 'take the eye cure'.

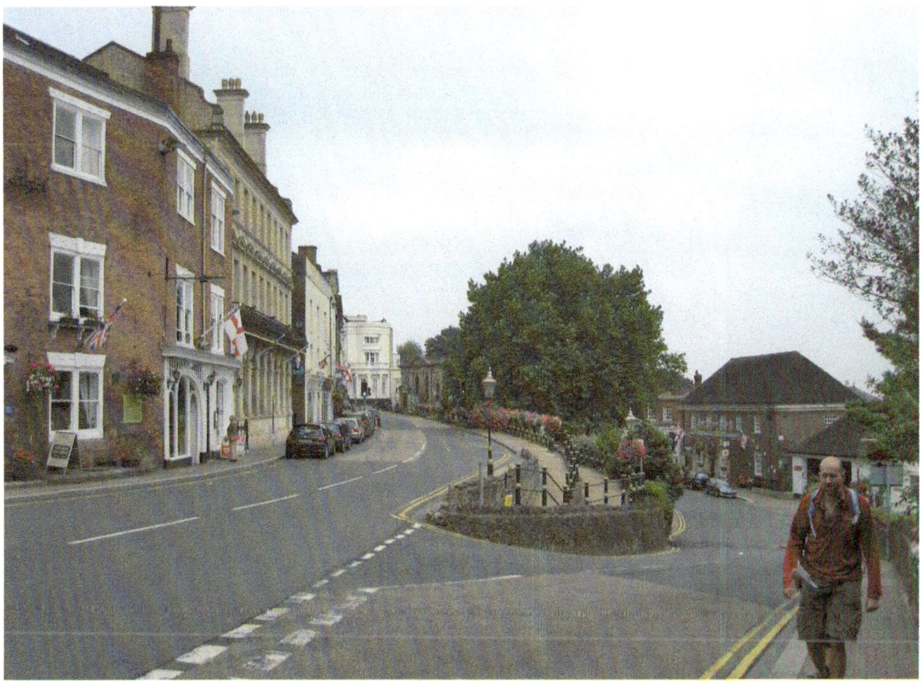

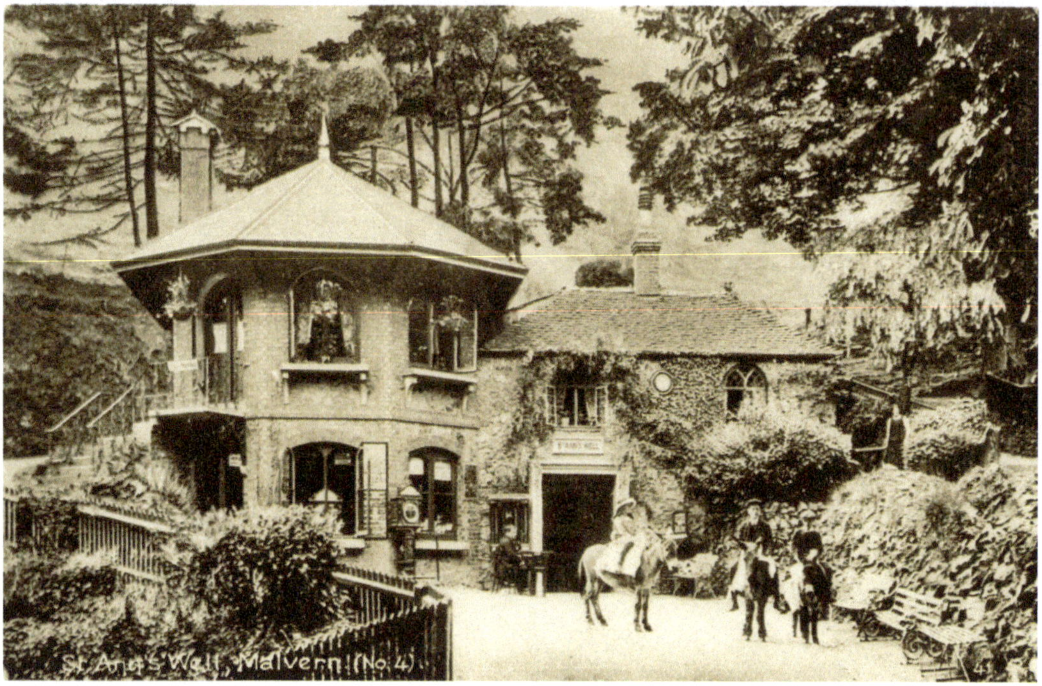

Holy Waters, Malvern

The medicinal values of the waters around Malvern have been appreciated by the local inhabitants for years. In fact, they go back centuries and in 1756, Doctor John Wall published a paper on the purity of these waters, which were well known for the successful treatment of people with eye problems.

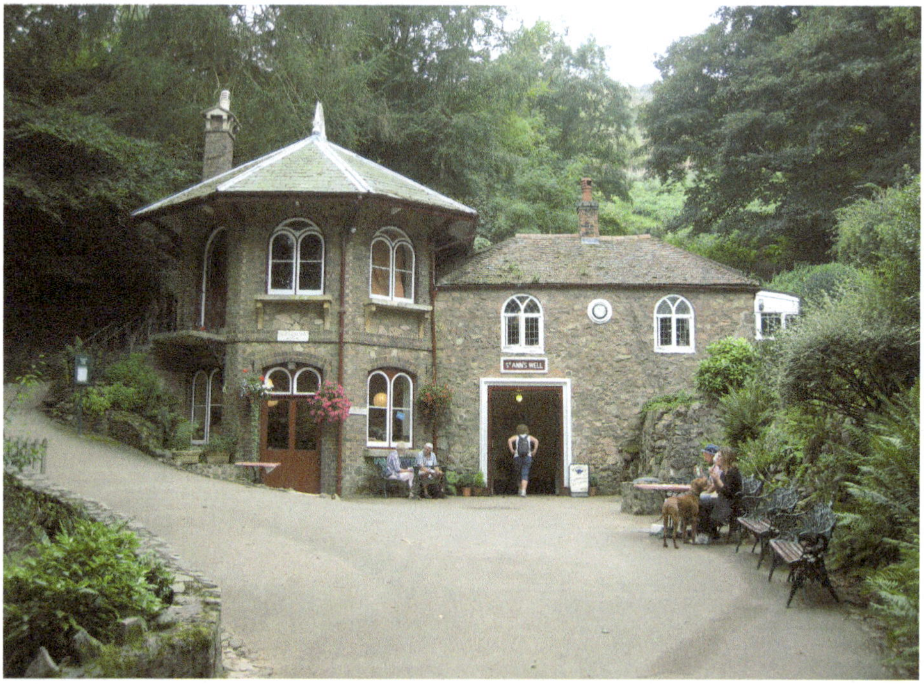

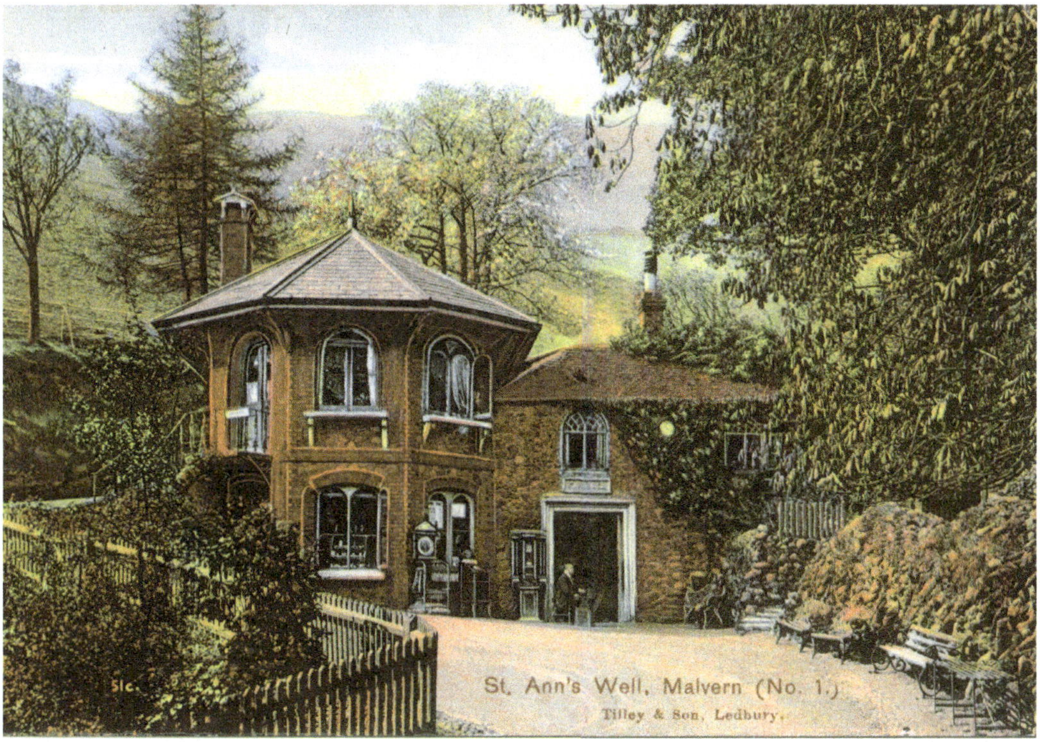
51c.
St. Ann's Well, Malvern (No. 1.)
Tilley & Son, Ledbury.

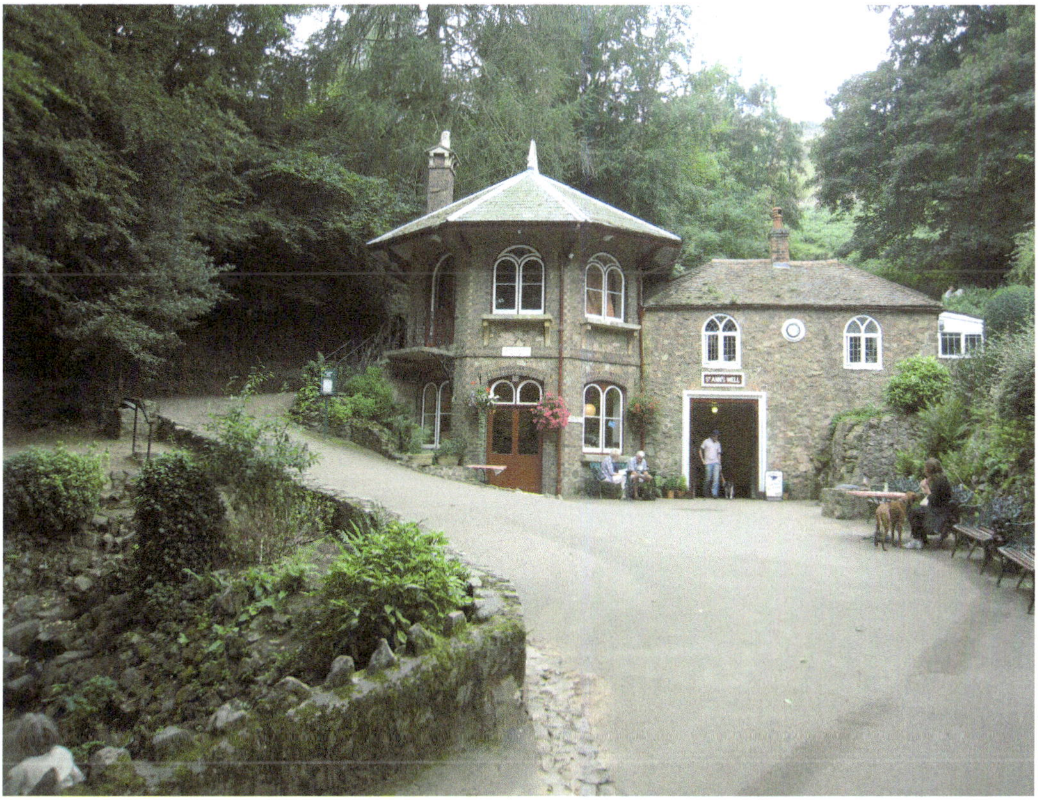

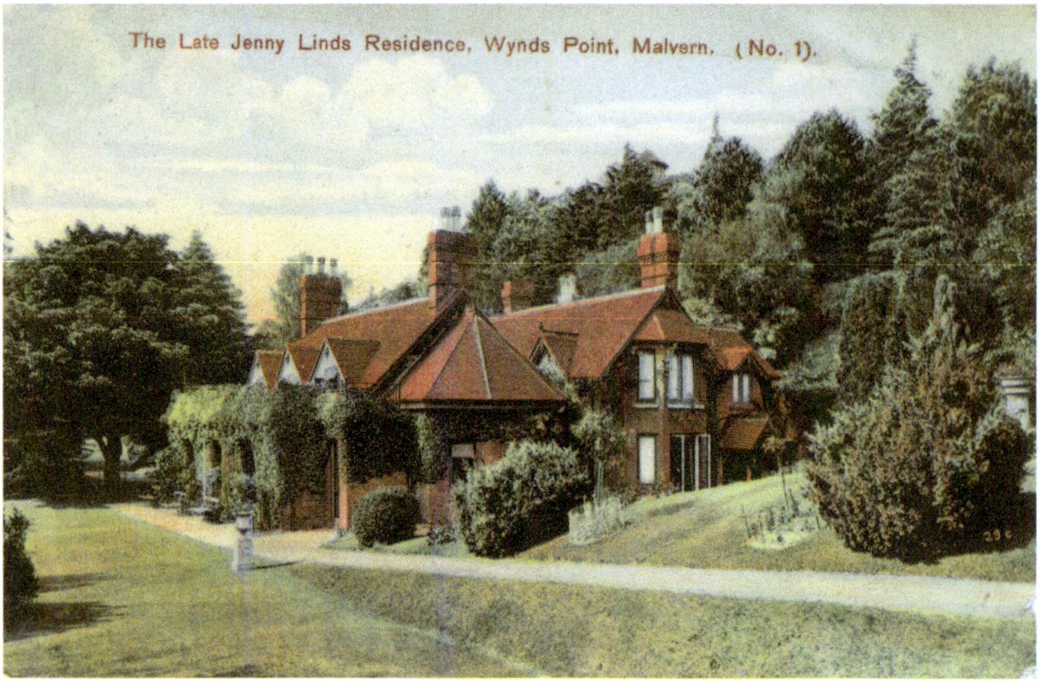

Wynds Point

Mention the 'Swedish Nightingale' and thoughts turn to Jenny Lind, a singer and musical patron, whose residence was Wynds Point on the Malvern Hills. Below, a view of Malvern from the hill behind St Ann's Well.

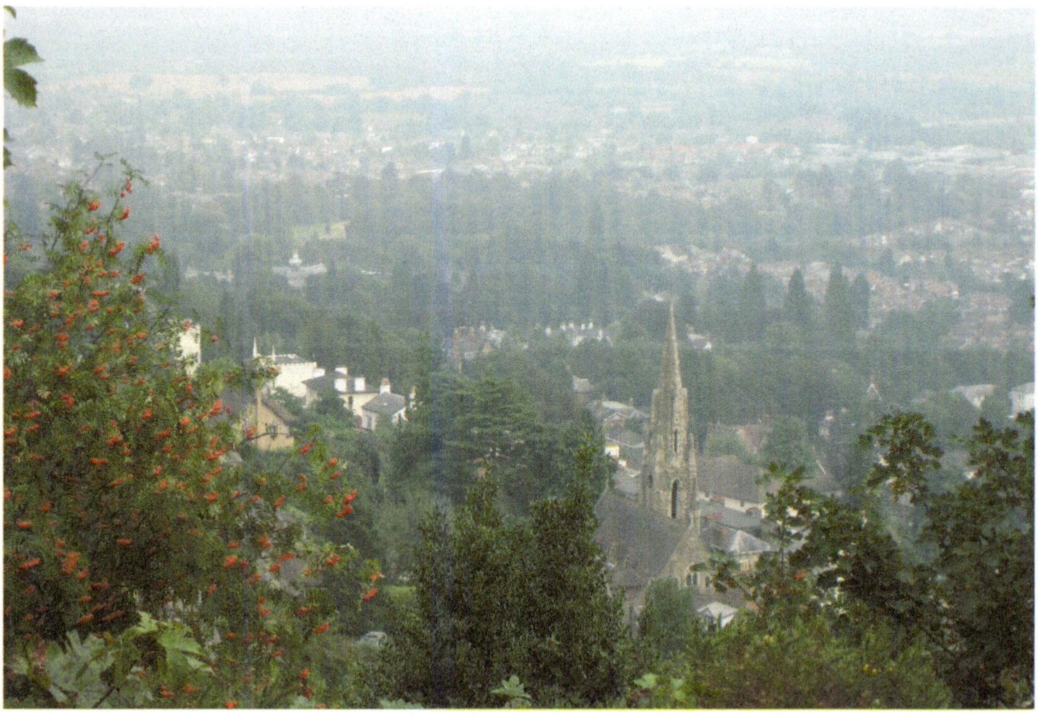

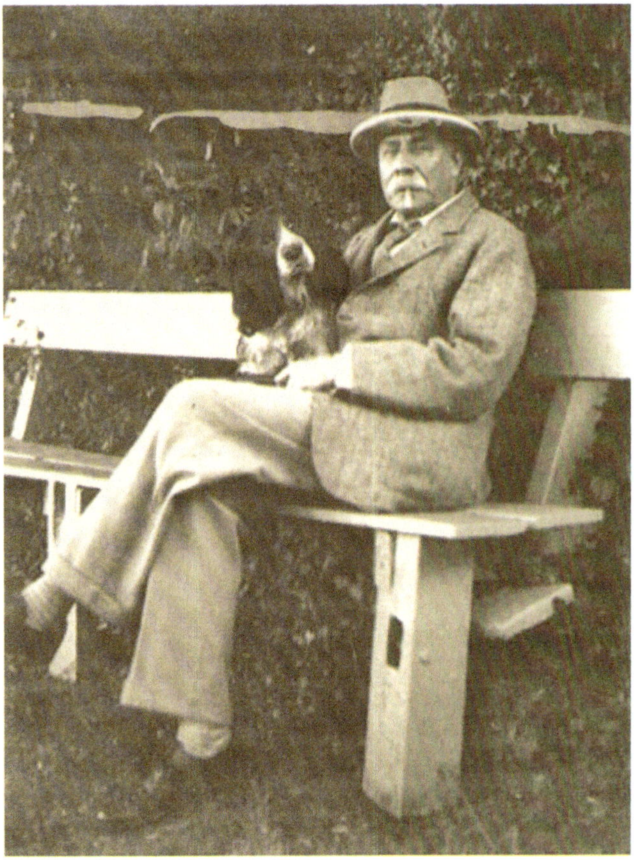

Sir Edward Elgar, Malvern
Think of the Malvern Hills and you think of Sir Edward Elgar and his *Enigma Variations*. One of the constants of Elgar's life was his love of the countryside, his native Worcestershire and his beloved Malvern Hills.

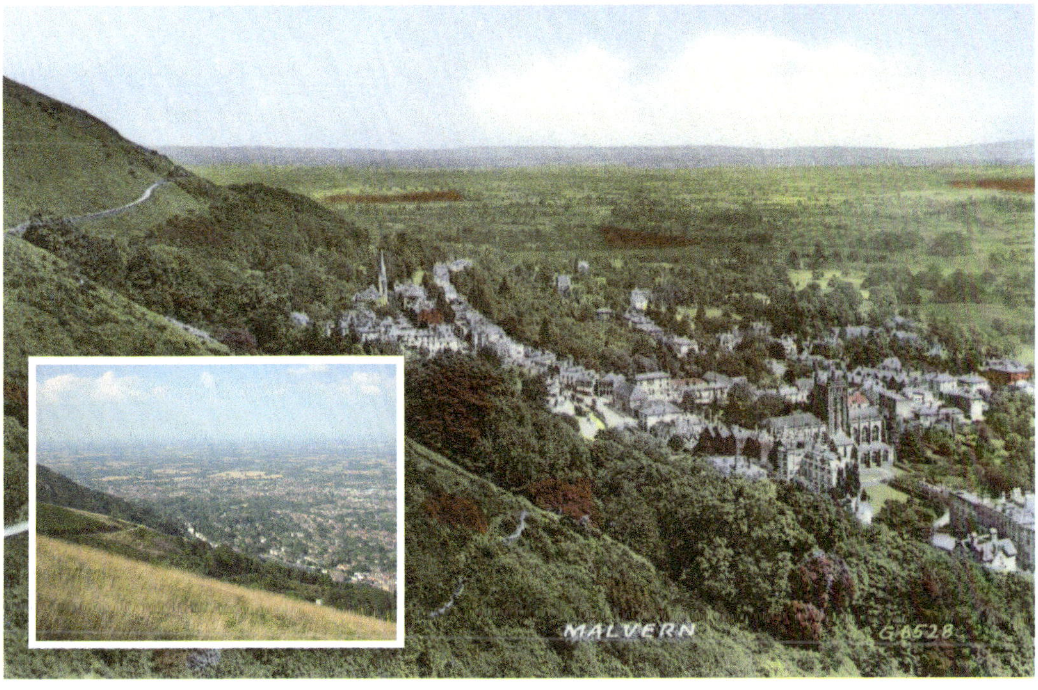

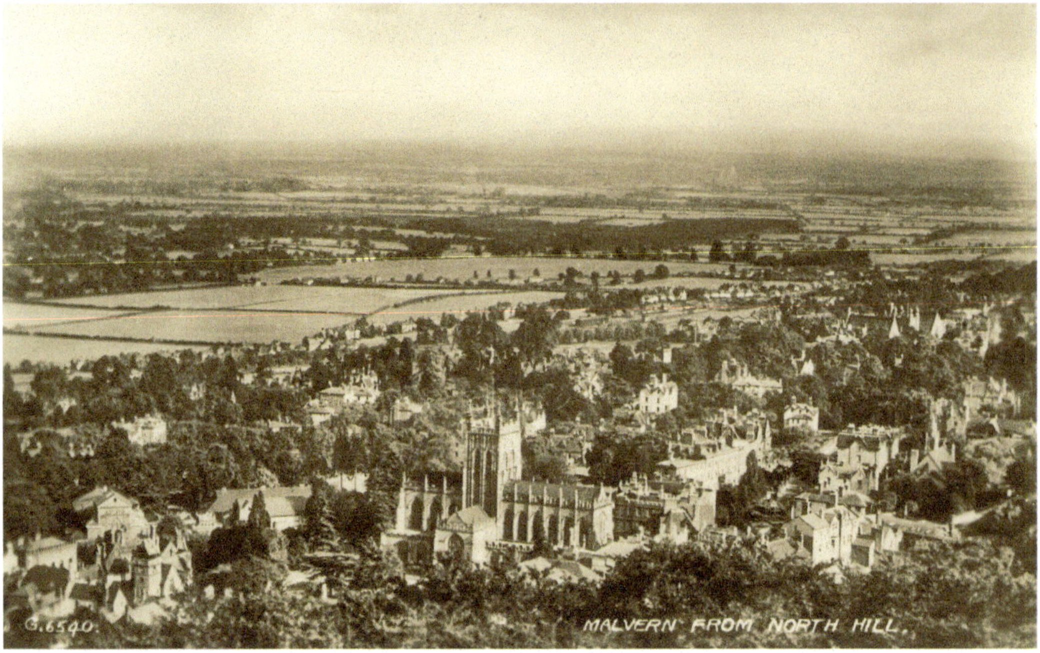

Malvern from North Hill

Malvern from the North Hill, 397 metres above sea level. Malvern has always been a tourist attraction and the bottom postcard, sent on 2 August 1916, is a fine example of a holiday card. The caption on the back of the postcard reads: 'Can't afford to send you anything much but hope this line will be useful to you.' My, how times change!

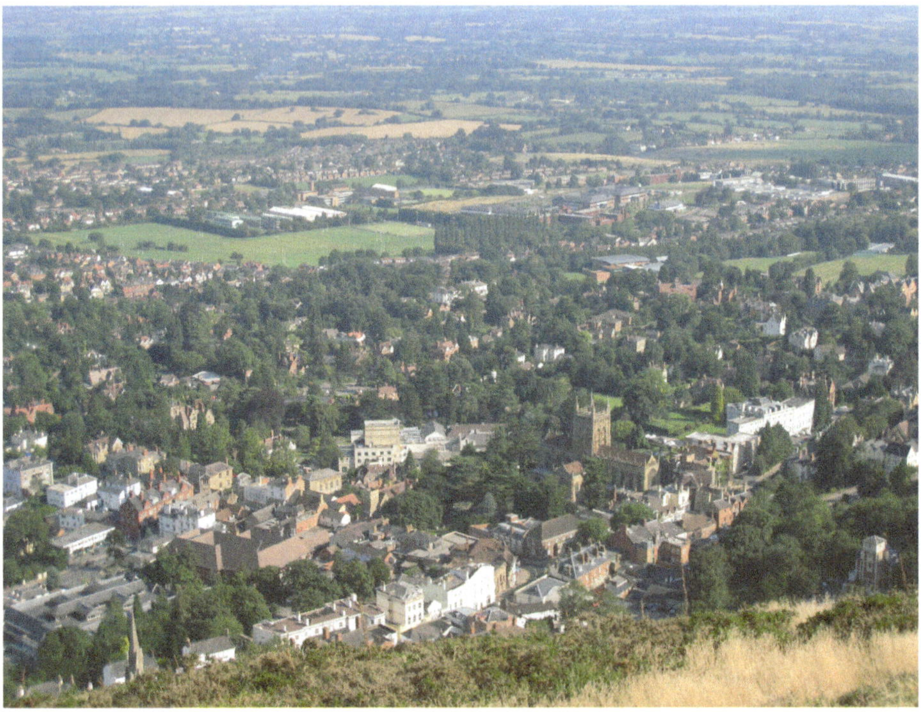

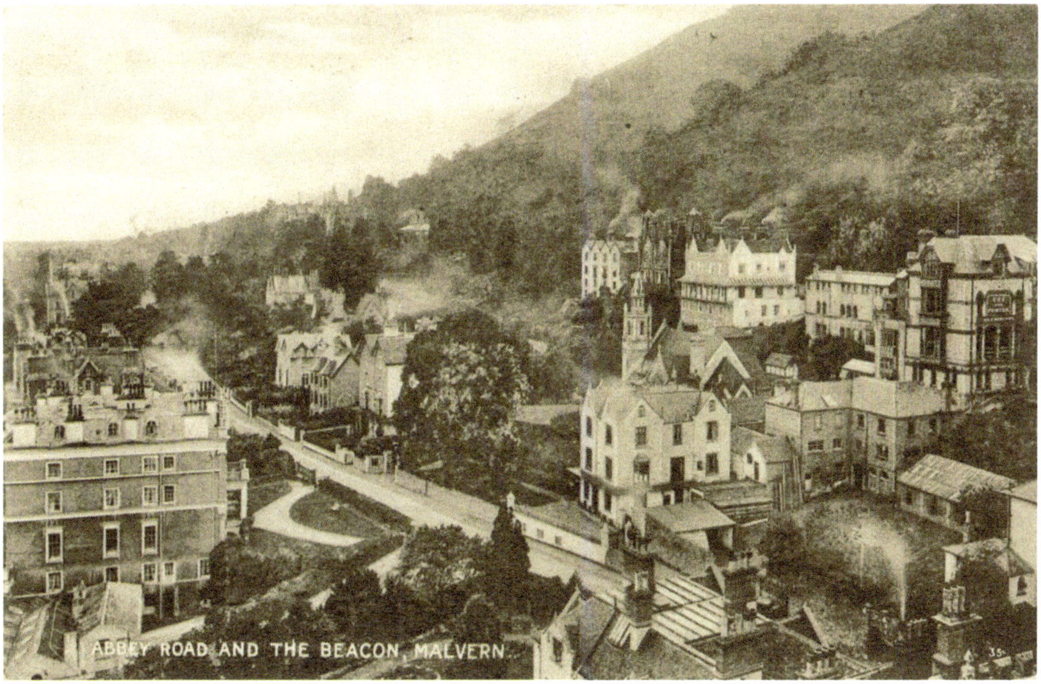

Abbey Road, Malvern

The Abbey Road and the Beacon, Malvern, provide a charming insight into early Malvern. The card was sent from the Foley Arms Hotel, Great Malvern. Below, a view of Malvern and the Beacon from North Hill.

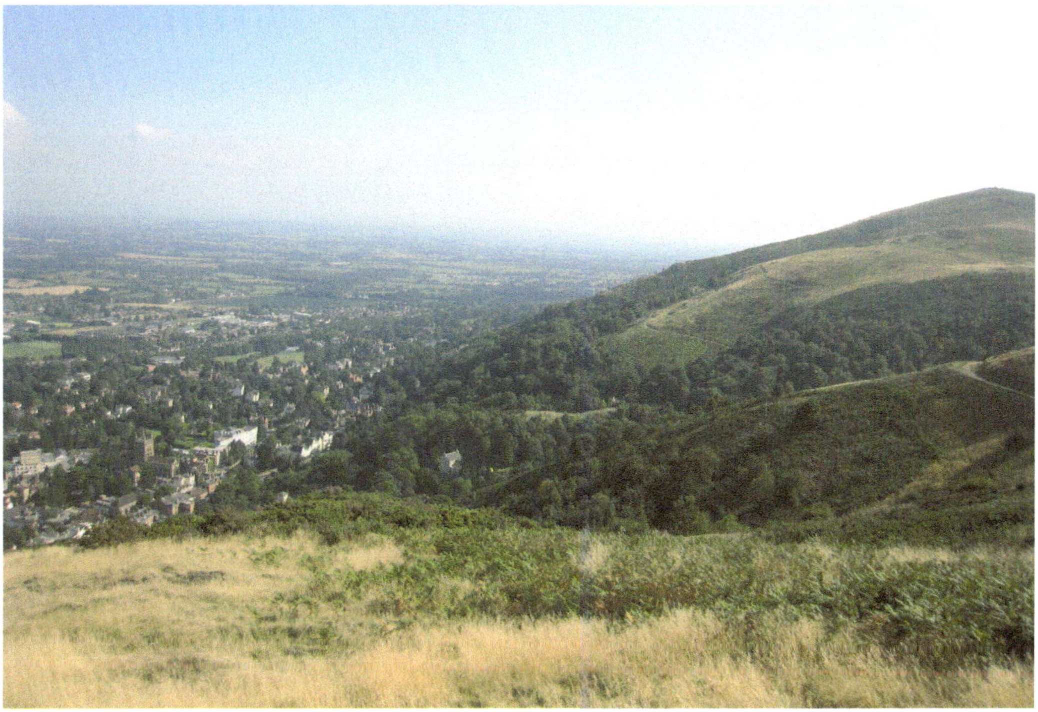

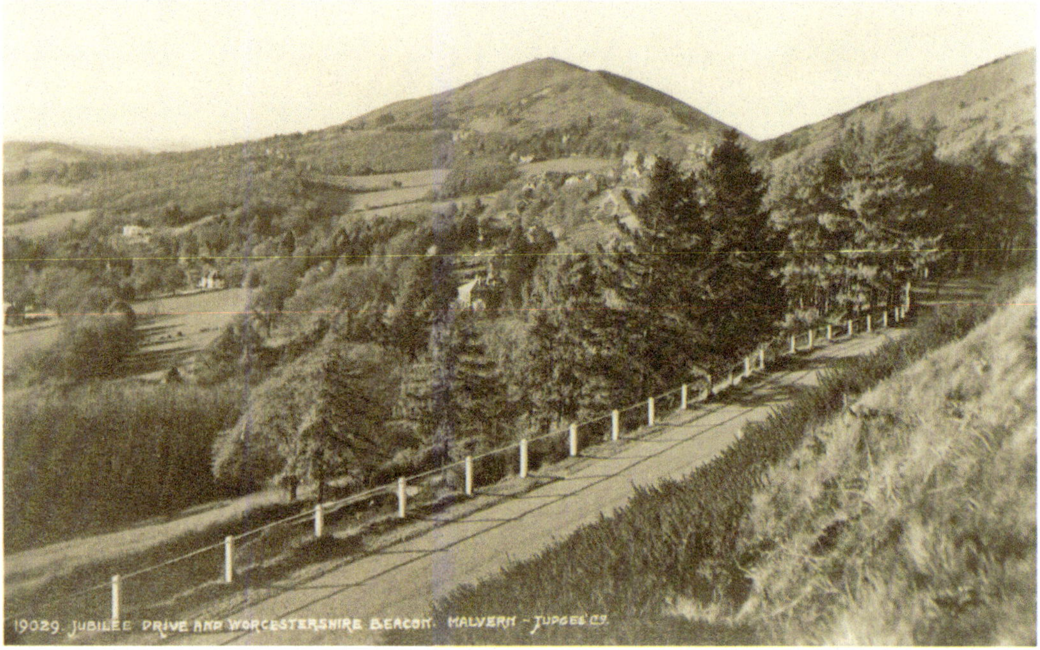

Jubilee Drive

A lovely view of the Jubilee Drive, which leads to the Beacon on the Malvern Hills. The arrival of the railway in the 1840s was to make Malvern its fortune, as it attracted visitors from all over the country.

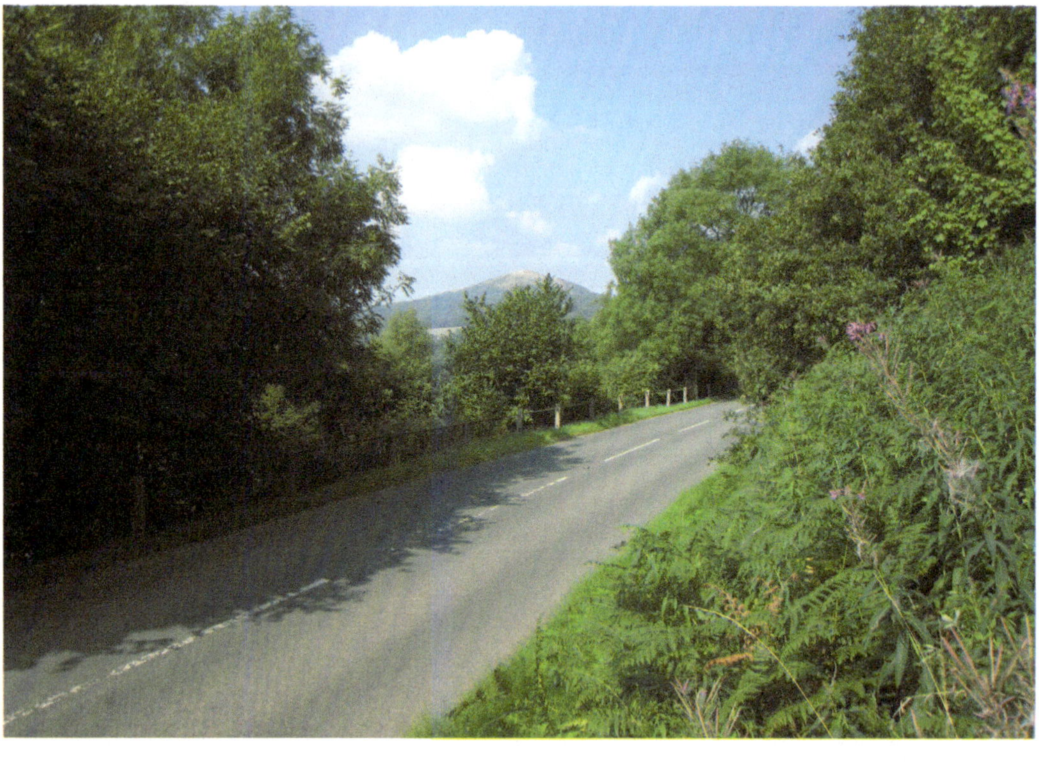

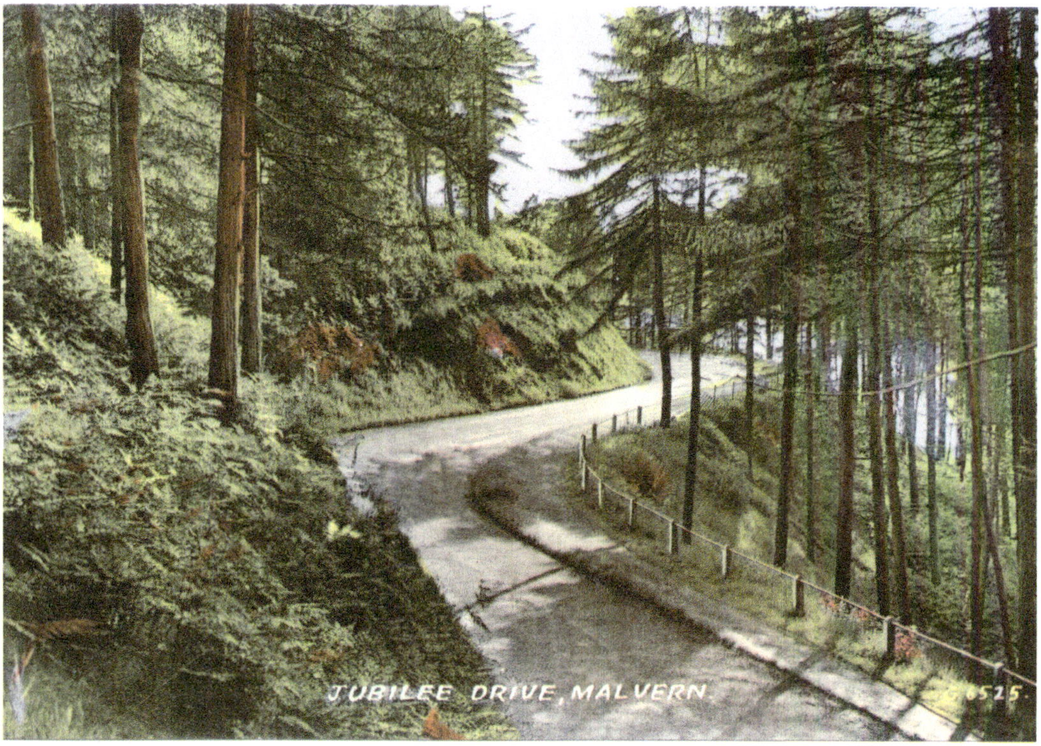
JUBILEE DRIVE, MALVERN
6525.

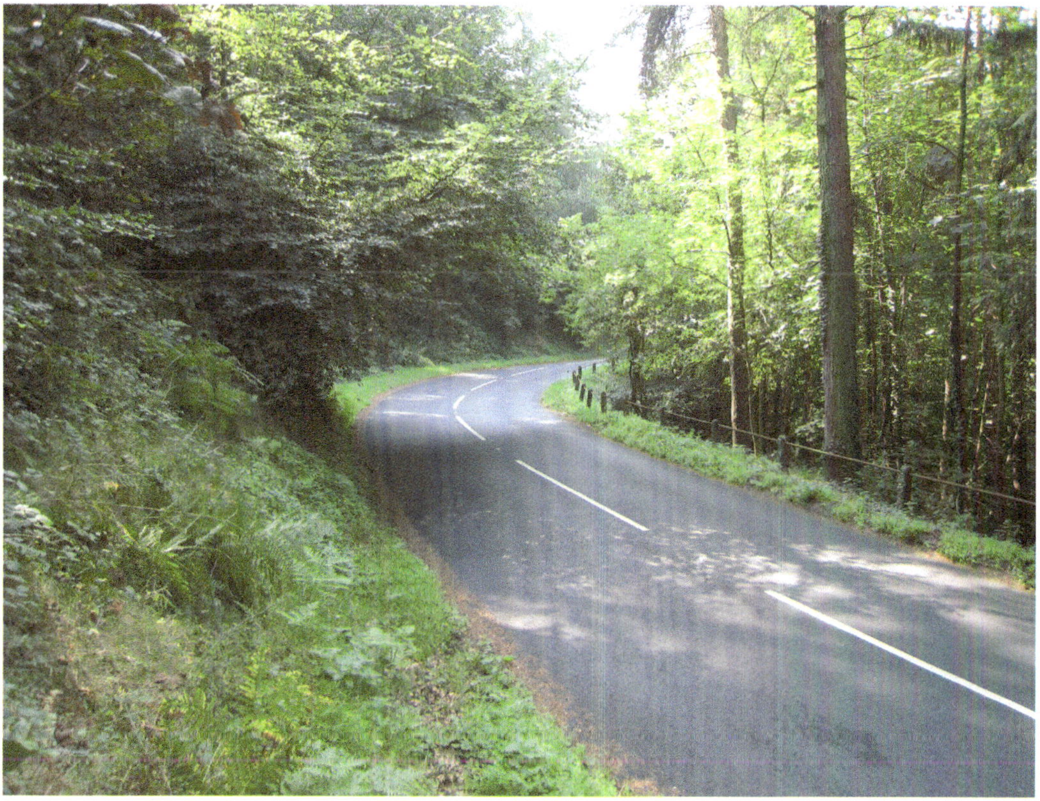

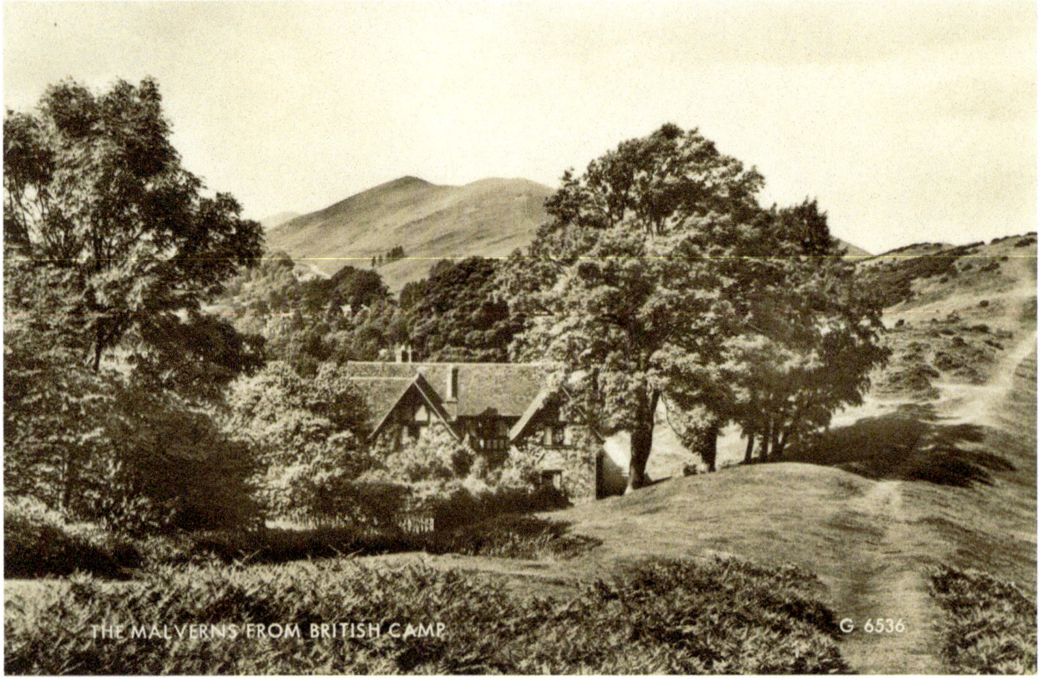

The British Camp

Here we see the Malverns from British Camp. The major tree growth has made the same view very difficult to replicate. The building can just be seen in the trees to the left, and more clearly in the inset.

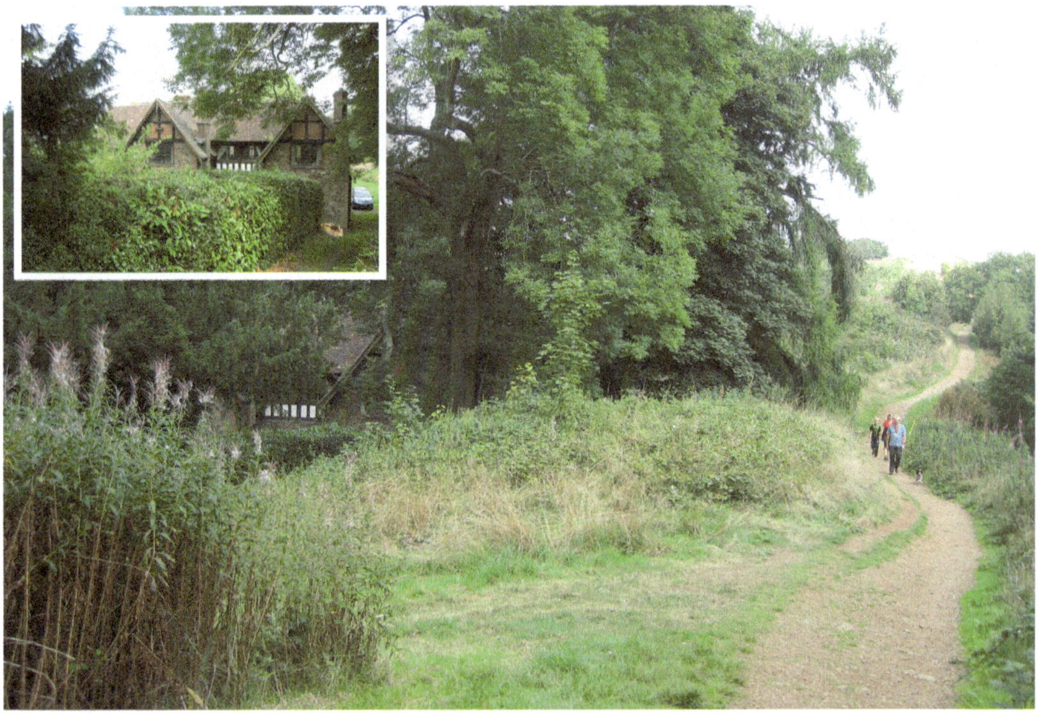

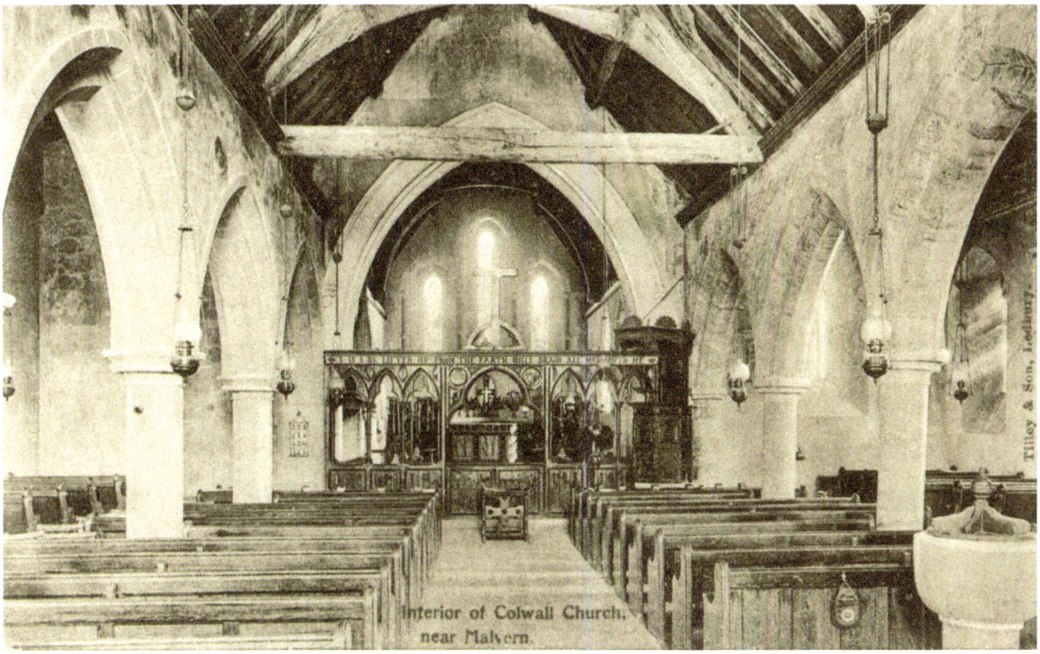

Colwall

Standing on the Herefordshire and Worcestershire border is the village of Colwall. The village nestles into the side of the Malvern Hills and commands a wonderful view of the Iron Age British Camp. The Colwall tunnels were dug beneath the Malvern Hills between 1856 and 1860, and there is a single track between Great Malvern and Ledbury railway station. Here we see the interior of Colwall church, near Malvern.

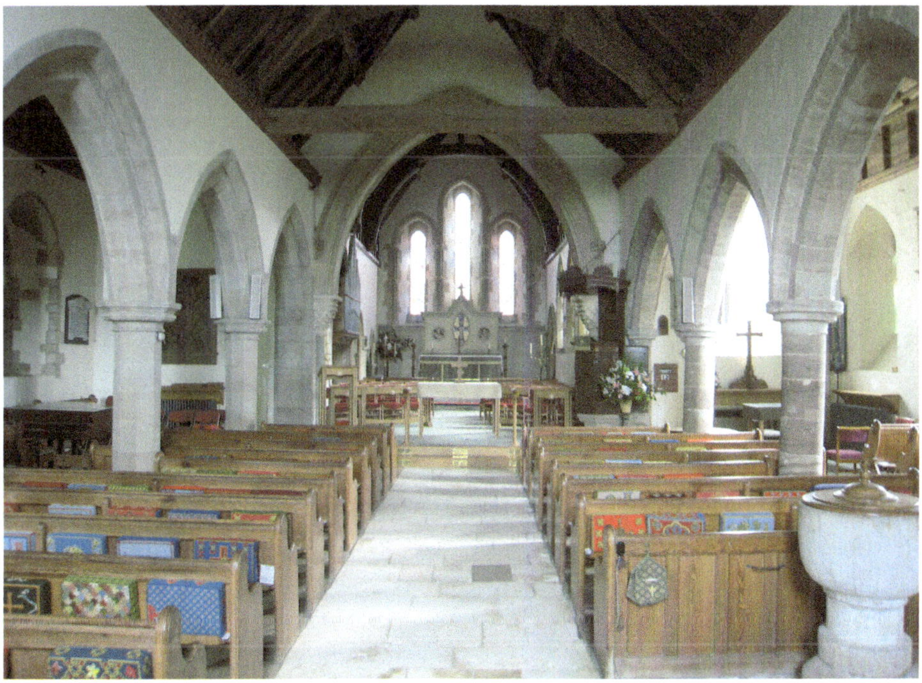

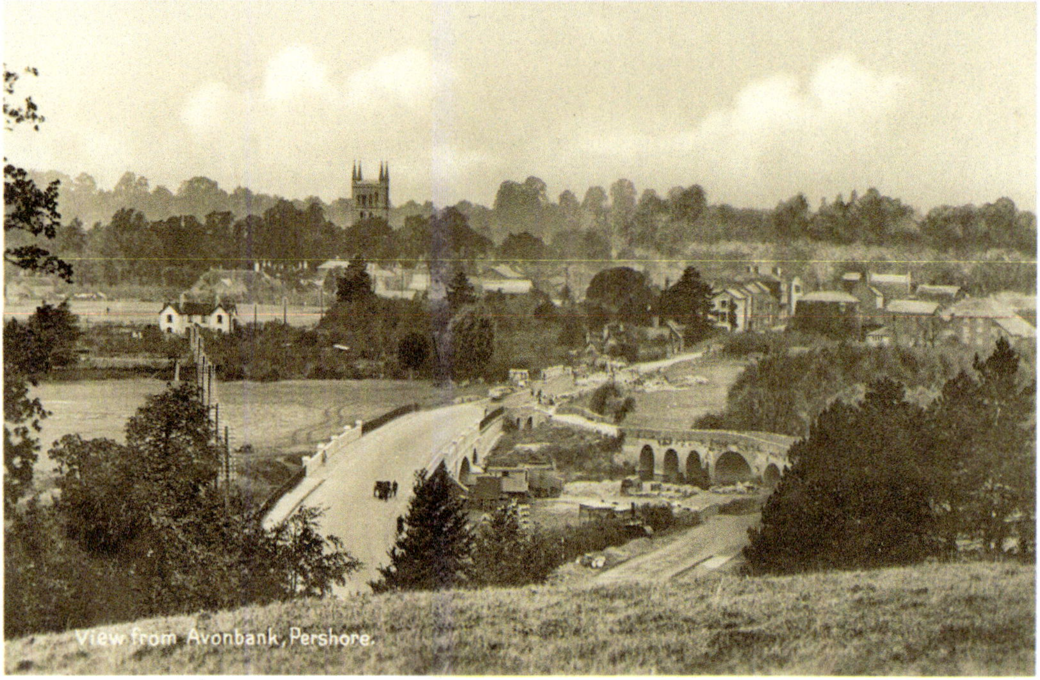

View from Avonbank, Pershore

Here we see a view of the River Avon from Avon Bank, Pershore. The market town of Pershore is well known for its abbey, college and plums! Part of the abbey dates from the eleventh century. The current structure of the abbey is smaller than the original building, due to the destruction of the nave during the reign of Henry VIII at the Dissolution. Below, the old and new bridges.

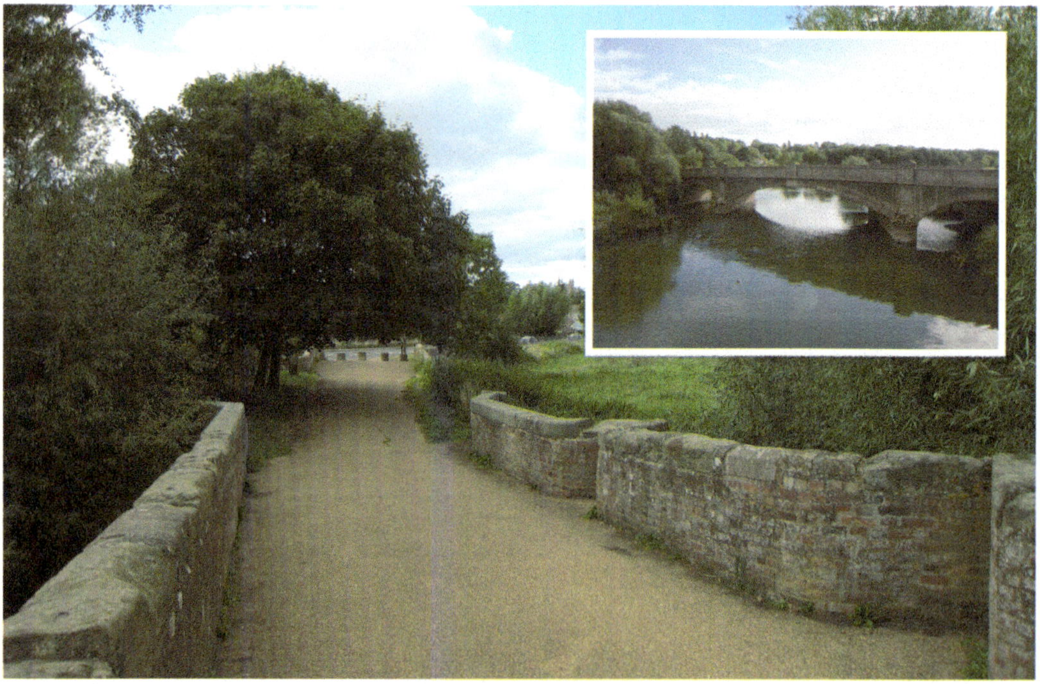

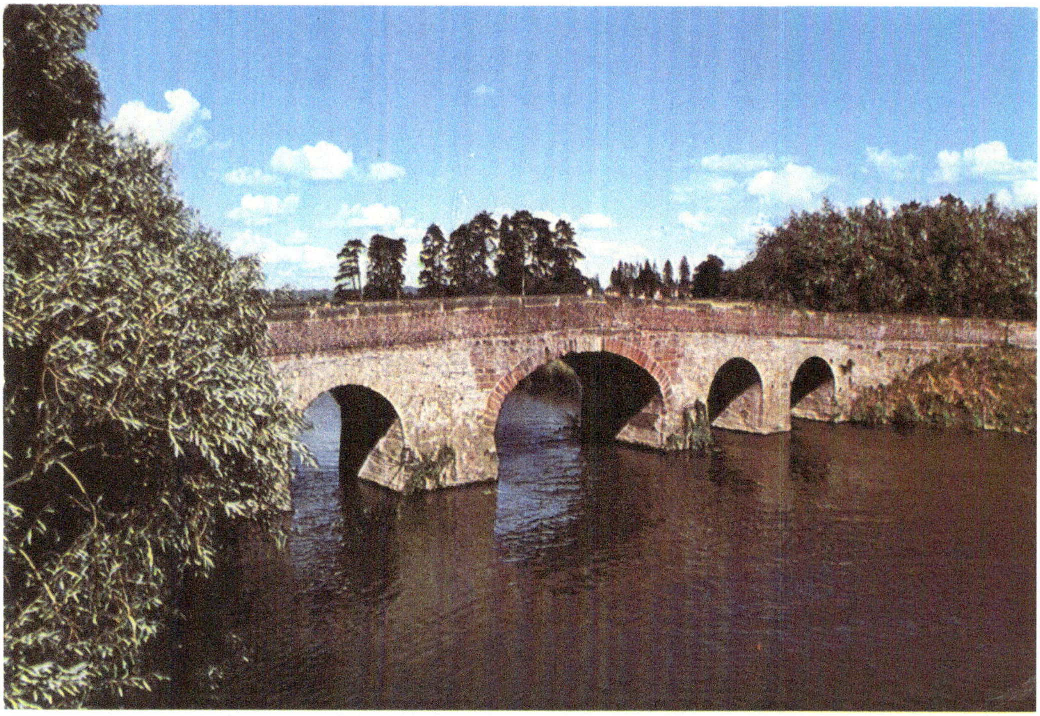

Old Bridge, Pershore
Situated 6 miles west of Evesham and 6 miles east of Upton-upon-Severn is the Vale of Evesham, and Pershore stands on the River Avon. A district rich in fruit and vegetables, the town lies midway between Worcester and Evesham. Here we see the old bridge that spans the River Avon.

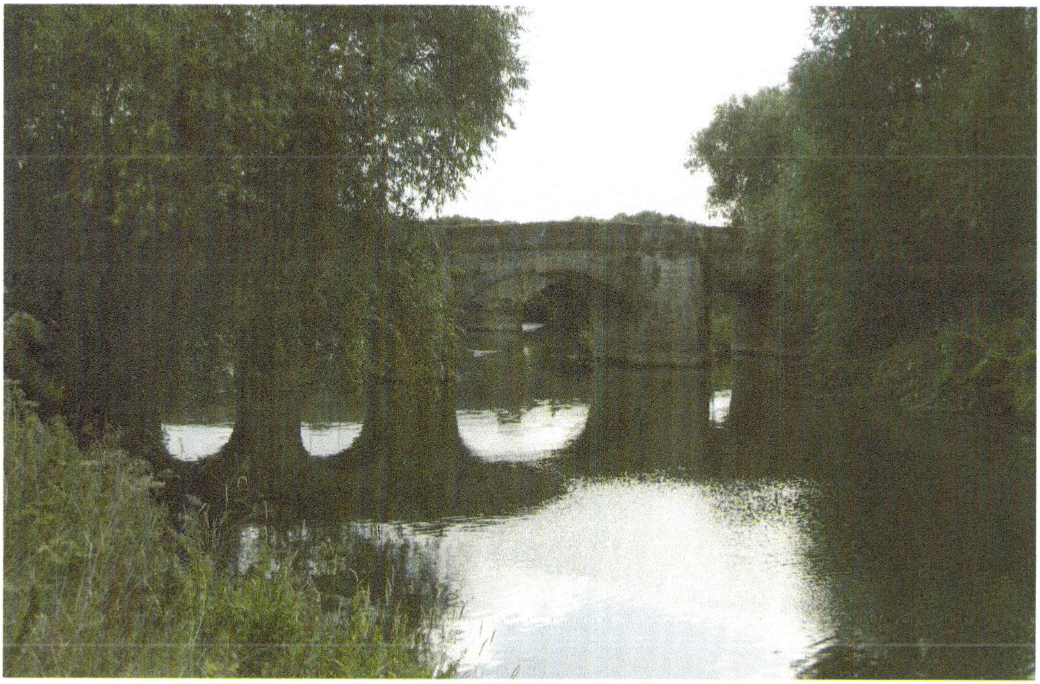

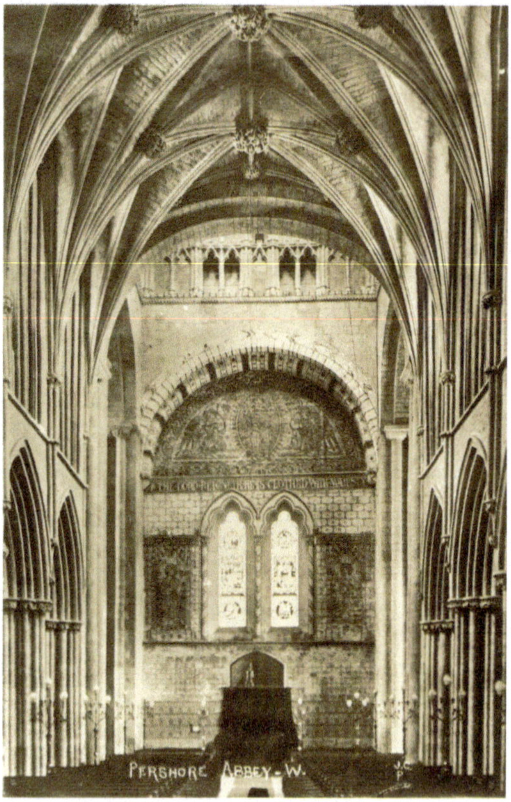

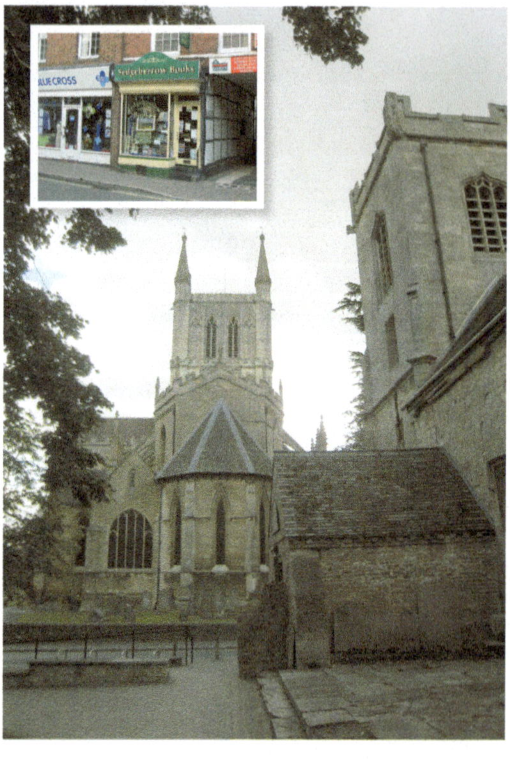

Abbey, Pershore

A religious house was founded in Pershore around 689. The Normans transformed the Benedictine abbey into one of England's greatest Christian establishments, but sadly all that is left today is a truncated church, a reminder of the great abbey that once stood there. The high street holds a number of shops, including Sedgeberrow Books.

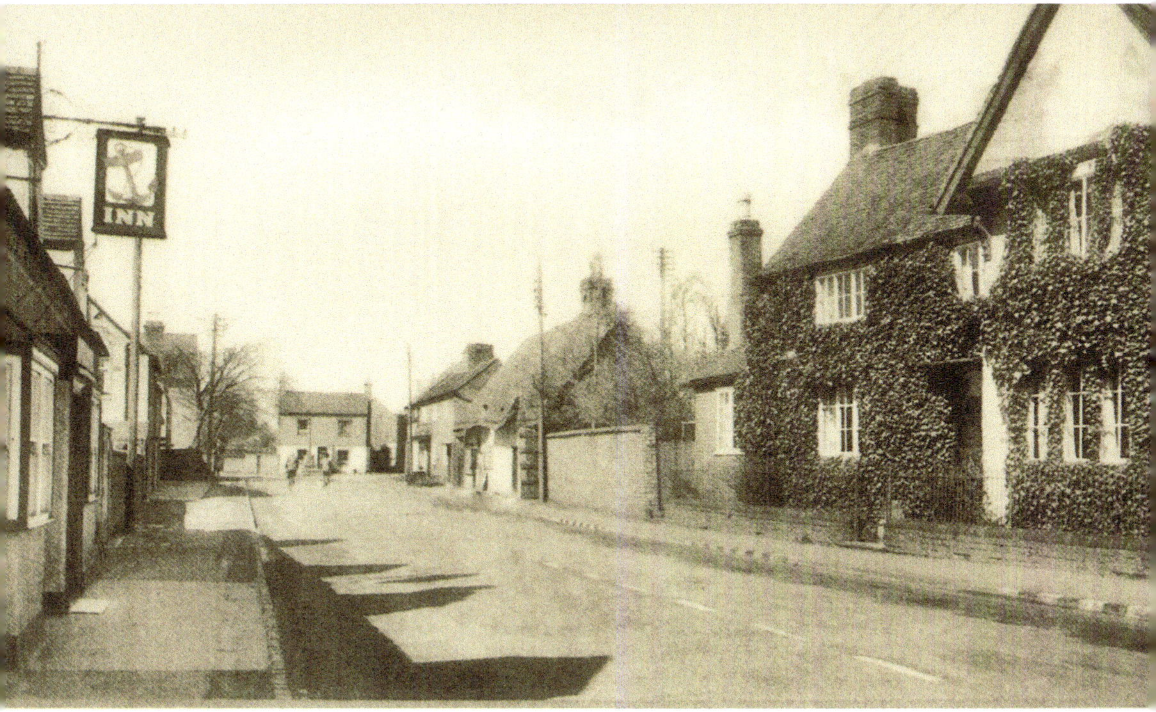

Wyre Piddle

As little girls, my sister and I would giggle away on the back seat of the car as our father drove us through Wyre Piddle! The village has changed considerably since those days, I hasten to say. The church was built on the site of a prehistoric burial ground in 1888. The font is twelfth century and some excellent examples of fifteenth-century glass can be found inside.

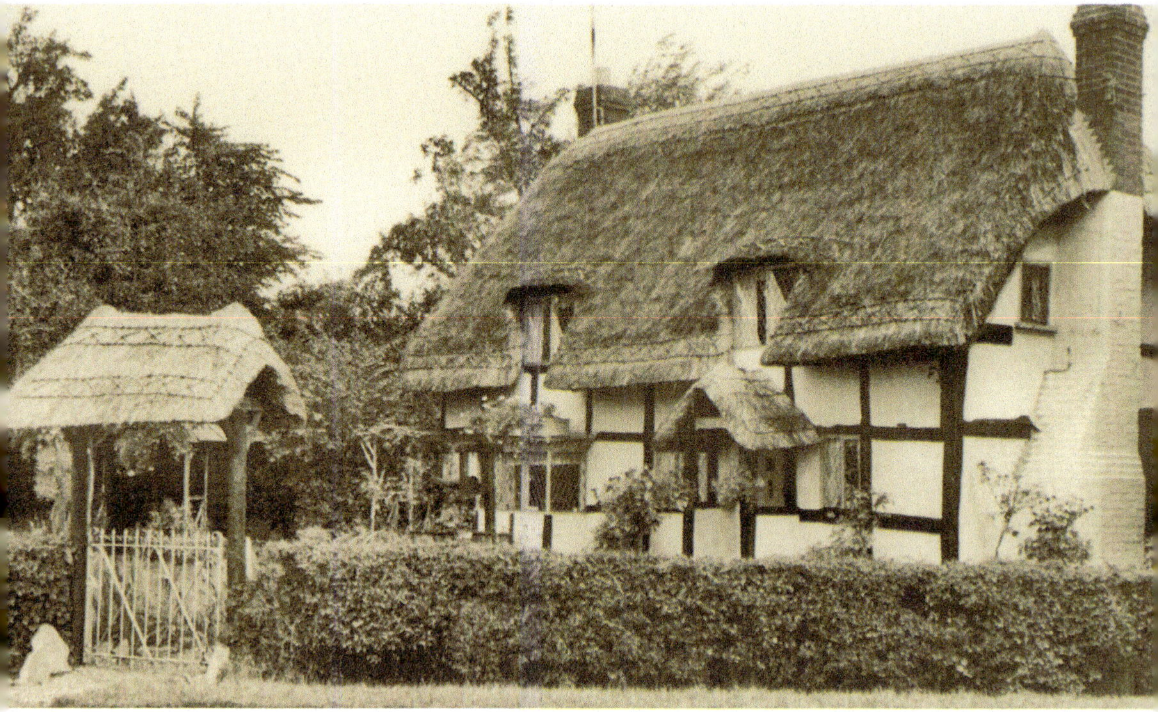

Great Comberton

I am always enthralled and enchanted with thatched cottages and this one is no exception. This charming old house stands in Great Comberton, a village whose old parish runs from the River Avon to the summit of Bredon Hill. The village library (*inset*) is well stocked.

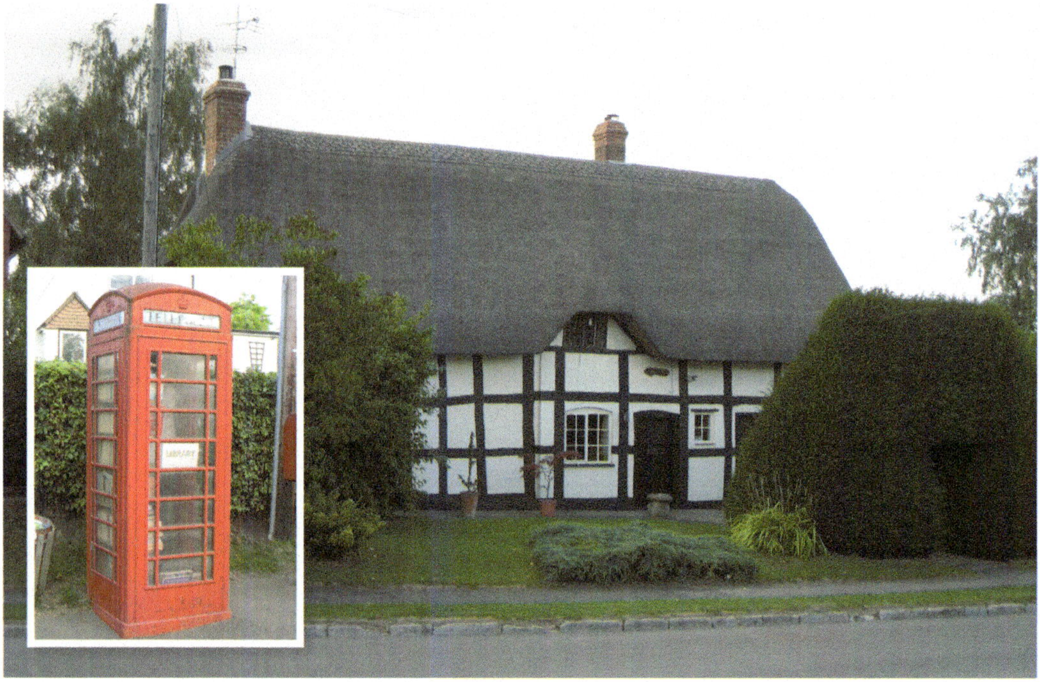

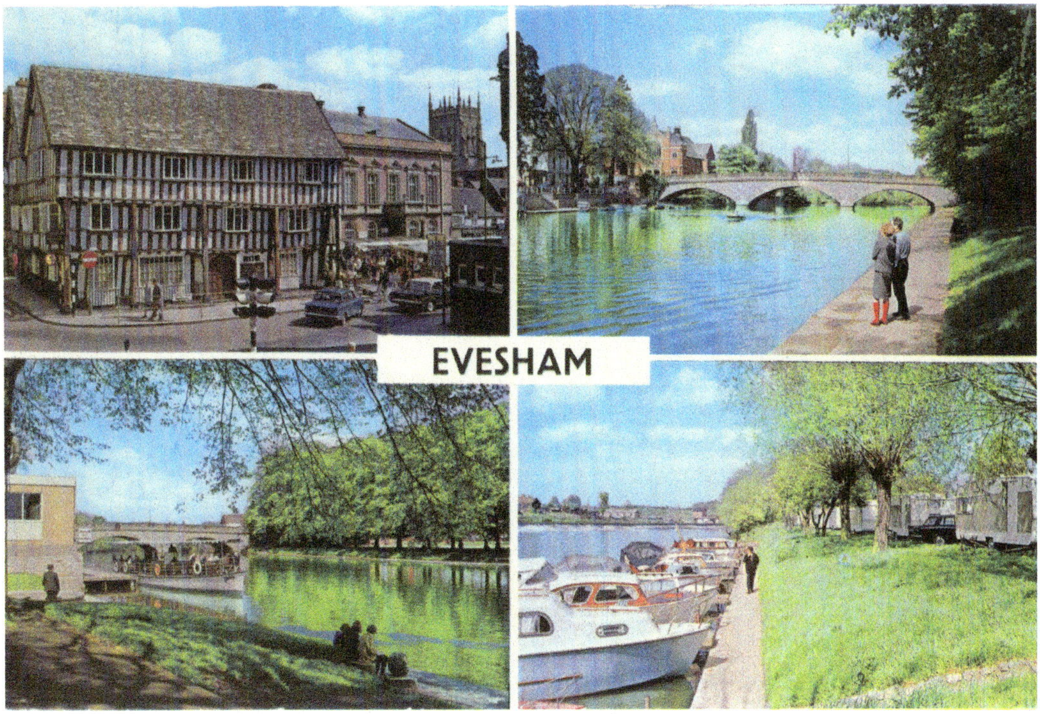

Evesham Multi-View

I love these old coloured postcards, which give four lovely examples of the area. Here we see Evesham, a lovely view of the Workman Bridge, which spans the Avon, and the beautiful Booth Hall.

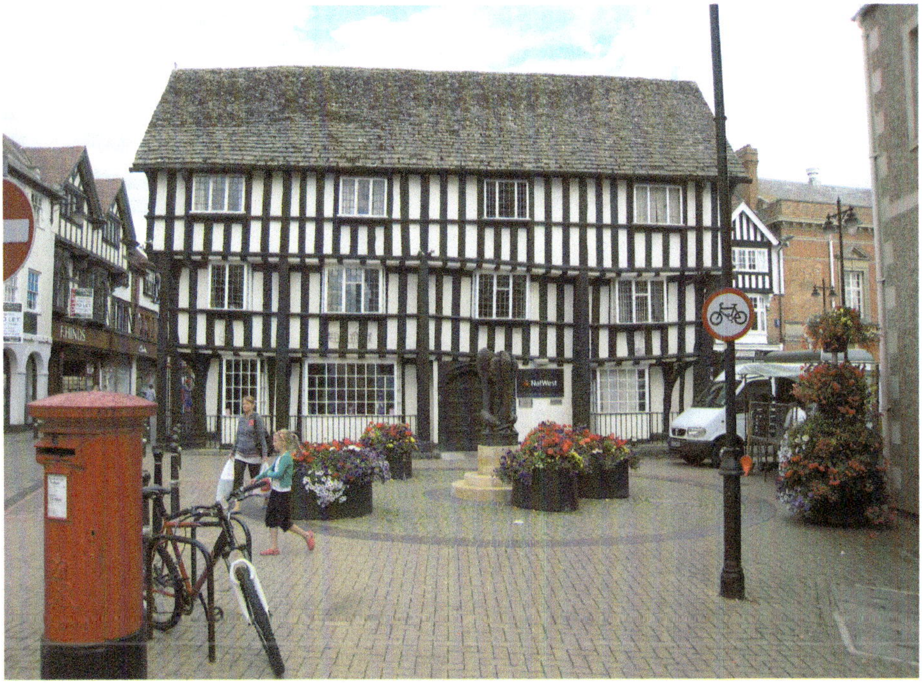

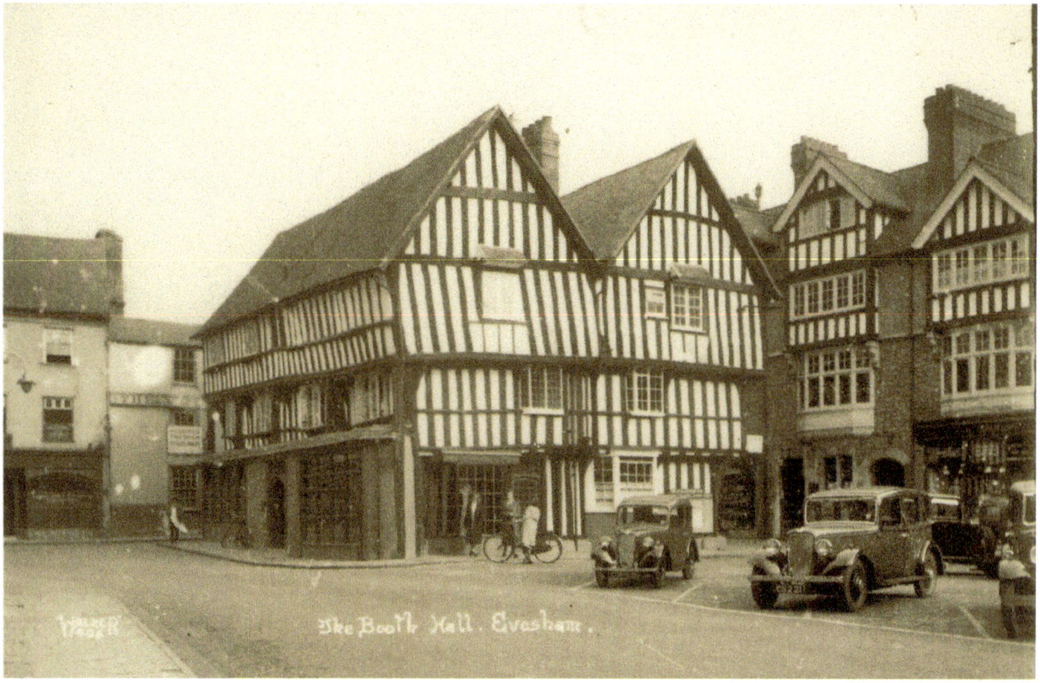

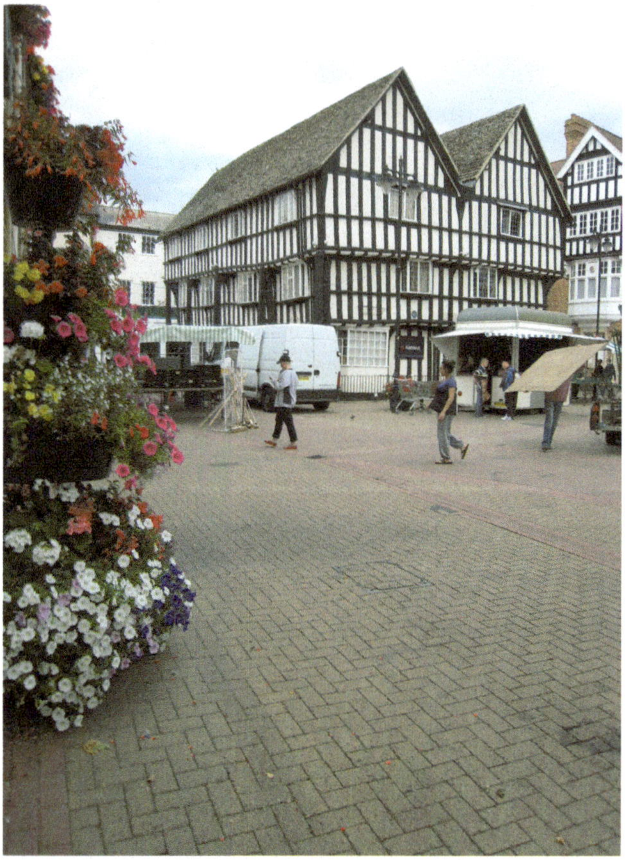

Booth Hall, Evesham

Evesham is a very picturesque town on the River Avon and boasts the beautiful Abbey Park. A market takes place each Saturday and enjoys a successful existence, with traders coming from across the UK. The fifteenth-century Booth Hall, with some lovely old motor cars parked adjacent, is known as the round house, although it is actually rectangular.

The Old Gateway, Evesham

Evesham is one of the county's prosperous market towns, and the Vale of Evesham is well known for its fruit-growing. A number of mills prospered on the banks of the River Avon, and the area has a wealth of market gardens. Here we see Abbott Reginald's Gateway, which symbolises the towns ecclesiastical past.

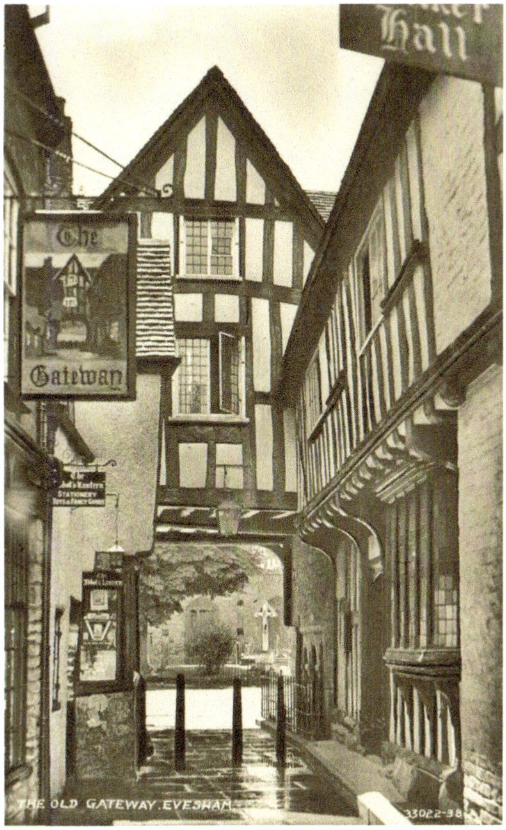

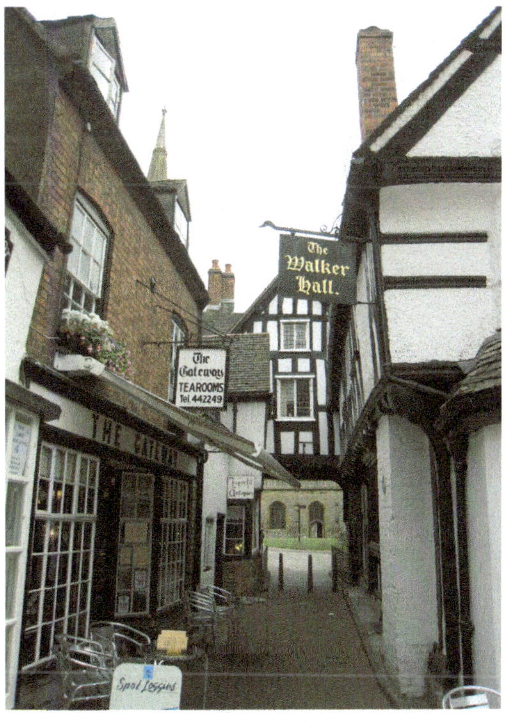

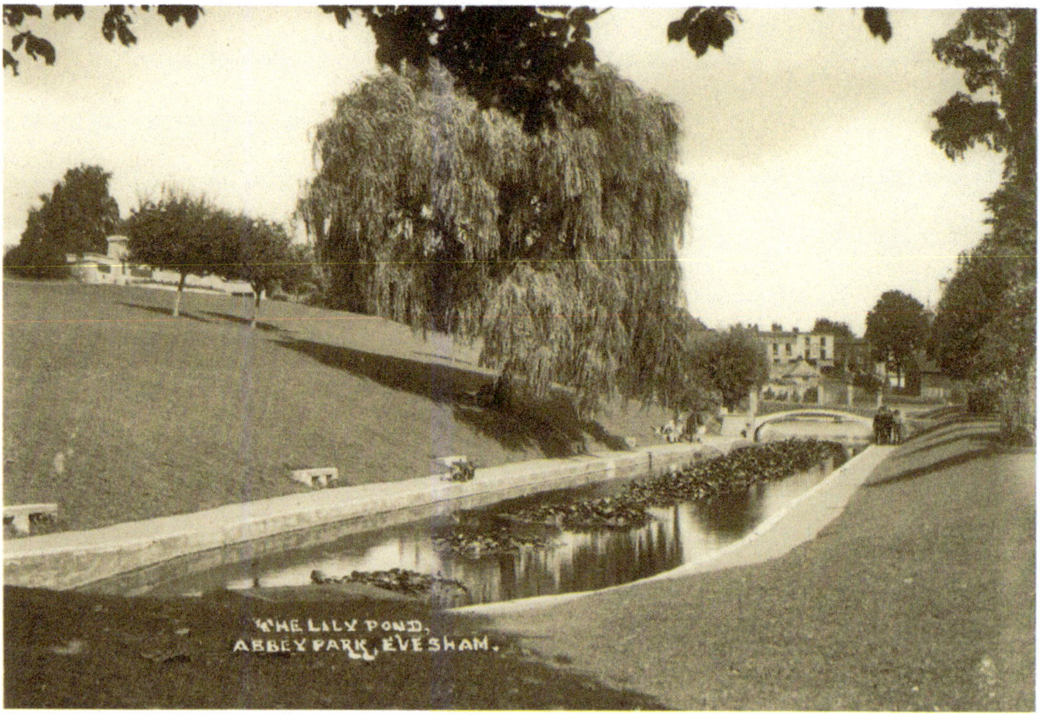

Abbey Park, Evesham

If you look across the green lawns of Abbey Park, you can see the remains of the Cloister Arch and some of the ancient surrounding walls. In the postcard we see the lily pond and the lawns of Abbey Park.

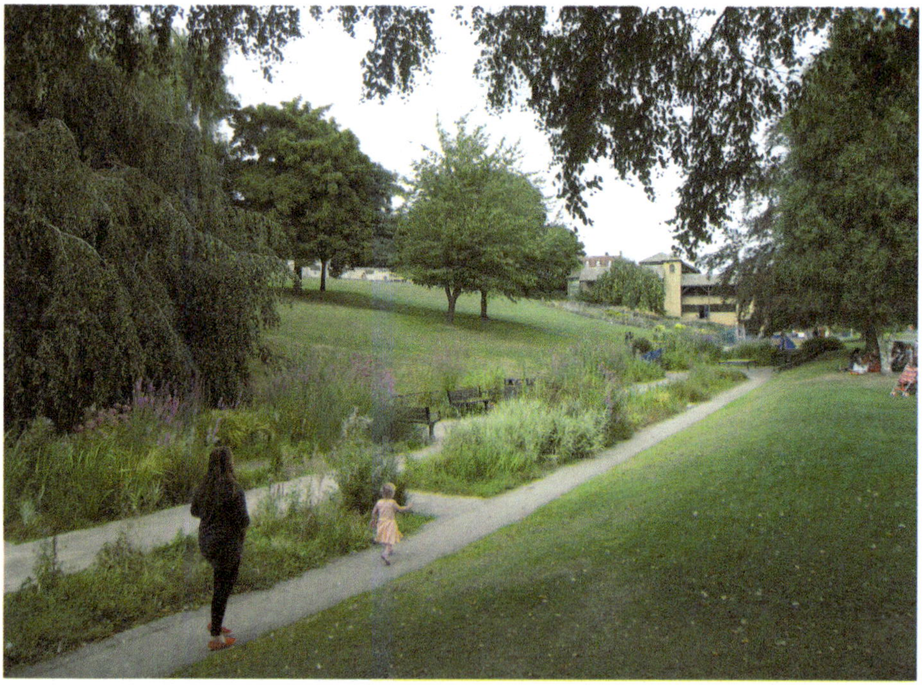

Bell Tower, Evesham

The impressive Abbot Lichfield's bell tower, which dominates the meadows of the River Avon, was built in 1539.

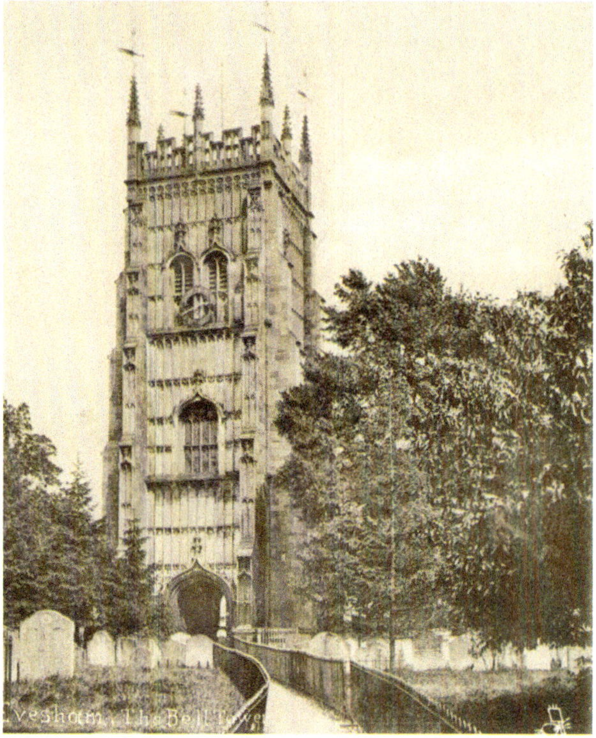

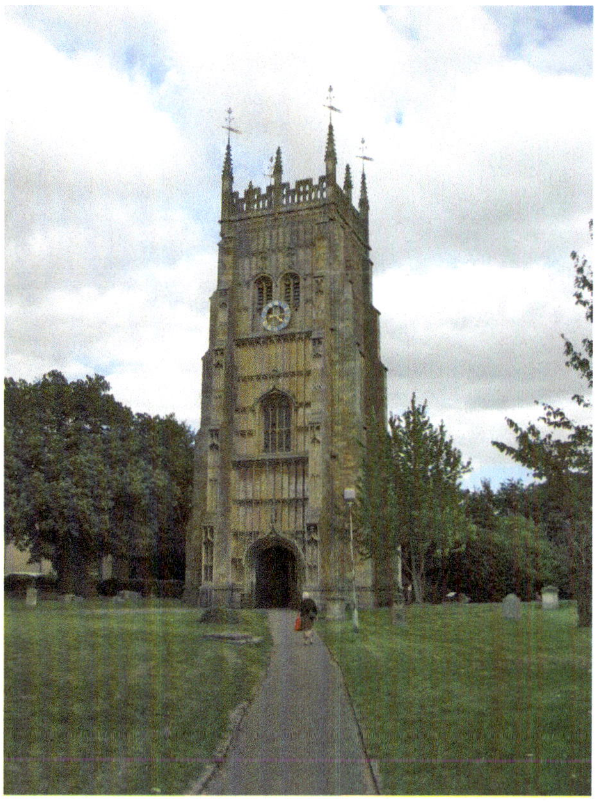

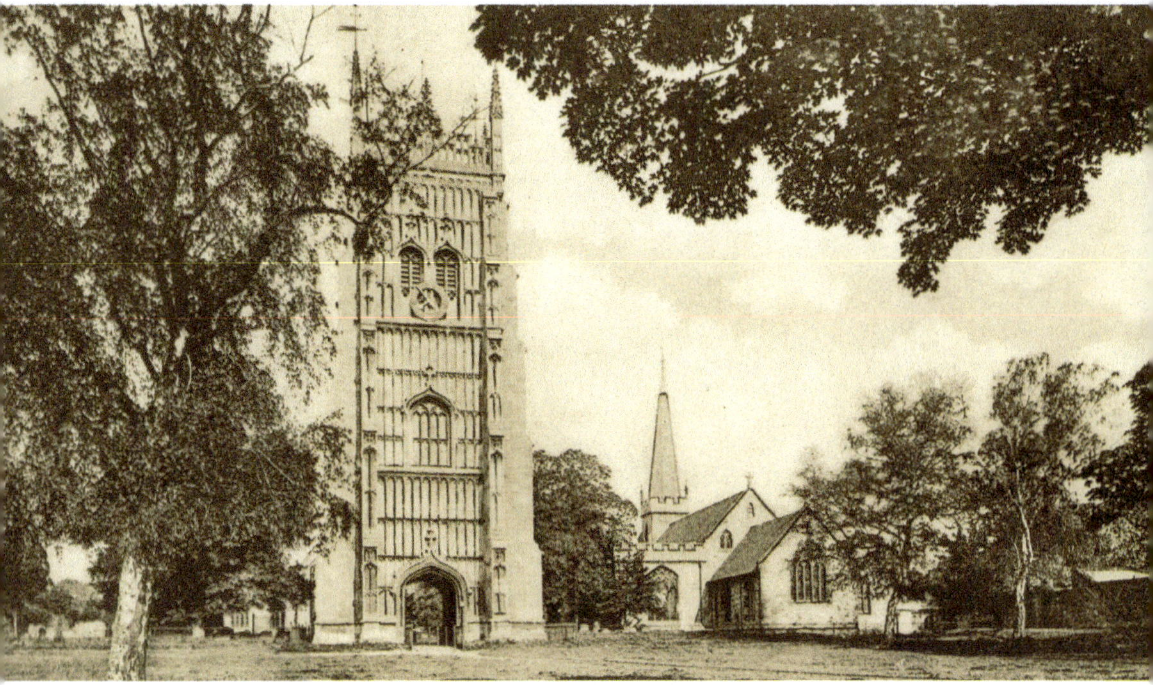

Bell Tower, Evesham

Alas, Evesham Abbey was dissolved by Henry VIII in 1539, the very year the tower was completed, and poor Abbot Lichfield had little time to enjoy his work.

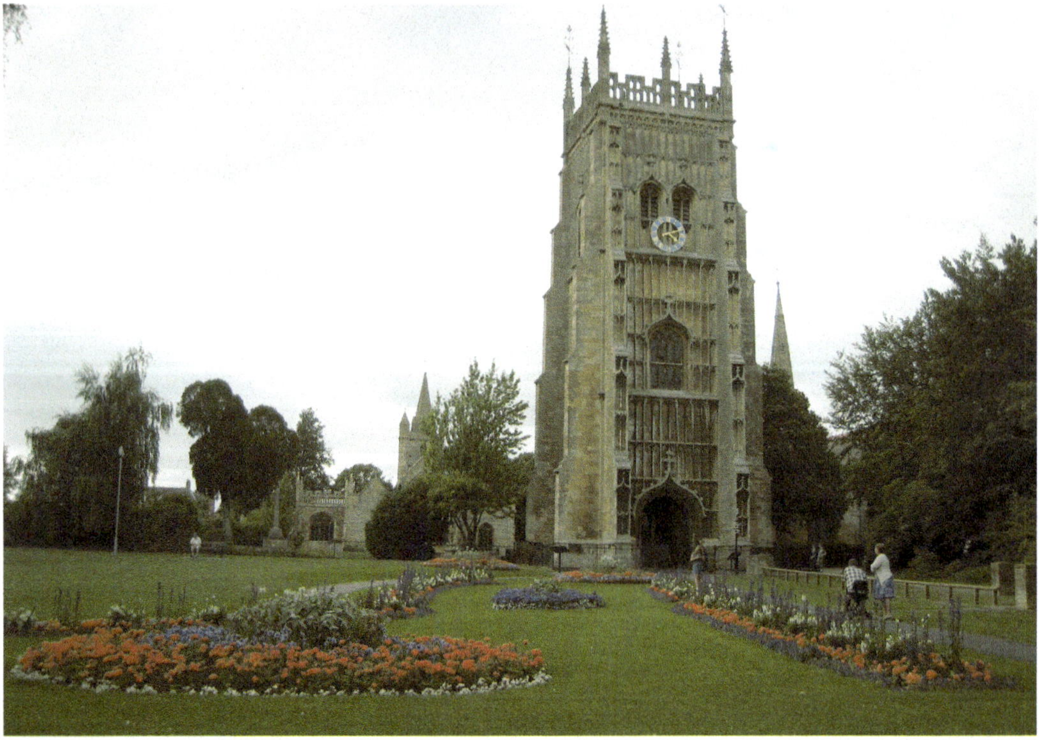

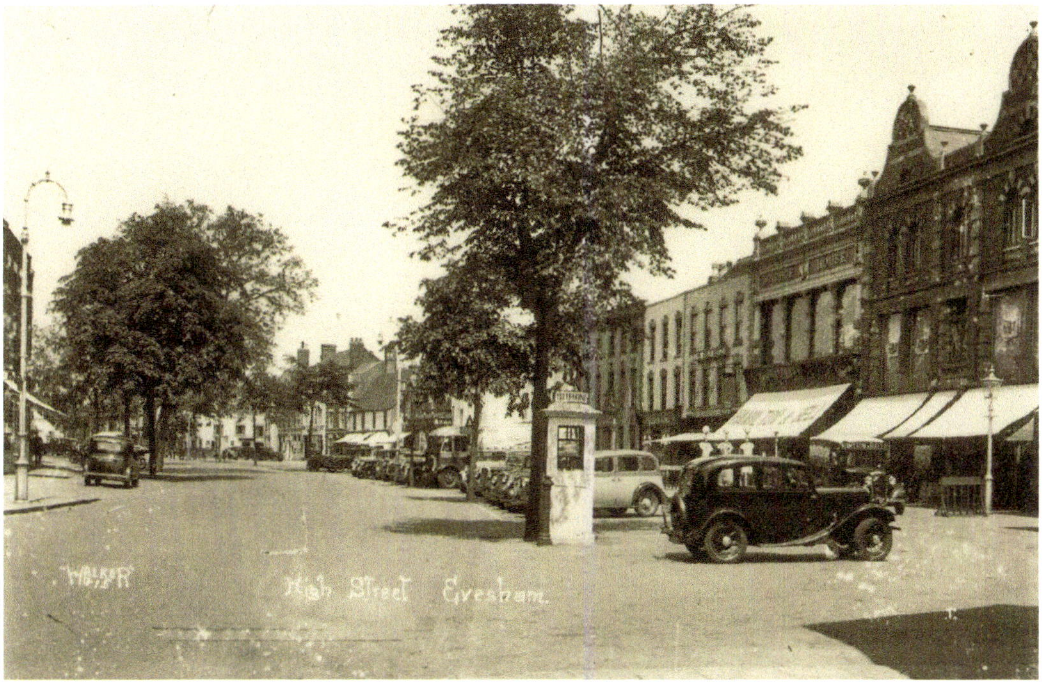

High Street, Evesham

The town centre has many modern and Victorian properties, with a smattering of ancient buildings. The High Street shows off Dresden House beautifully and the River Avon sweeps through the town to one side, with the town centre above it.

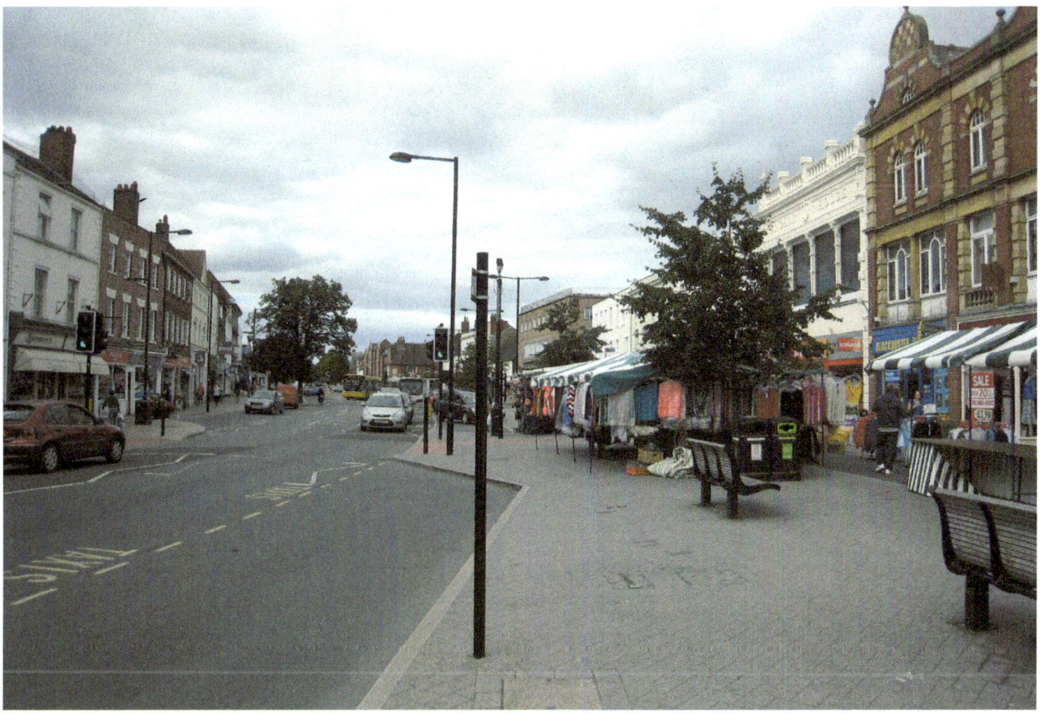

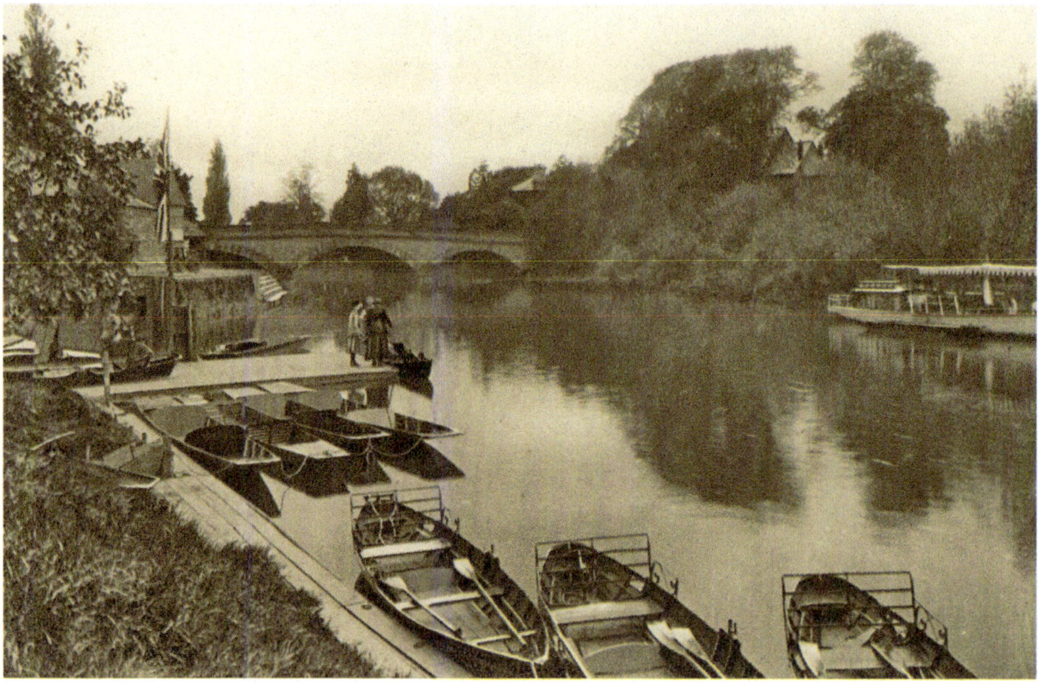

The Workman Bridge, Evesham

Here we see the Workman Bridge and the boats ready for hire. On the eastern bank near to the Workman Bridge is the recently renovated public quay. For centuries, this was the loading stage for goods that had travelled via the River Severn at Tewkesbury from the sea.

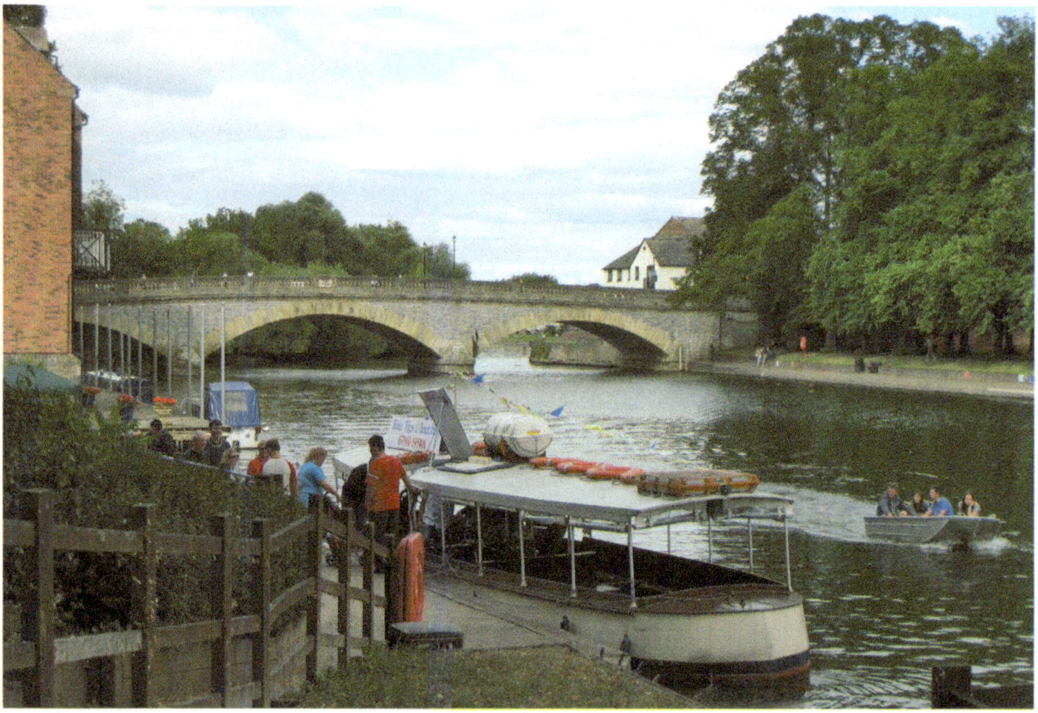

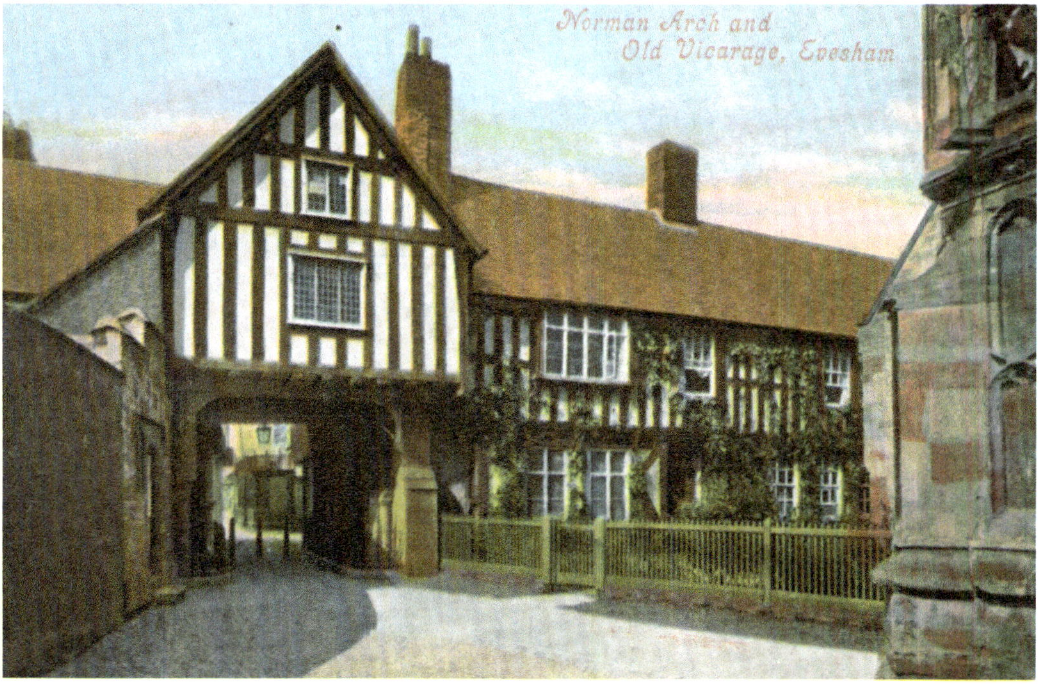

Old Vicarage, Evesham

The Norman Arch and Old Vicarage, Evesham, where two churches share the same churchyard. The street patterns of Evesham have changed very little over the decades, and we can see the lost glory of the town from the buildings still standing in the town centre. The River Avon runs through the town and flooding remains a problem.

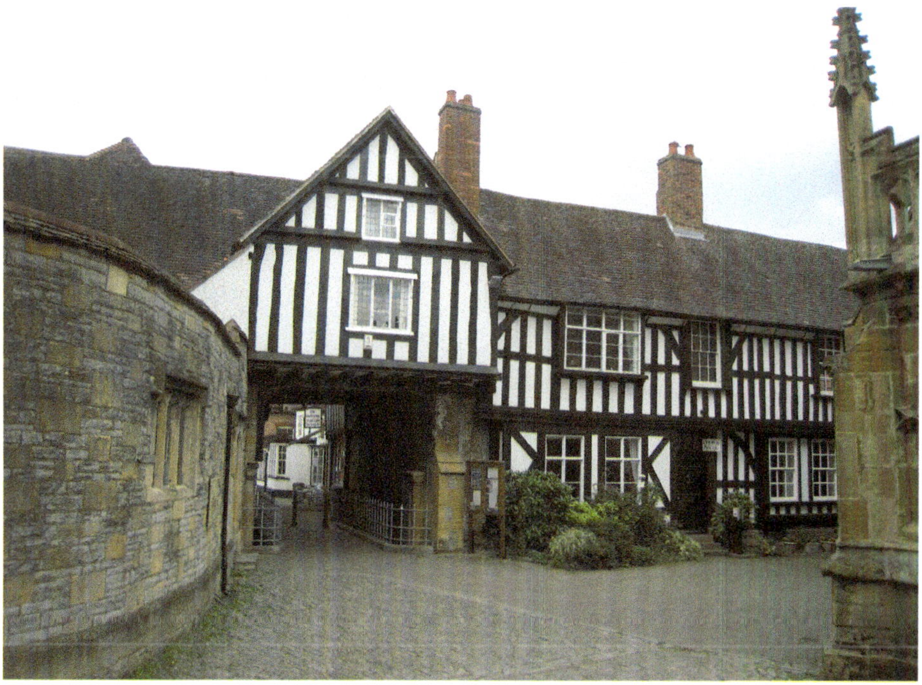

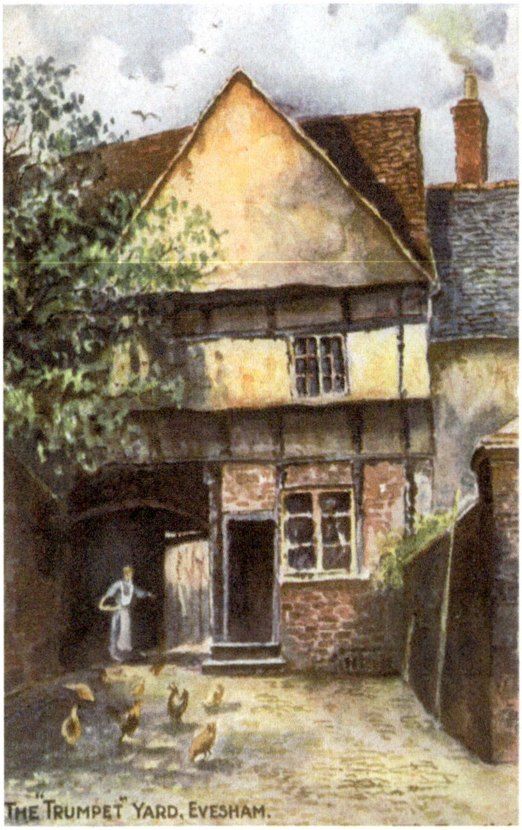

Trumpet Yard, Evesham

Evesham is a good central point for exploring the vale around the River Avon. It is also close to the Cotswolds. Now a peaceful spot, Evesham had a chequered history. At the Battle of Evesham on 4 August 1265, during a thunderstorm, Henry III defeated the rebel barons led by Simon De Montfort. De Montfort and his son perished, along with over 4,000 others. This lovely old postcard reflects more peaceful times and shows the famous Trumpet Yard. Below, shops in the town centre.

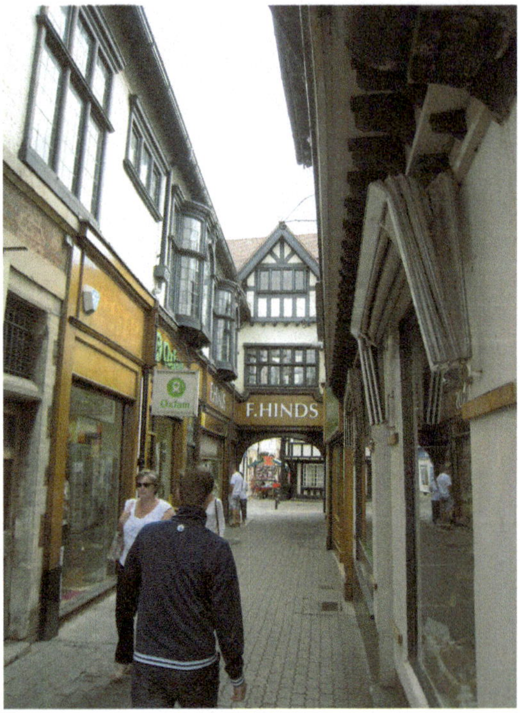

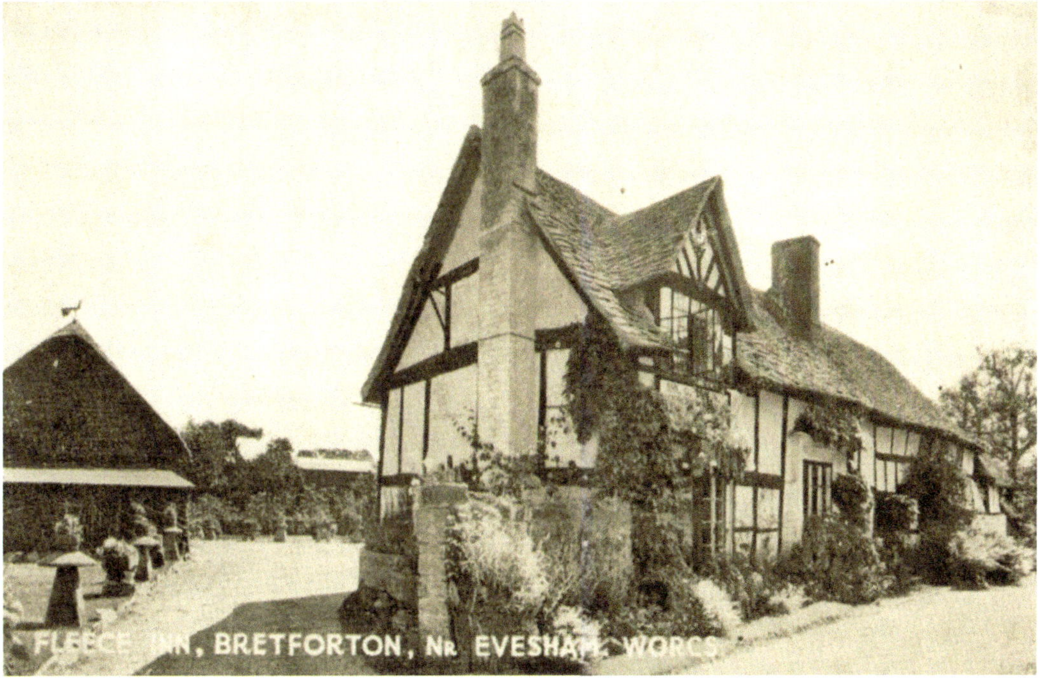

The Fleece Inn, Bretforton

The Fleece Inn at Bretforten, near Evesham, is a half-timbered medieval farmhouse that was originally used by a farmer and his stock. The fourteenth-century English inn is owned by the National Trust. First licensed in 1848, it houses a precious pewter collection.

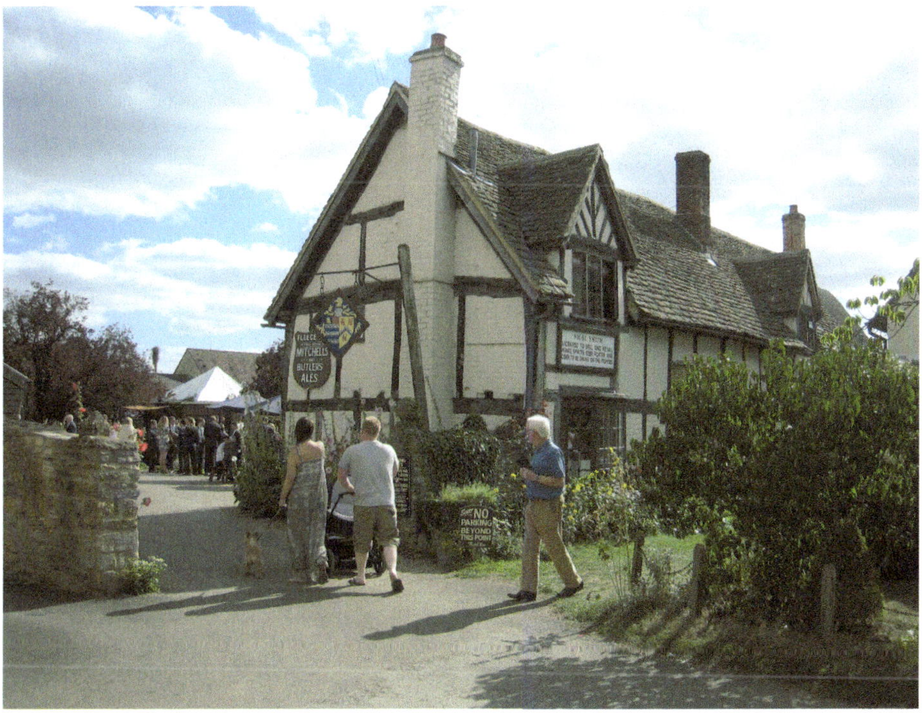

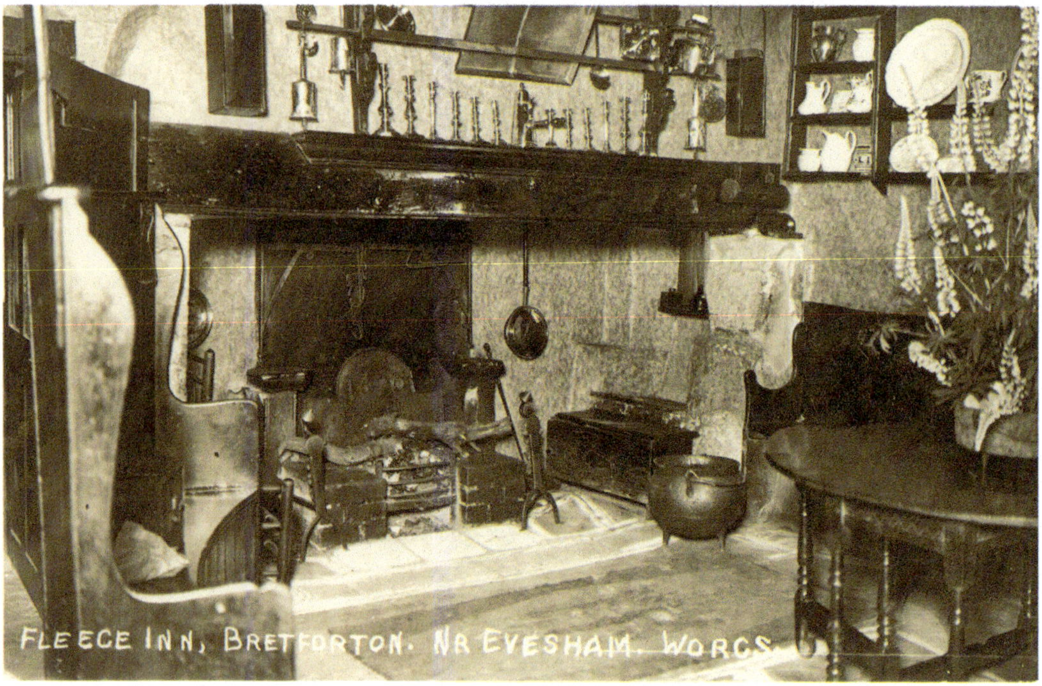

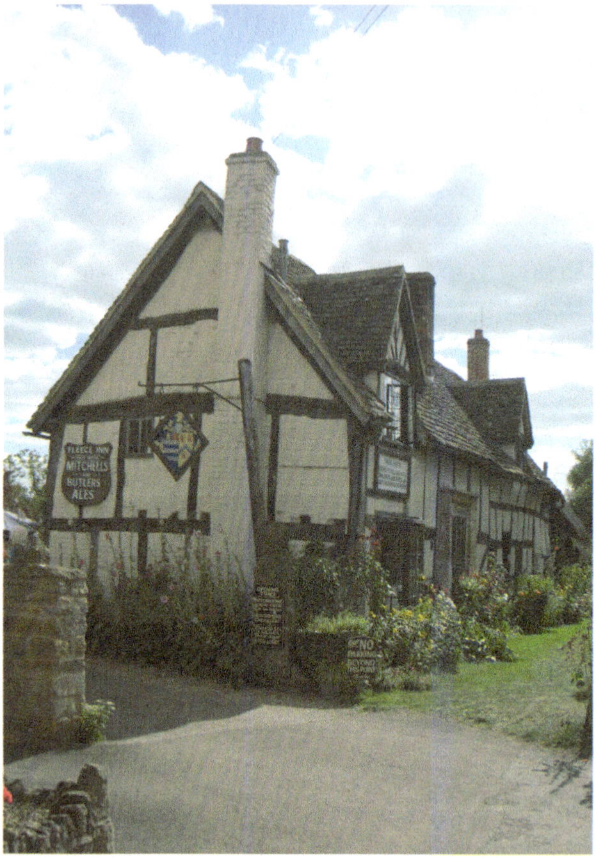

The Fleece Inn, Bretforton

The Fleece Inn is a fine example of the old-fashioned drinking houses in and around Worcestershire. This fourteenth-century inn is said to be haunted by former landlady Lola Taplin. Bretforton has one of the nicest village squares, complete with an old inn, cottages and grand houses.

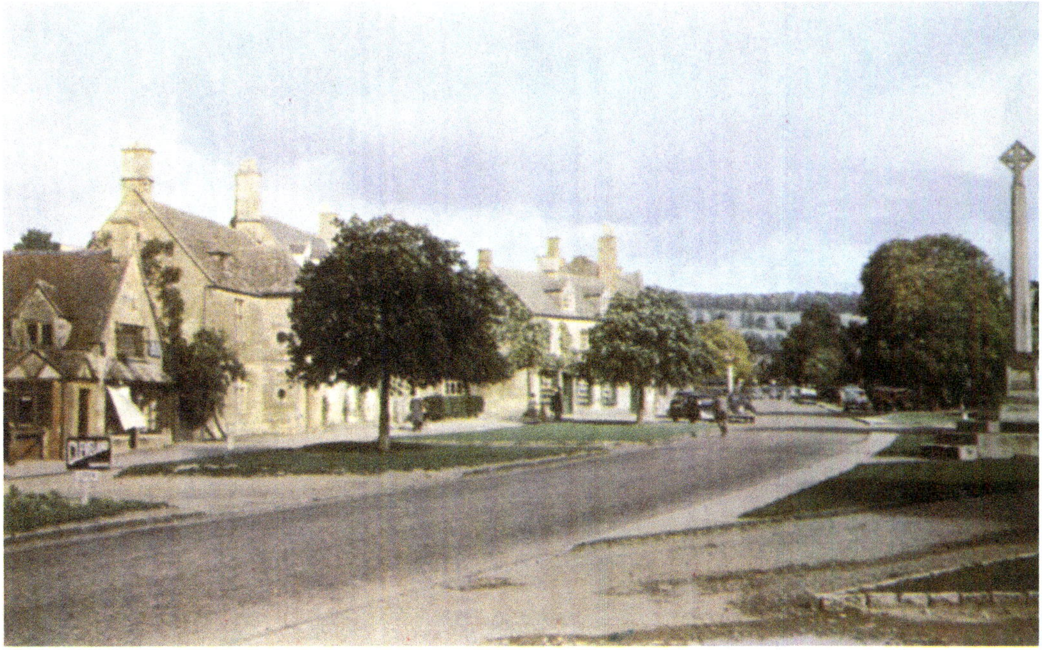

Main Street, Broadway

This charming view looks up the village from the Green. During the Civil War, Charles I and Oliver Cromwell stayed in the village. Over time, colour was introduced to postcards, and as you can see by the models in the postcards, the bottom picture has moved forward in time.

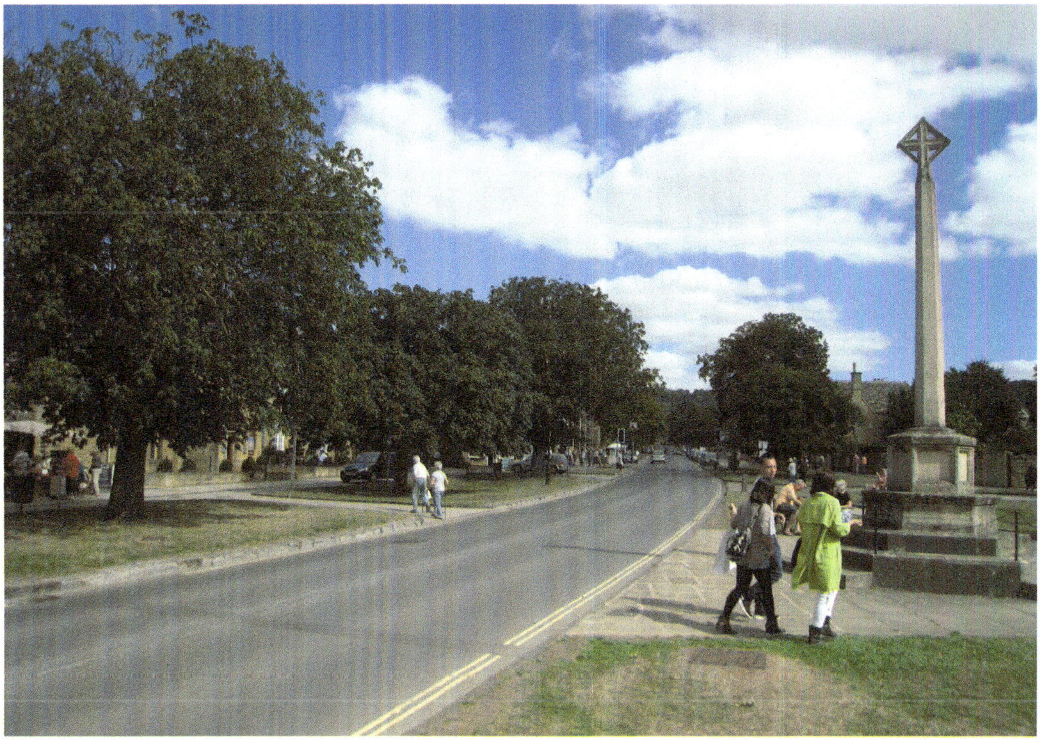

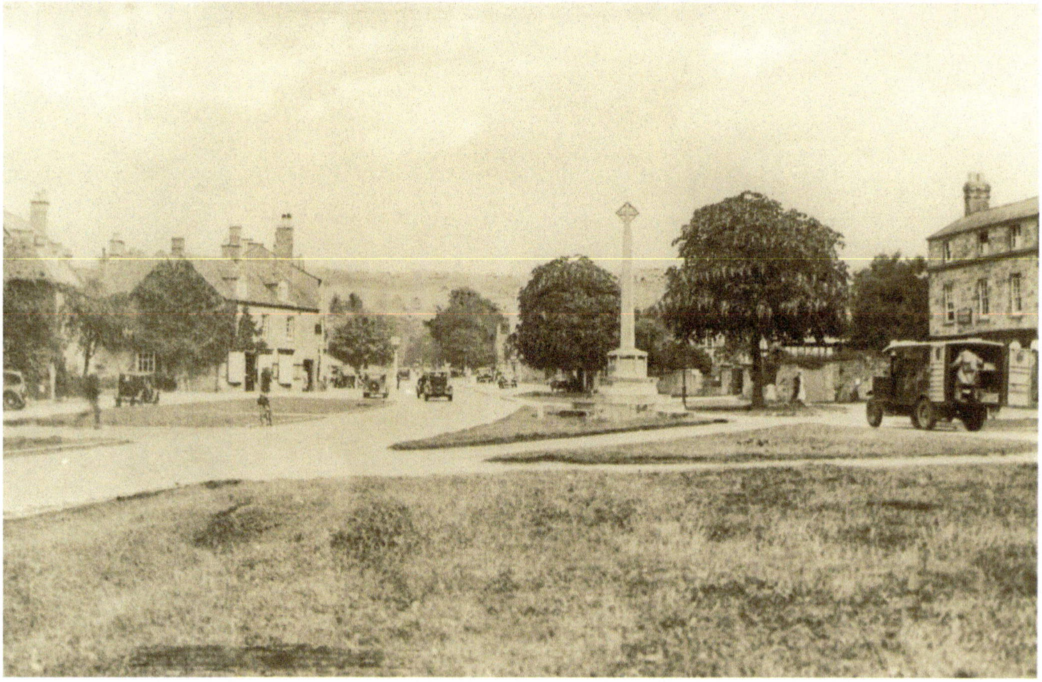

Broadway

Broadway is described as an exceptionally beautiful Worcestershire village. Mainly constructed from warm local stone, the village attracts tourists from all over the world.

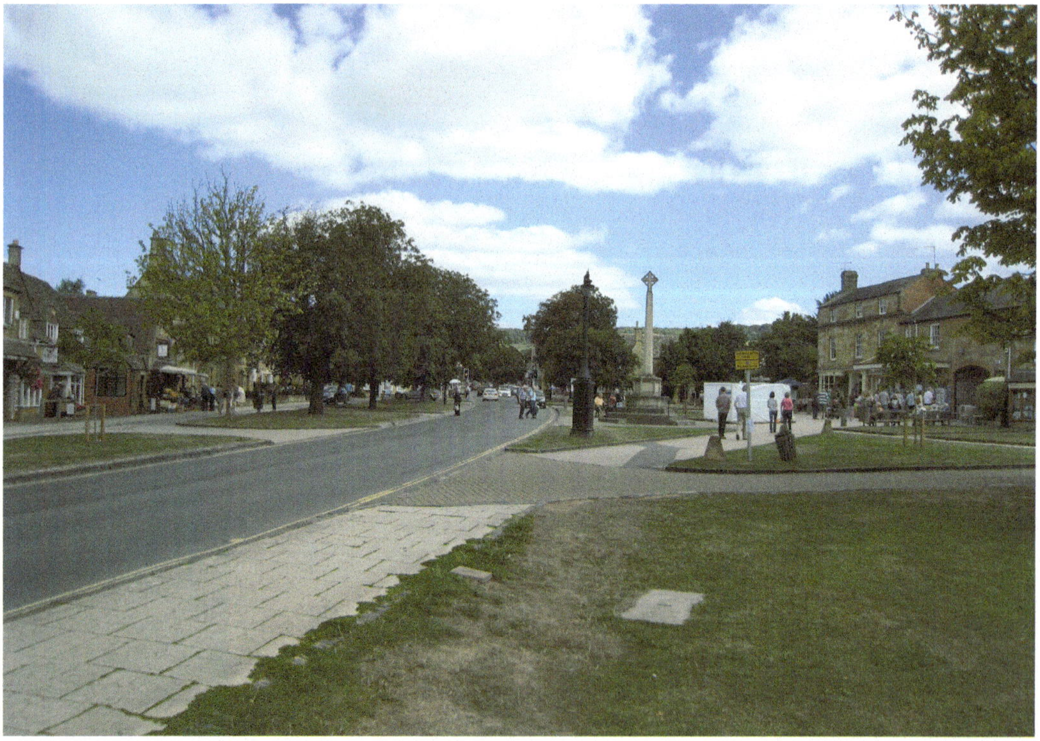

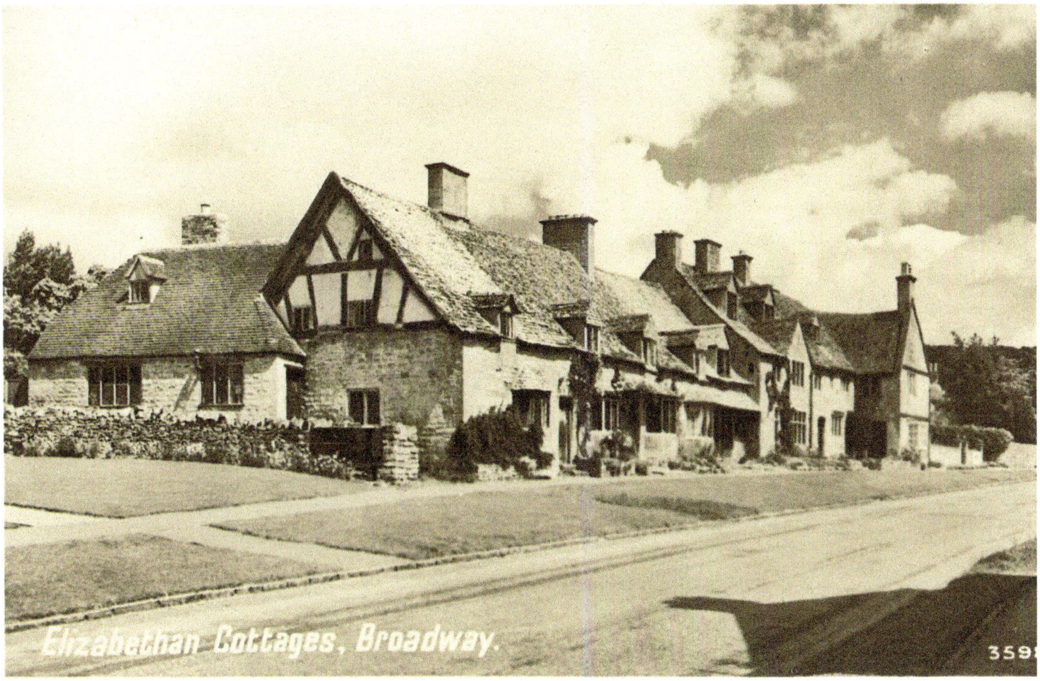

Elizabethan Cottages, Broadway

These images of Elizabethan cottages were taken in Broadway. A number of these older houses were originally inns, since Broadway lay on the coaching route between Worcester and London. This lovely postcard shows Broadway before the days of the motor car, which today paints a different picture, with a steady flow of traffic passing through the village.

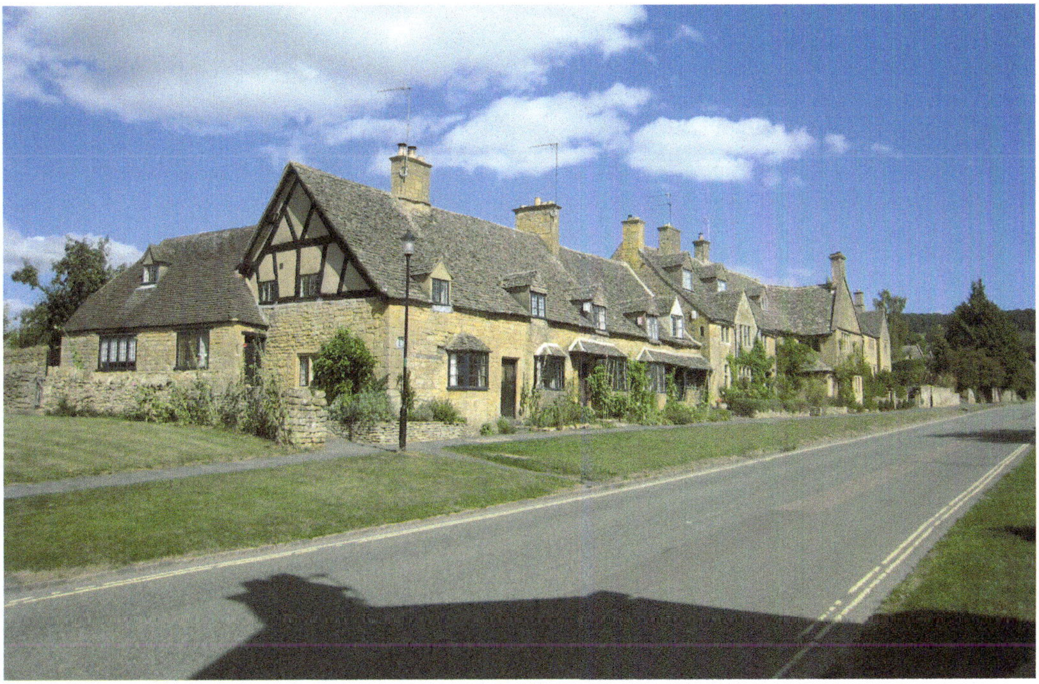

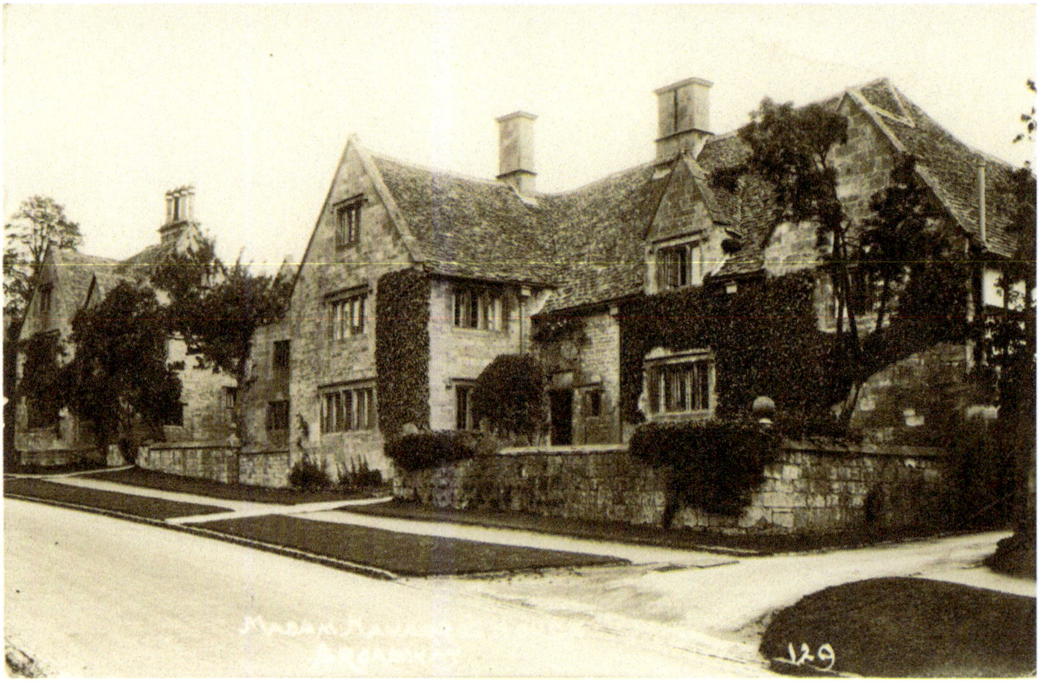

Madame de Navarro's House, Broadway

Broadway is an exceptionally beautiful Worcestershire village, mainly constructed from warm local stones. Today, the village attracts tourists from all over the world. Madame de Navarro's house is a fine example of the architecture to be found in Broadway.

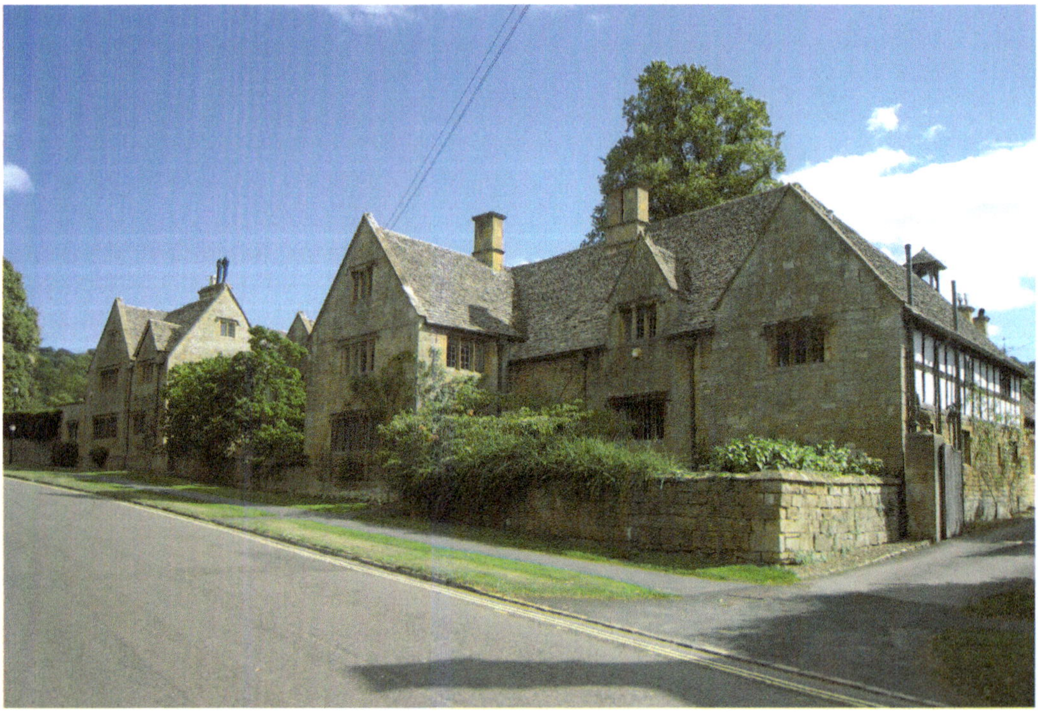

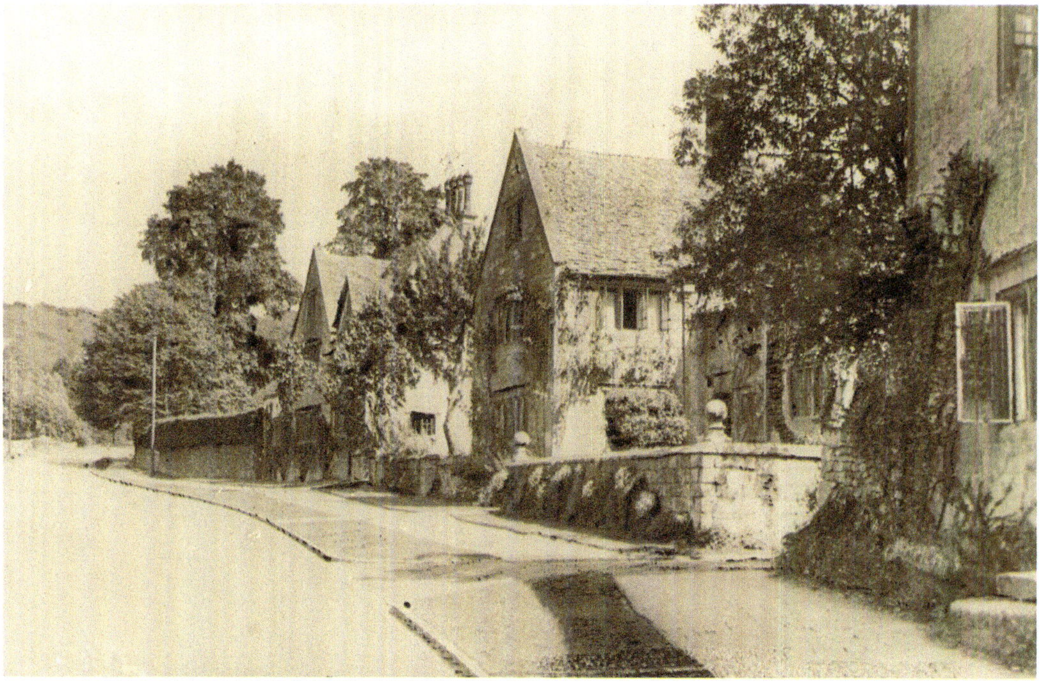

Madame de Navarro's House, Broadway

More views of Madame de Navarro's residence in Broadway. Broadway lay on the London to Worcester coaching route and consequently a number of older properties in the village were originally inns.

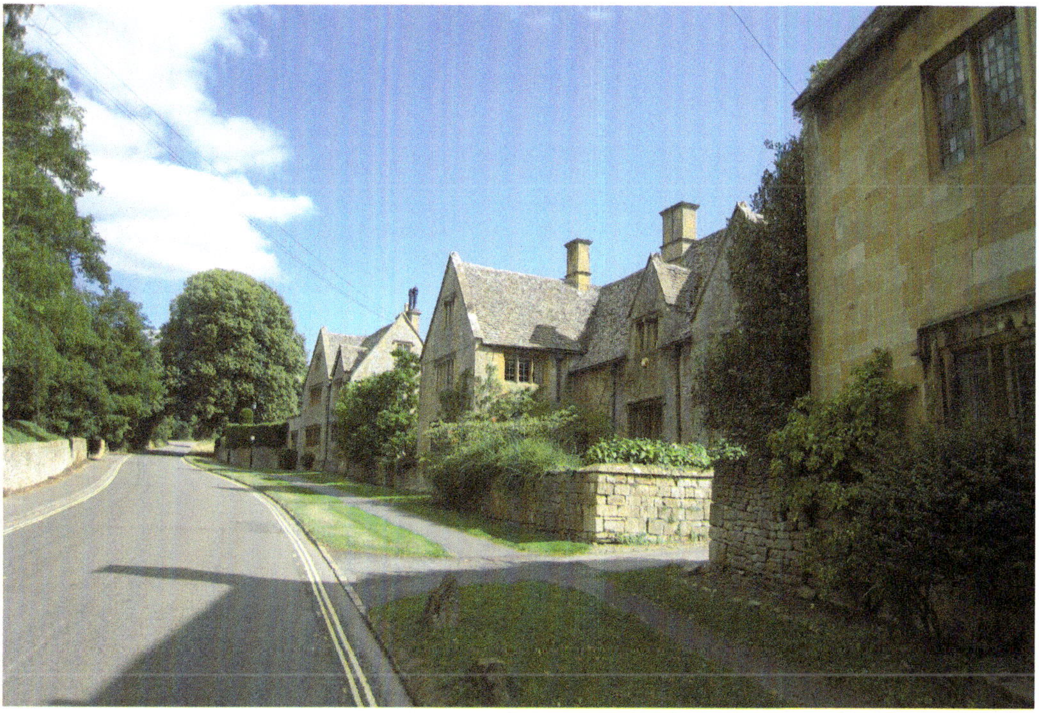

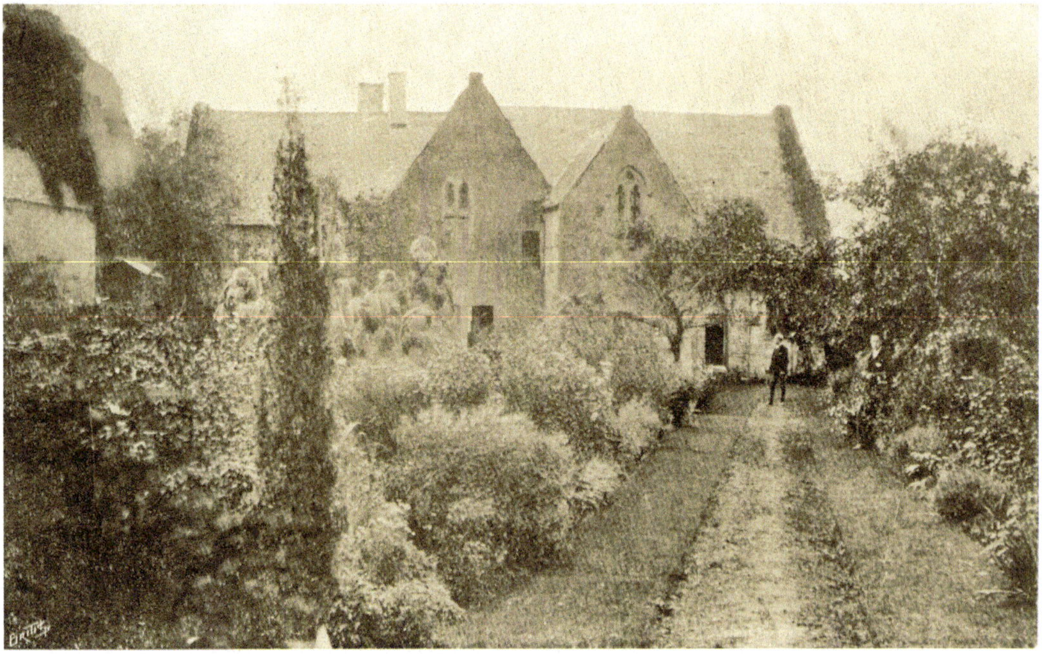

The Old Priory, Broadway

Today, Broadway is full of antique and craft shops and a haven for tourists. It is also an exceptionally beautiful Worcestershire village and home to the Old Priory and garden.

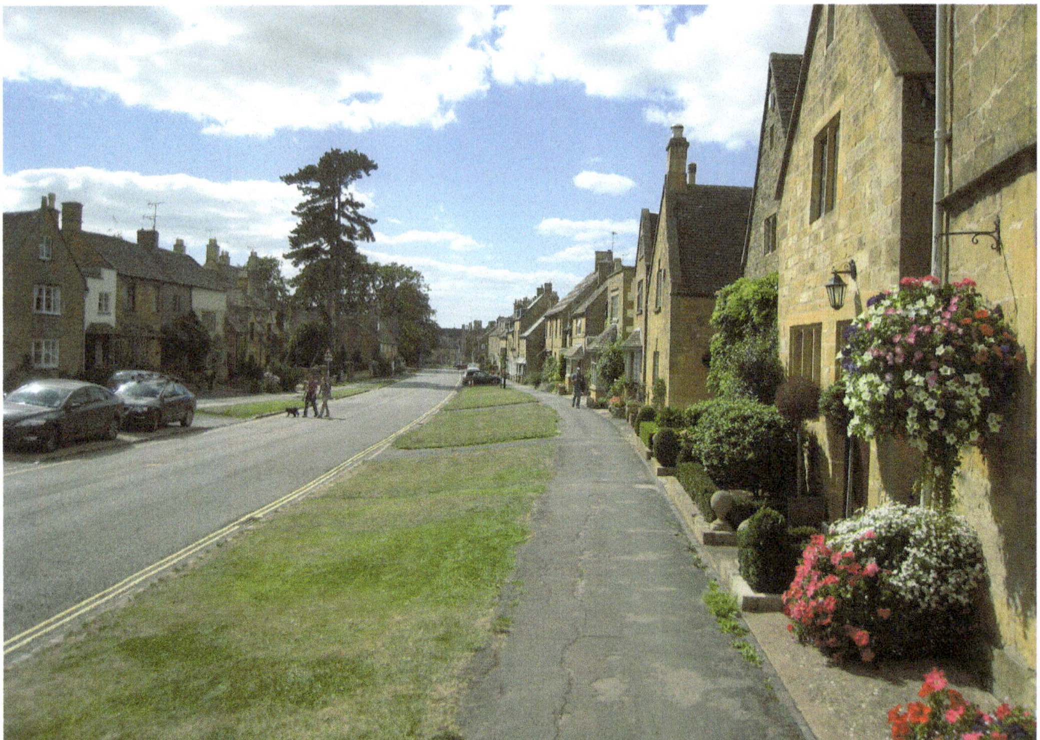

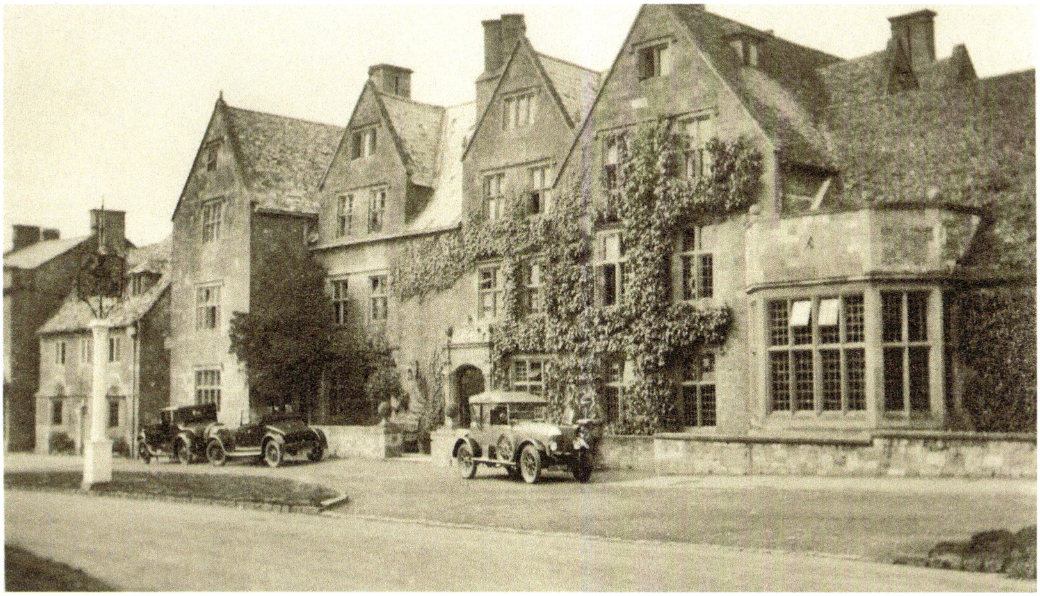

Lygon Arms, Broadway

One of the most prestigious hotels in Broadway is the Lygon Arms. Here we see the Great Hall (*inset*), showing the Tudor fireplace and the minstrels' gallery. It is like taking a step back in time, and is a pleasure to visit and a joy to behold. Above is a lovely old postcard view of the Lygon Arms. I love the old cars and the charisma of the early days of the motor car. I believe the car in the centre is an early Vauxhall, though I may be mistaken. Little has changed today, except the type of motor cars.

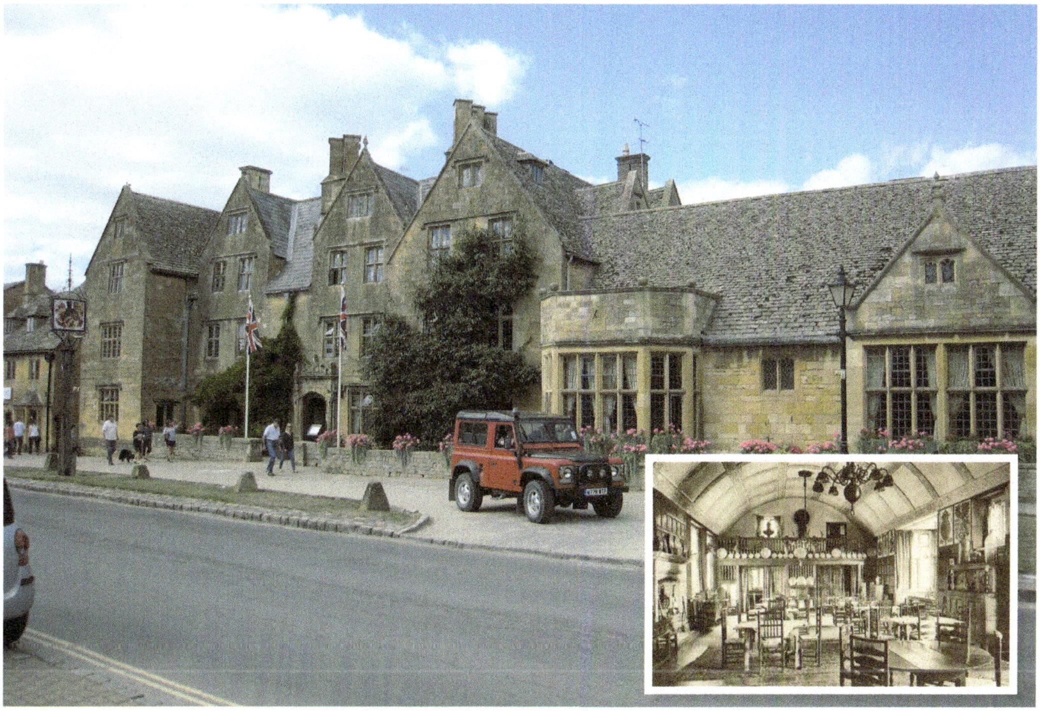

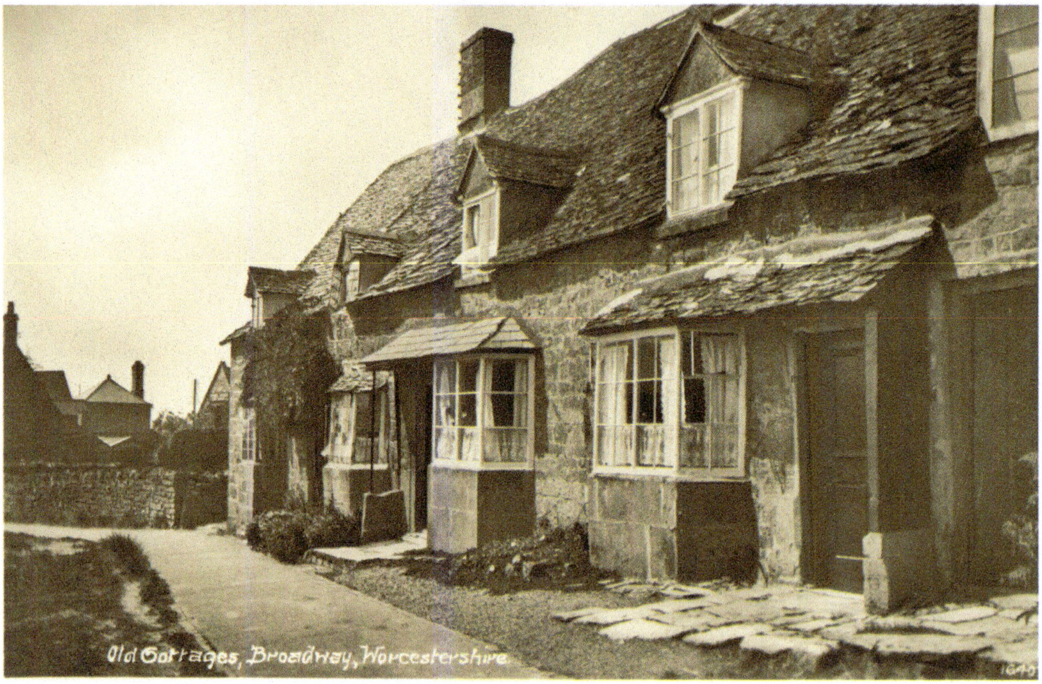

Old Cottages, Broadway

A fine example of some lovely old cottages in Broadway. Many of these older houses were inns in the past, at a time when Broadway lay on the London to Worcester coaching route.

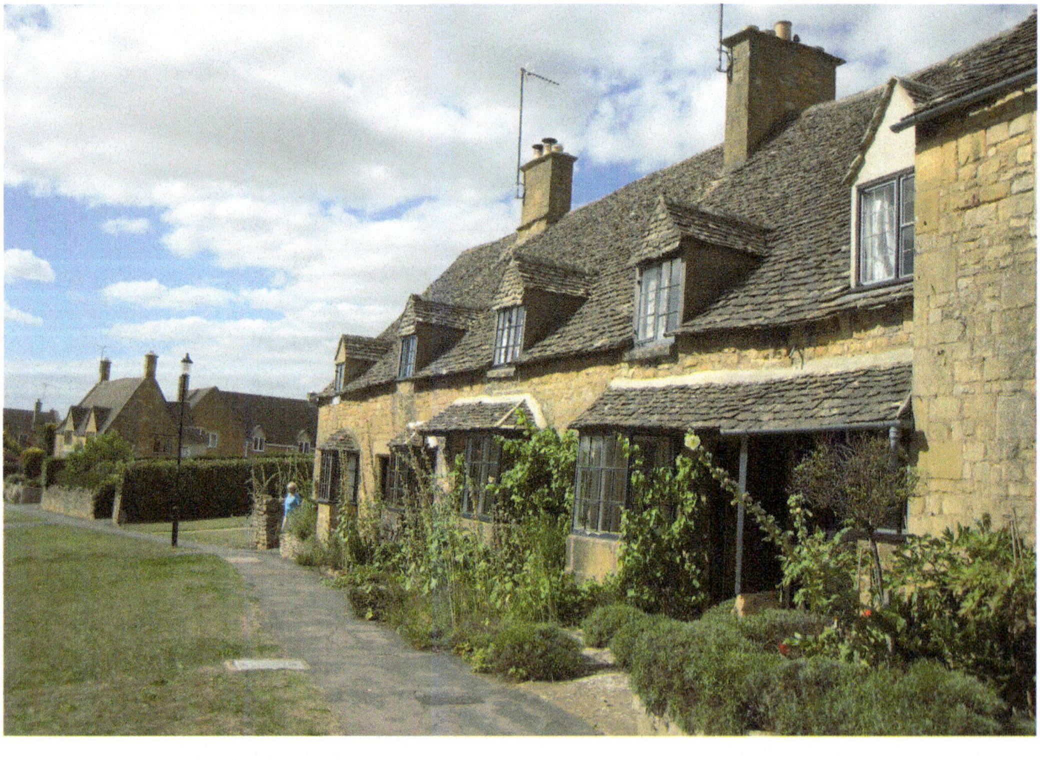

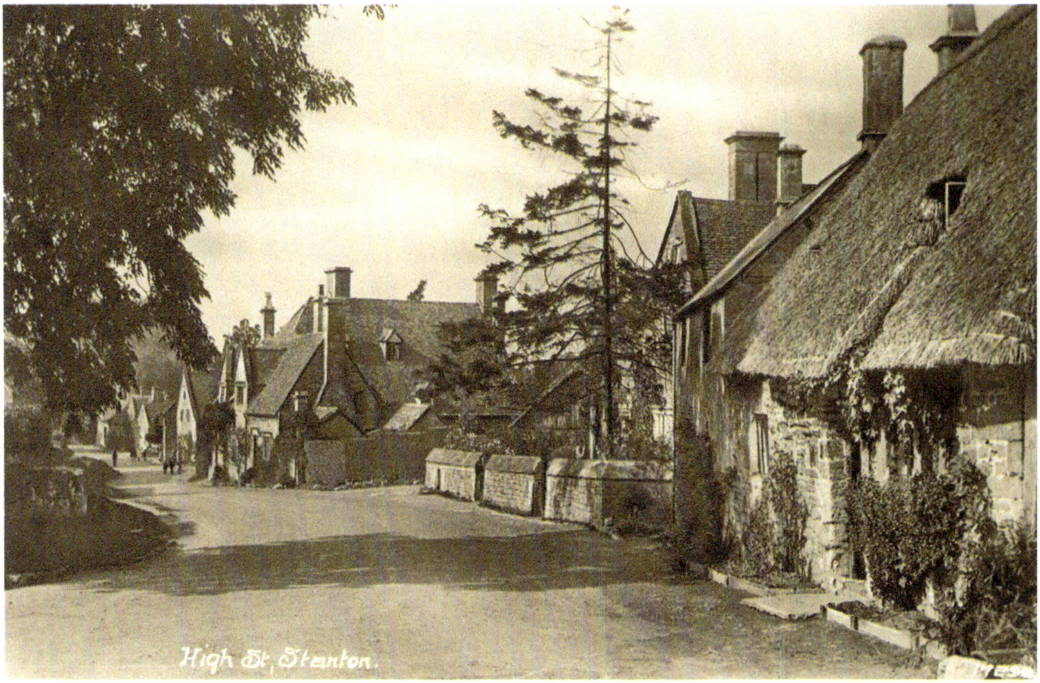

High Street, Stanton

This picturesque little village nestles below the slopes of Shenbarrow Hill, and has changed very little over the past 300 years. The parish church is St Michael's, and many of the houses in the village are sixteenth and seventeenth century. Stanton is a lovely village where time has stood still, and is a delight to visit. While technically in Gloucestershire, it is in touching distance of Broadway.

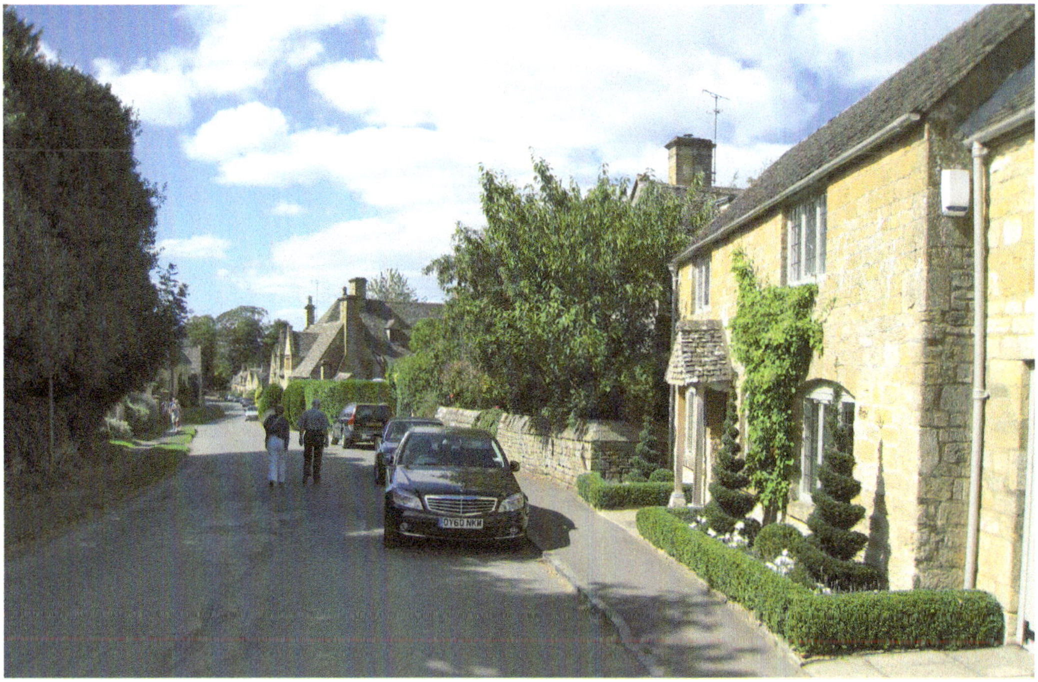

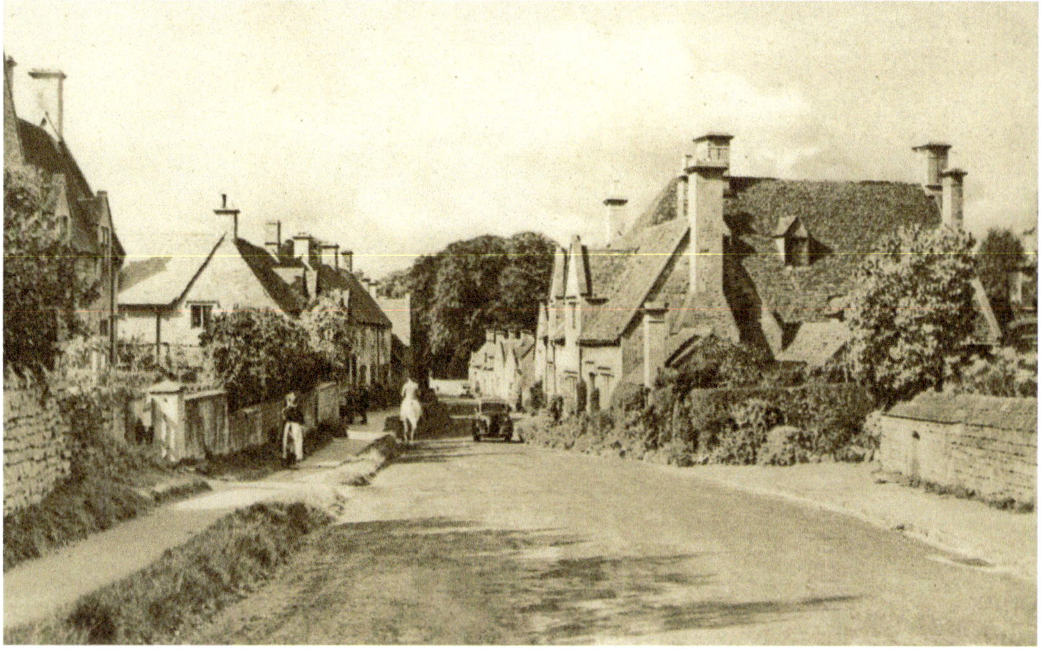

High Street, Stanton

Situated 4 miles from Broadway and nestling below the slopes of Shenbarrow Hill is one of the prettiest villages in the Cotswolds, Stanton. Stanton's church is St Michael's, and a well-worn figure of St Michael with a sundial stands above the door as you enter.

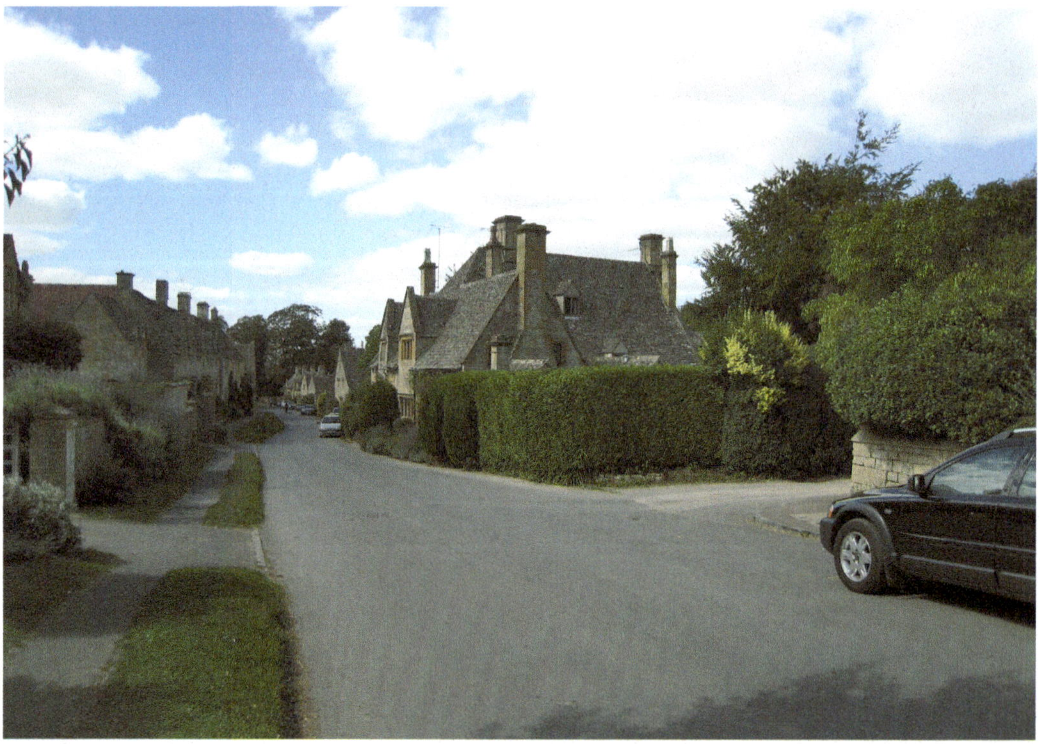

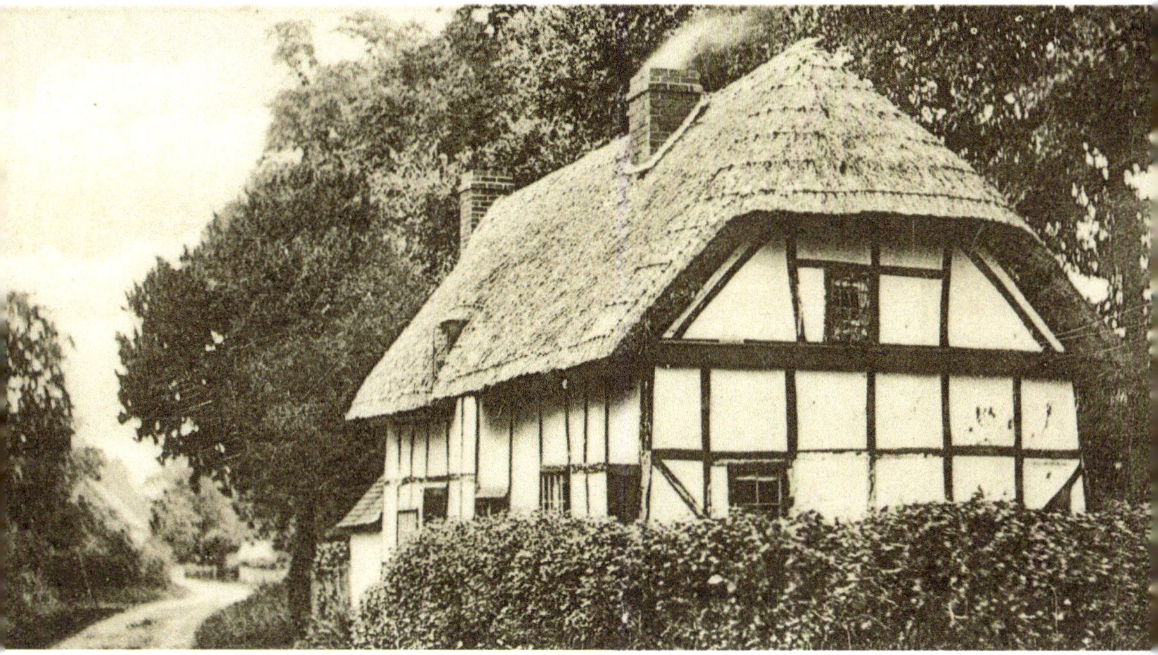

Rous Lench

The Rous family were Lords of the Manor from 1397 to 1876 and gave their name to this part of the Lenches. The unusual half-year dating on Lady Rous's tomb can be seen in the annexe within the church of St Peter. On the back of the postcard it reads: 'A New Year message from my heart, though you and I are far apart. May health and Happiness unite to make your New Year Glad and bright.'

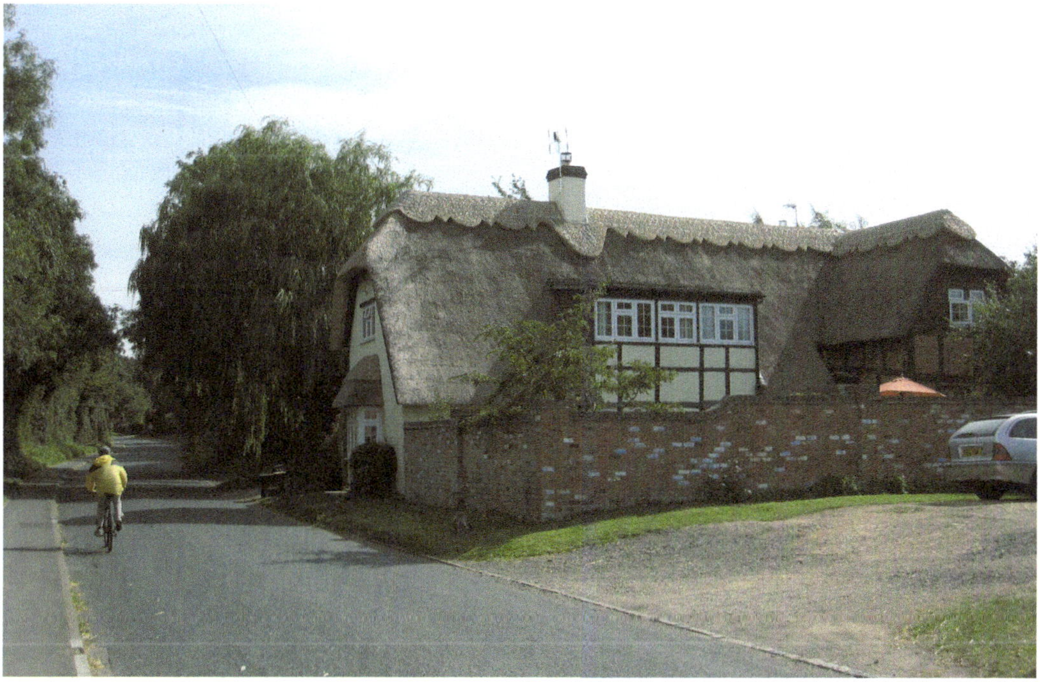

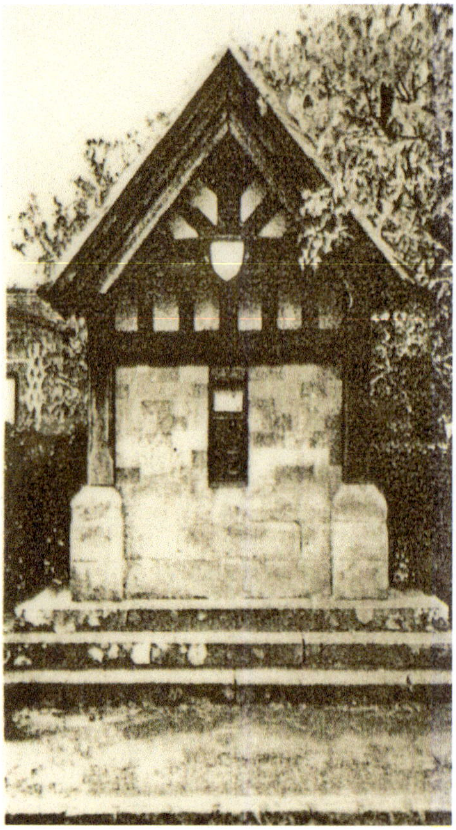

Rous Lench

Dr Chaffy, a local parson, built two pillar boxes around 1890, one at Rous Lench and the other at nearby Radford. Standing high on their plinths, they resemble miniature summer houses, with each box having the Chaffy coat of arms beneath its eaves. To post your letter you have to go up the shallow steps, which form the base of the plinth.

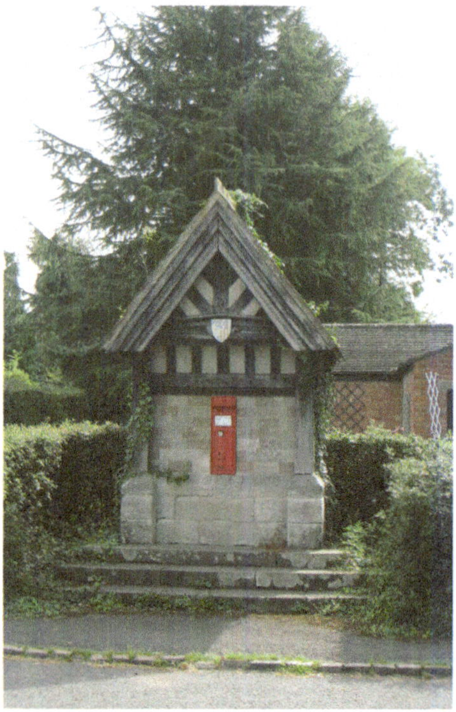

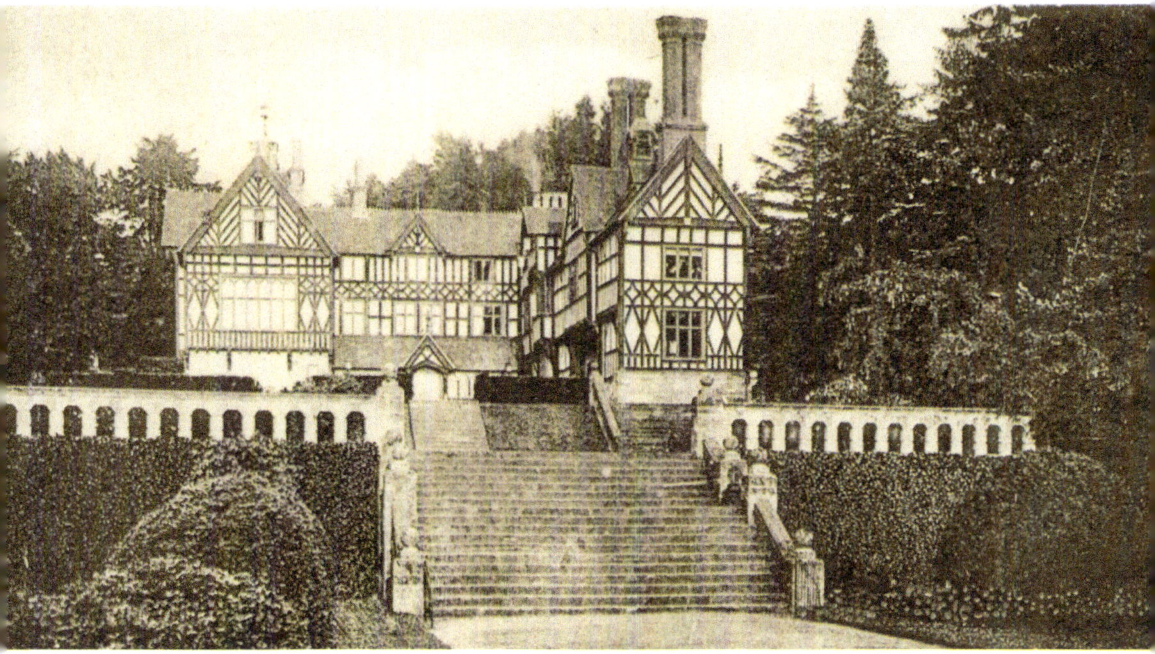

Lench Court and Gardens, Rous Lench

Rous Lench is the largest of several Lench villages in the Vale of Evesham. The village church contains Saxon and Norman fabric, with ornaments of a later date. The main house in the village is Lench Court, a black-and-white sixteenth-century building. Below, the beautiful yew garden can be found within the grounds of Rous Lench Court. There are several Lench villages, all of which are in the Vale of Evesham. Rous Lench is the largest.

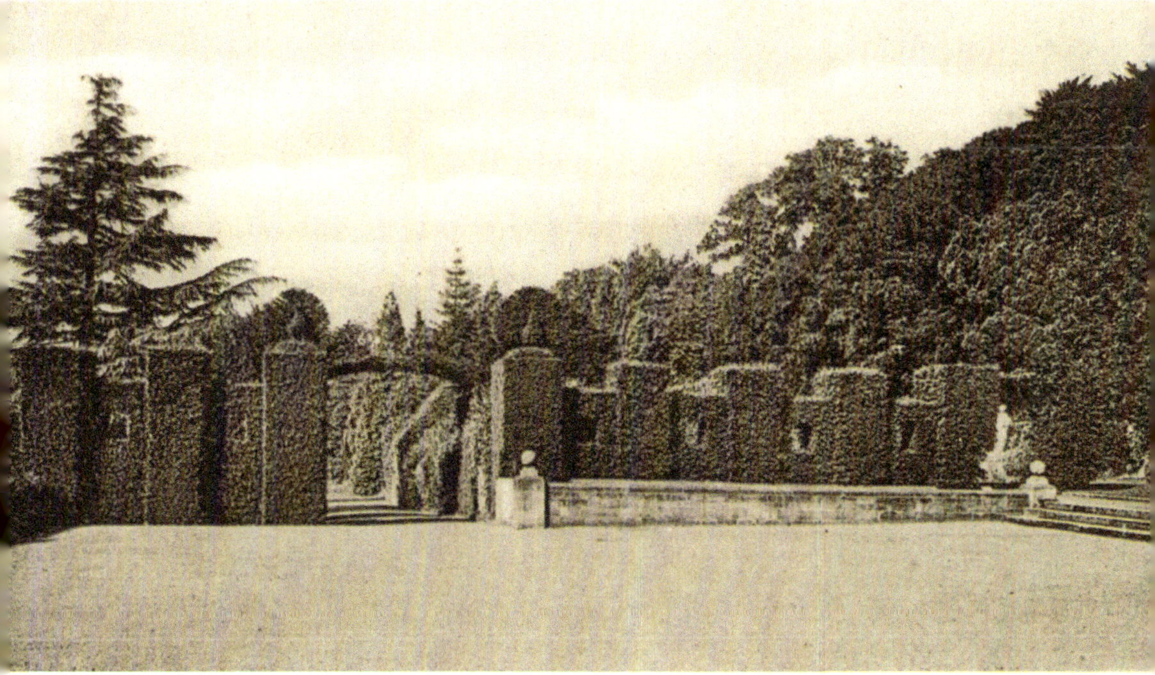

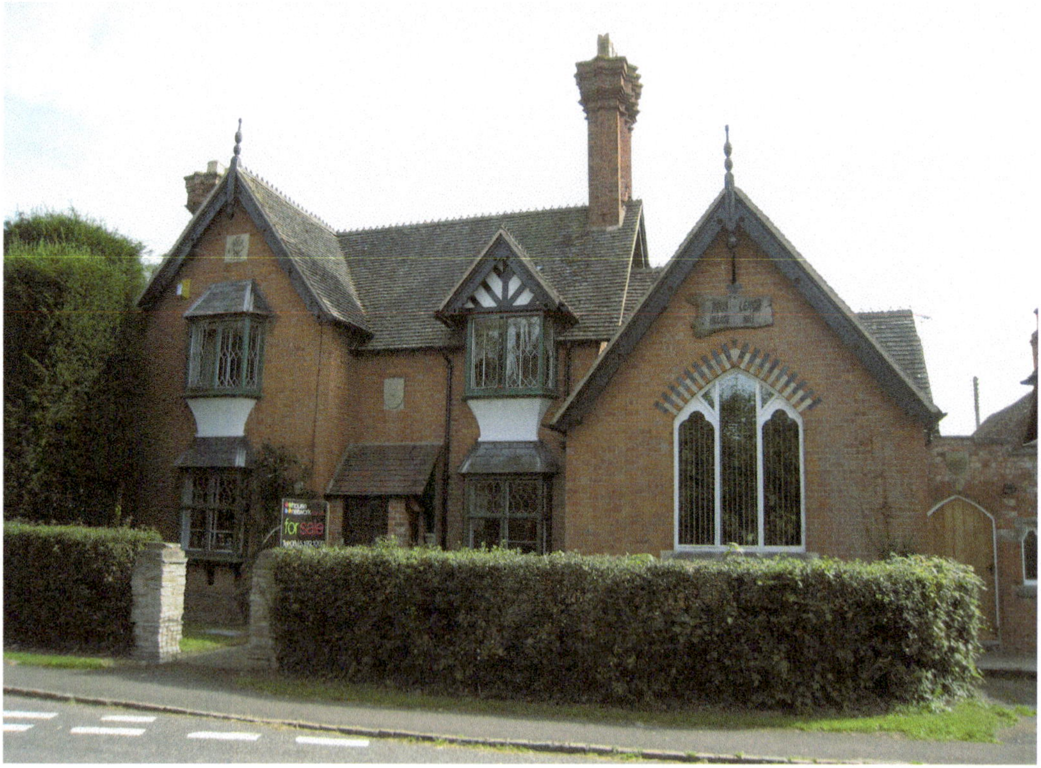

Village Hall, Rous Lench
A view of Rous Lench Village Hall and cottages.

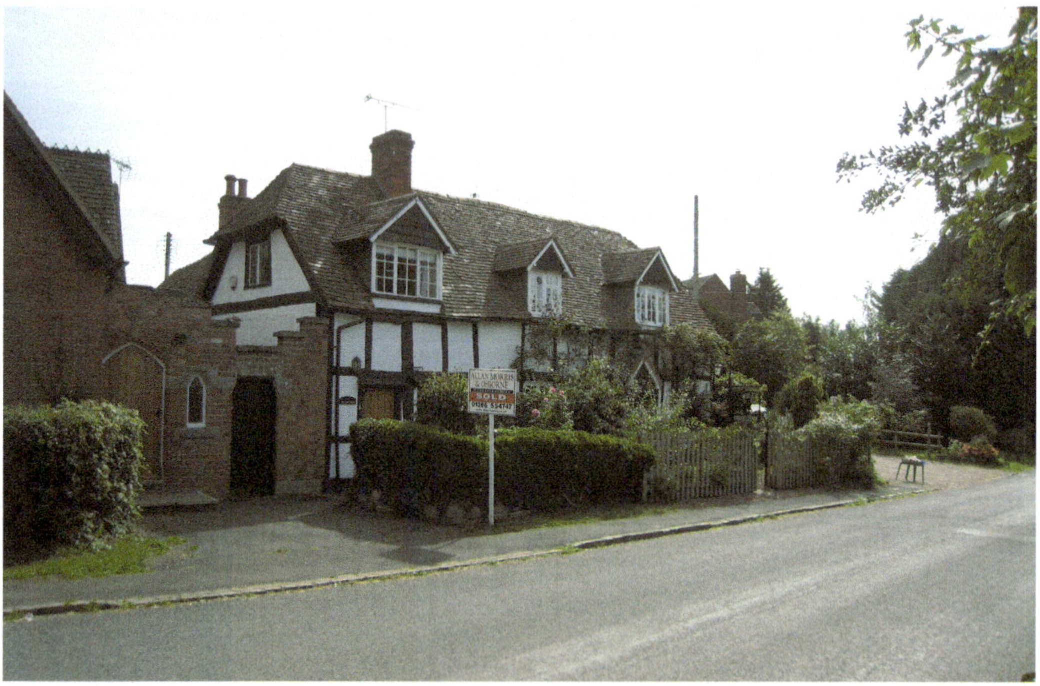

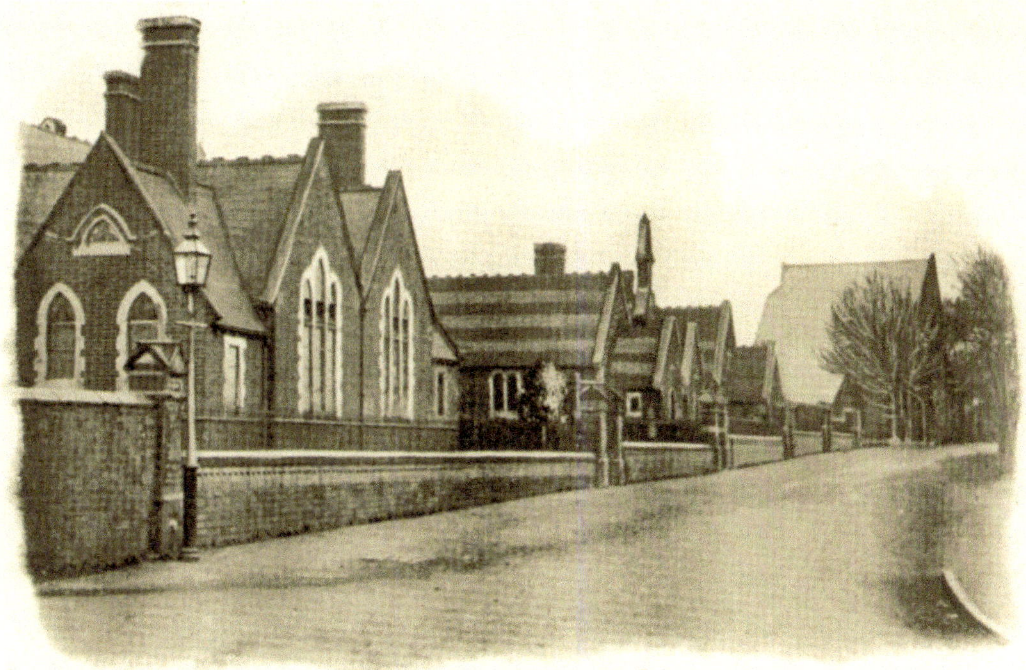

COUNCIL SCHOOLS, ASTWOOD BANK.

Astwood Bank

Astwood Bank is a village on the outskirts of Redditch and lies on the Worcestershire and Warwickshire border. Sadly, the railway was closed in 1964 and the station building known as Studley and Astwood Bank was converted into a dwelling house. The village has been very successful, its knock-out cricket team having played twice in the final at Lord's.

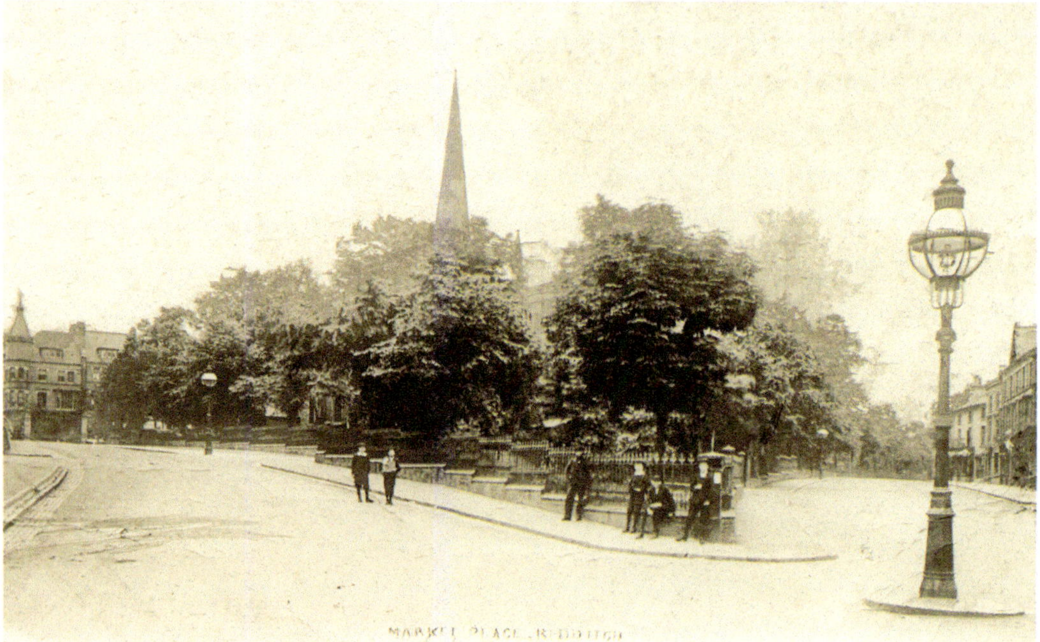

Redditch

Redditch sits on the River Arrow and was renowned for its needle making, although fishing tackle and bicycles were also manufactured later. Redditch always appears to be Victorian. Beside the town is the site of the Cistercian monastery of Boardesley, a house founded in 1138.

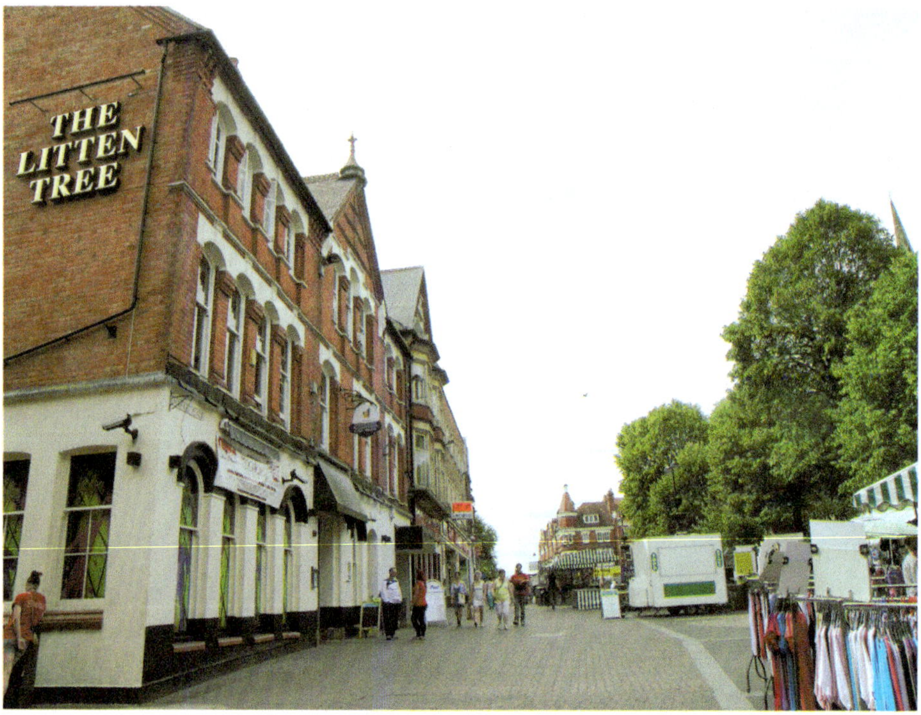

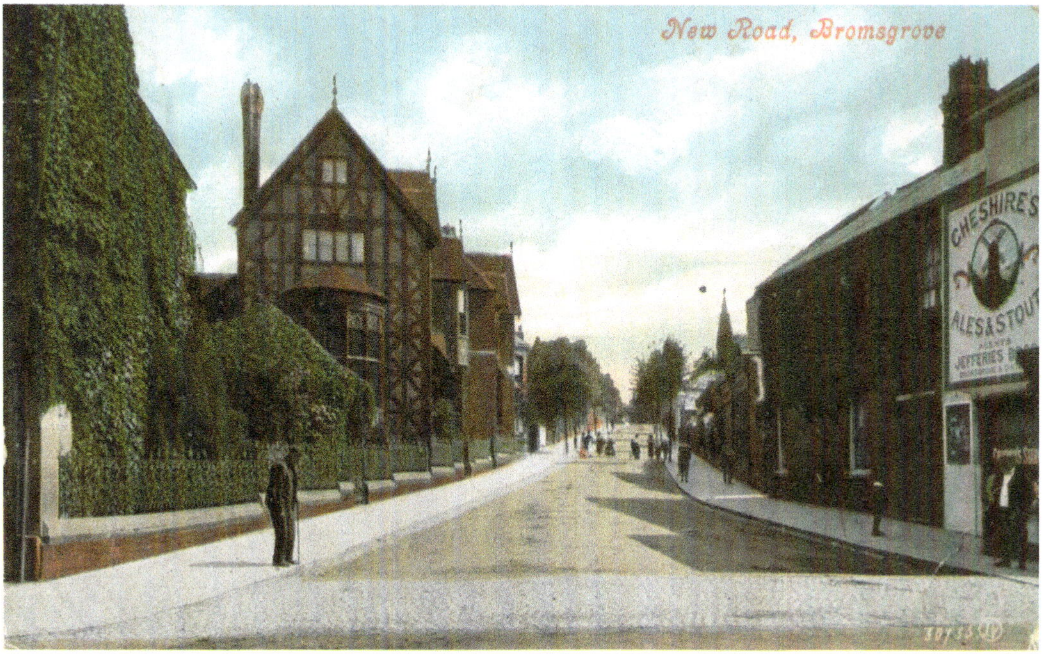

New Road, Bromsgrove

This old market town on the slopes of the Lickey Hills was famed for the manufacture of nails. The monuments of Thomas Scaife and Joseph Rutherford, who were killed in a railway accident, are located in Bromsgrove churchyard. Their epitaph reads: 'My engine now is cold and still, no water does my boiler fill, my coke affords its flames no more, my days of usefulness are o'er.'

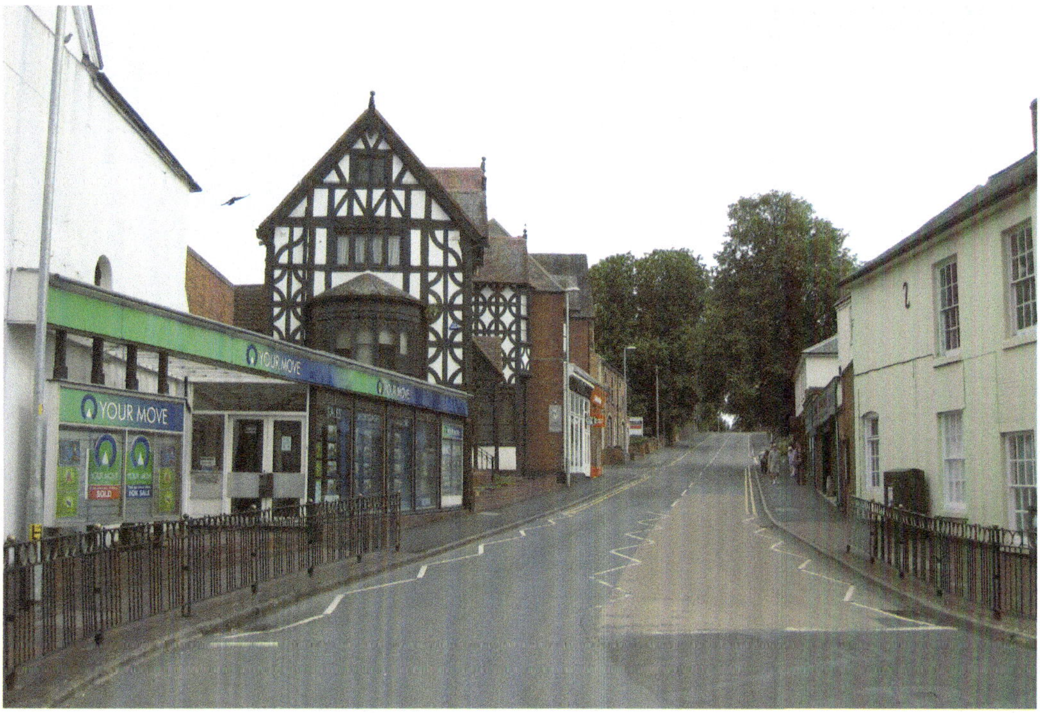

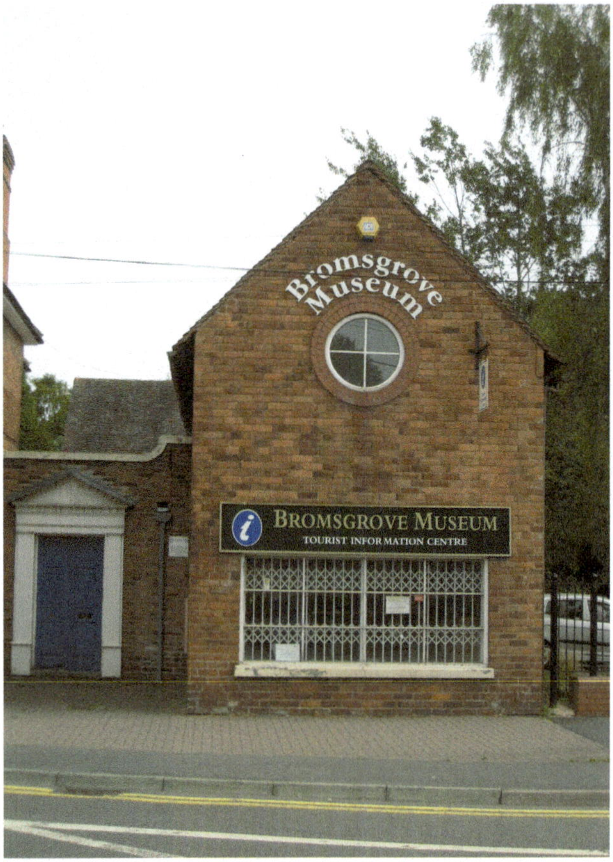

Bromsgrove Museum and High Street

Bromsgrove is an industrial and market centre. The fourteenth-century parish church has a 200-foot spire. Inside the church is a lovely collection of monuments and tablets to the local worthies. Here we see Bromsgrove's museum and a view of the high street.

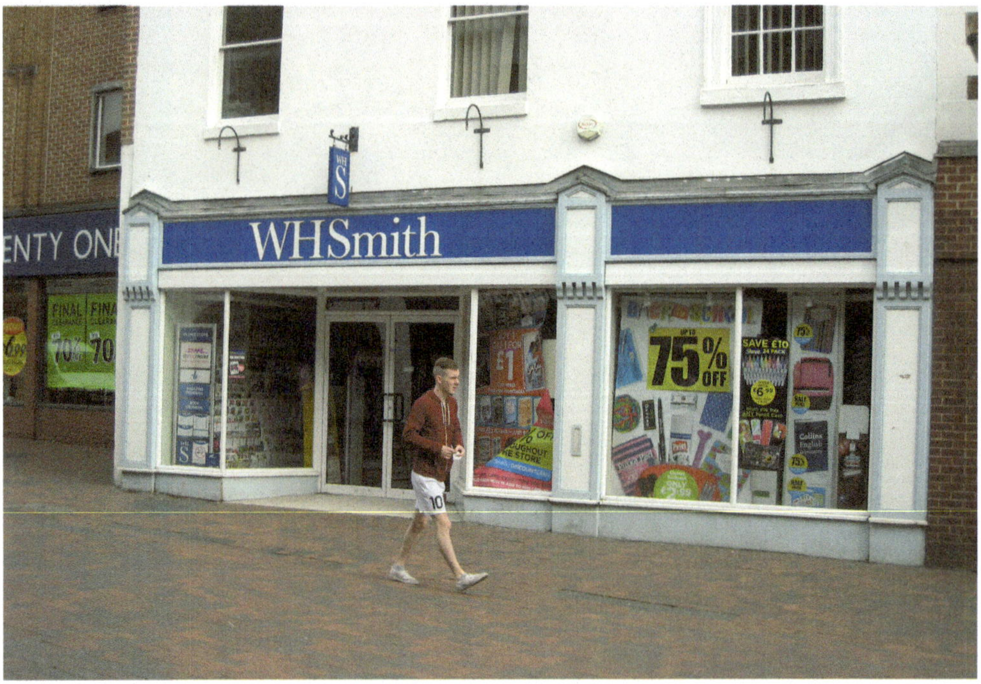

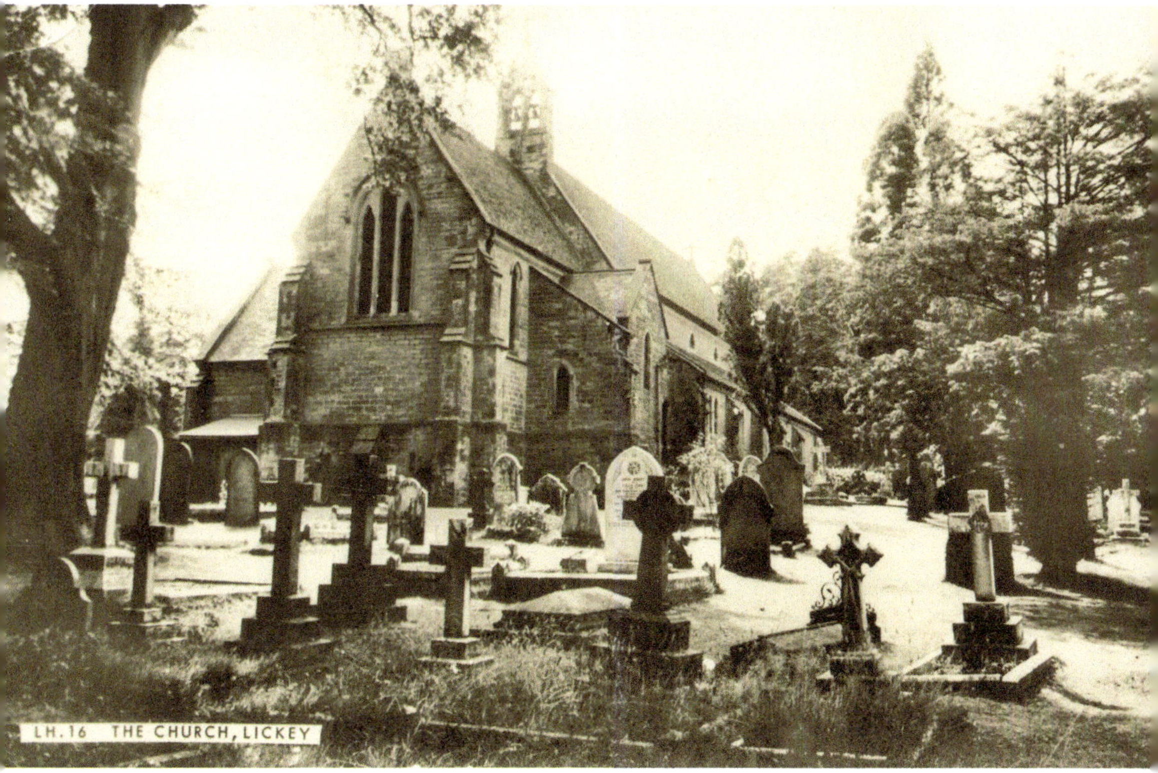

Lickey

On the edge of Lickey Country Park, at the junction of Old Birmingham Road and Monument Lane, stands Lickey church. During the reign of Queen Victoria, there was much development of the railways, schools and churches in the area.

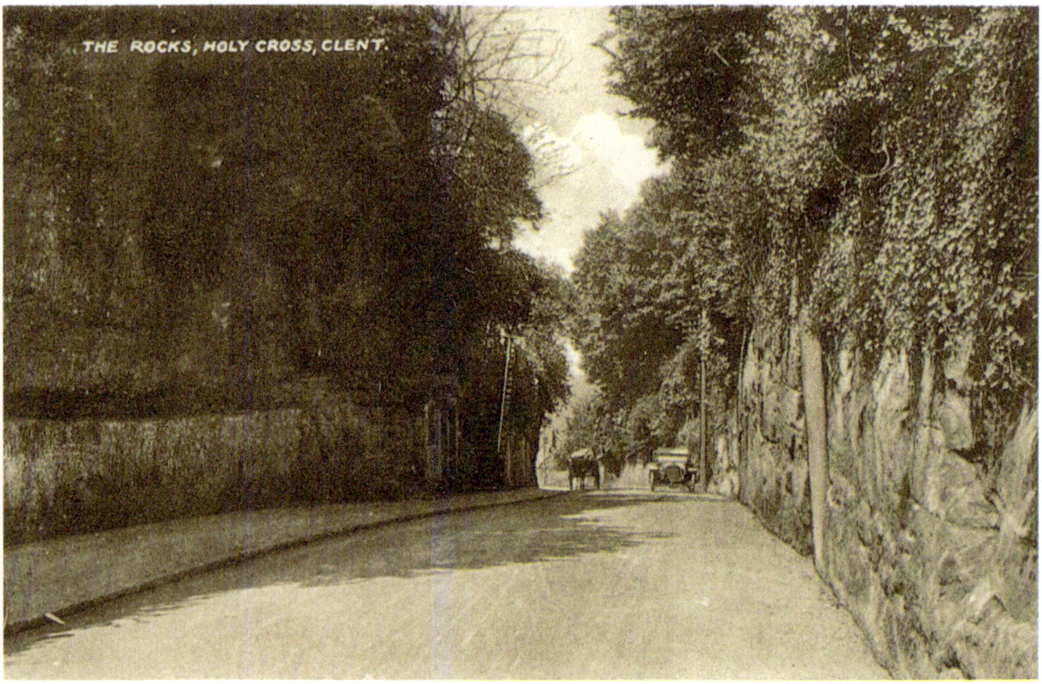

Clent

Above the village of Clent are the Clent Hills, with their great, open, grassy mounds and quaint farms. On the back of this delightful postcard of the rocks, Holy Cross, Clent, is written: 'It is very wet here again today, some fields of hay have lain so long that they have started to burn it because it is spoiled.' What a lovely insight into the past! Below, a view of the Mount, Clent.

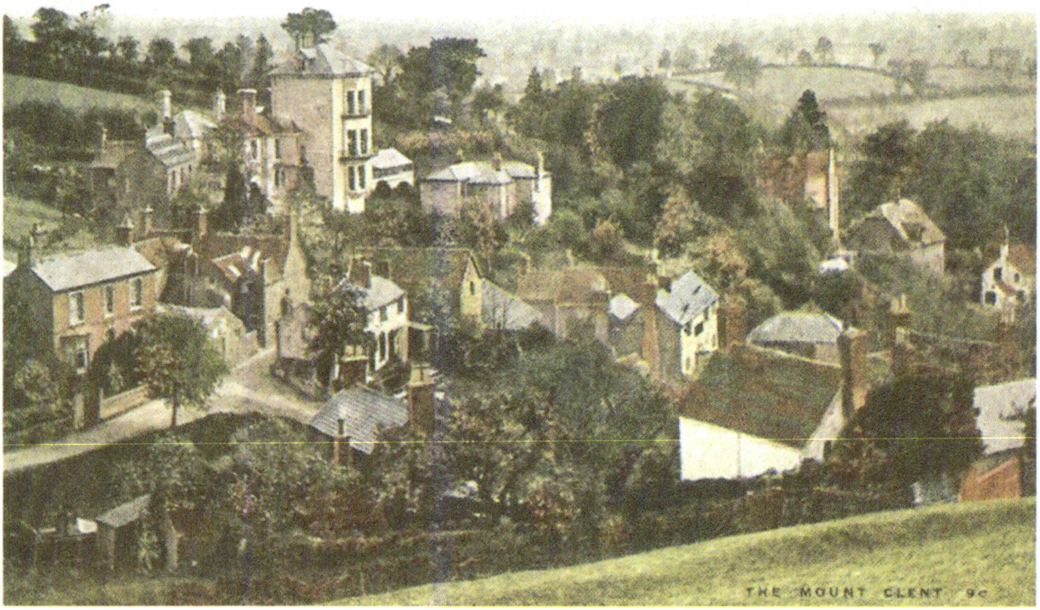

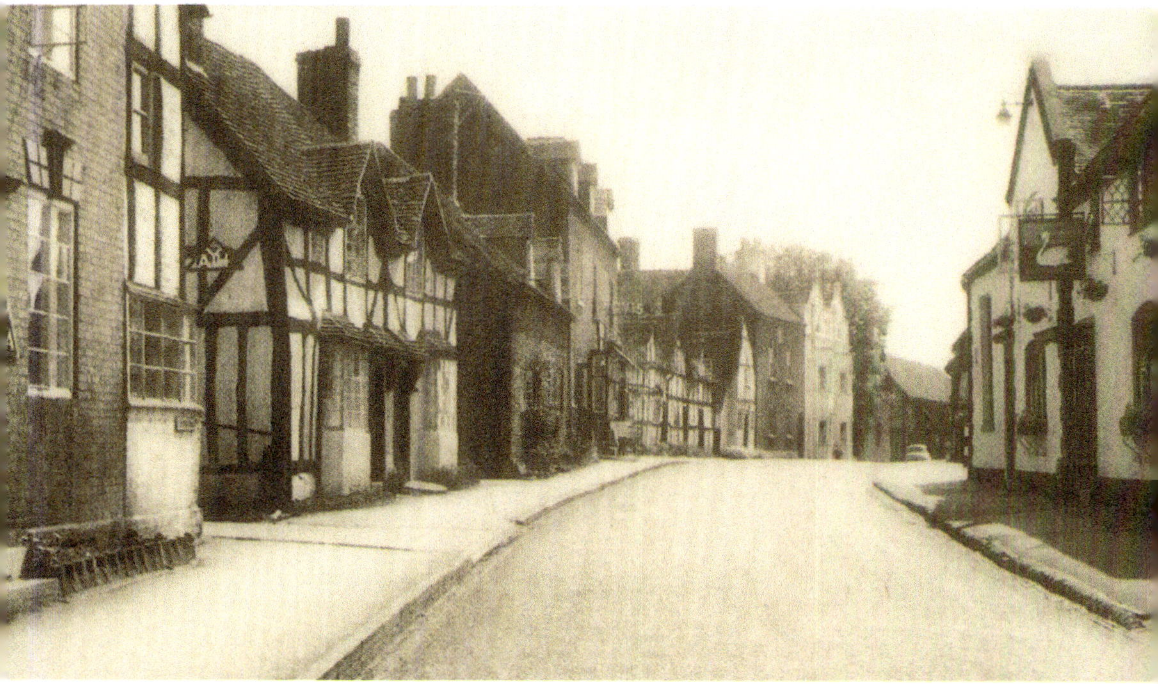

Chaddesley Corbett

The Swan Hotel stands on Chaddesley Corbett's only street. About a mile from the village is Harvington Hall, which dates back to the sixteenth century. At the time of the Catholic persecution, priests would hide in the many secret chambers to be found in the house.

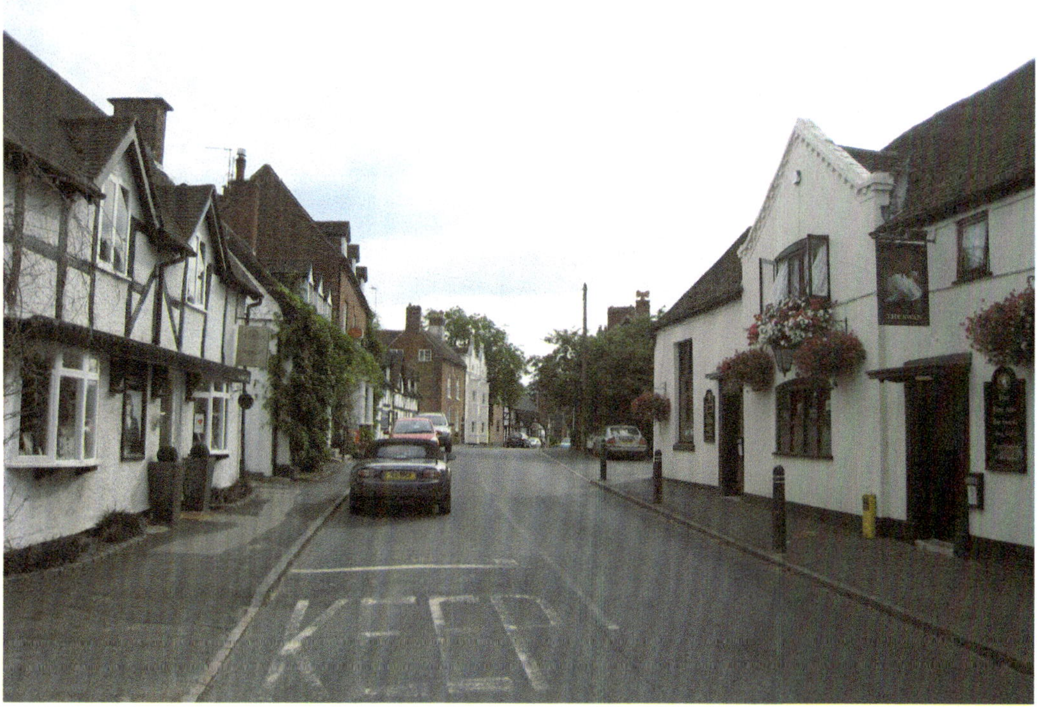

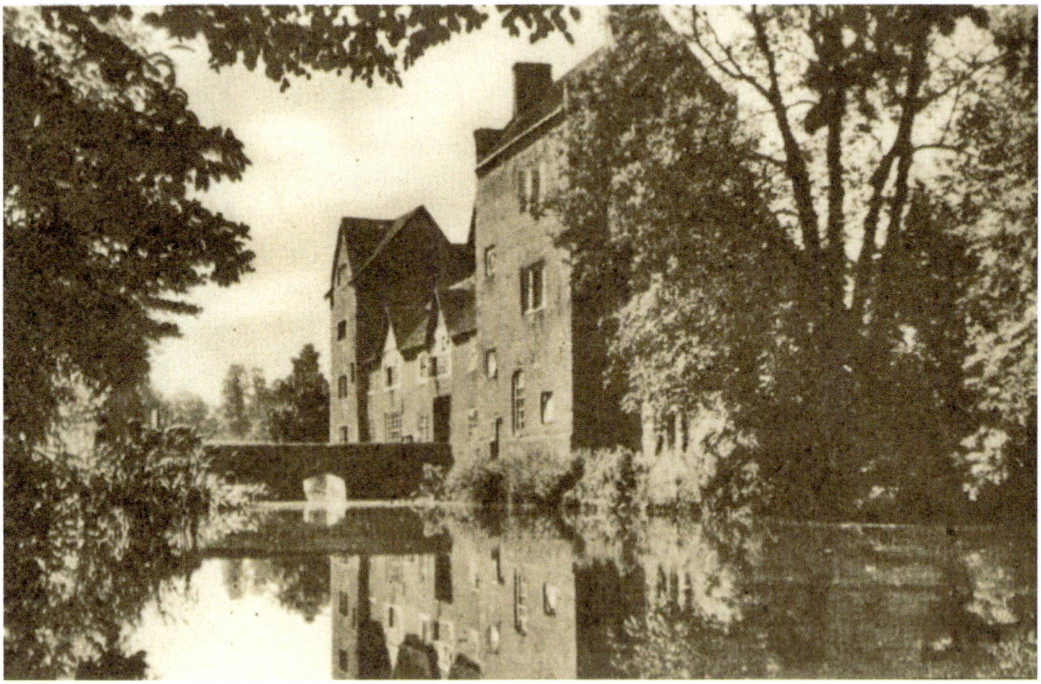

Harvington Hill

Once home of the Pakingtons, a family of staunch Roman Catholics, Harvington Hall had seven priest holes at a time when your faith could see you killed. It is a gabled and mullioned Elizabethan home, all in red brick and complete with its own moat. On the day the modern pictures were taken, a pilgrimage was taking place, seen through the trees in the inset.

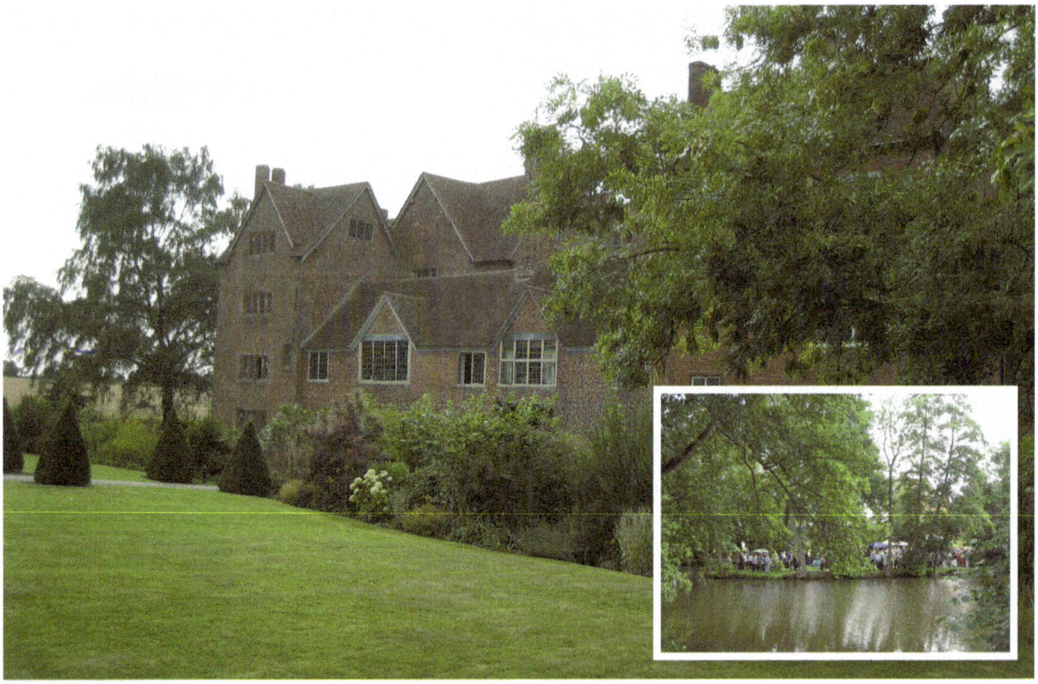

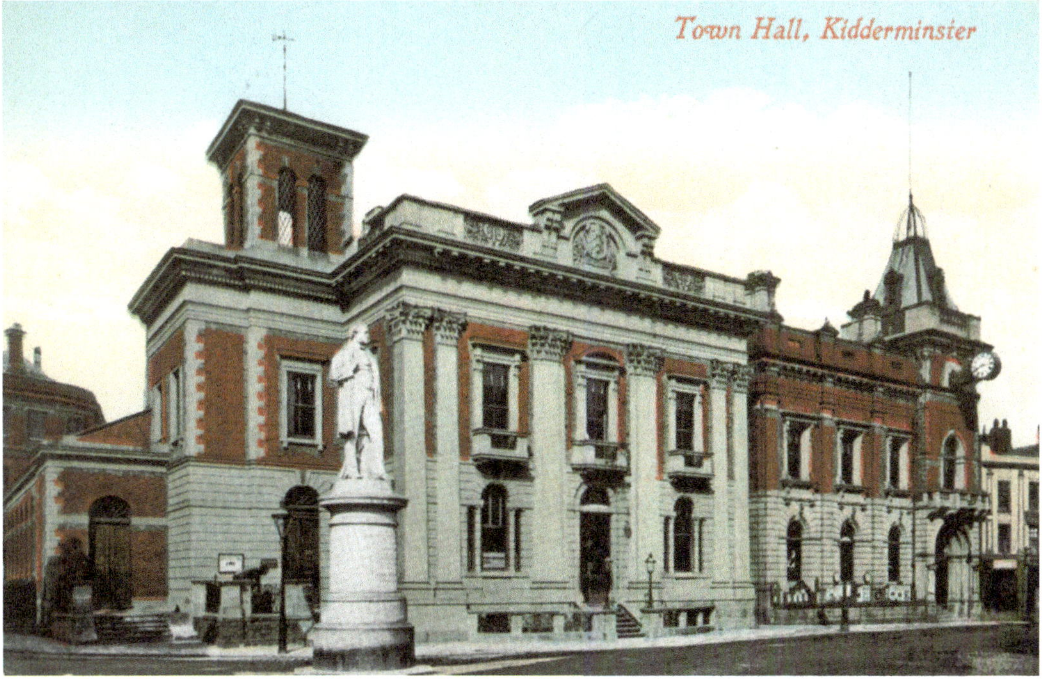

Town Hall, Kidderminster

In the thirteenth century, Flemish weavers arrived in Kidderminster, and it was around this time that the town became a borough. Here we see the town hall with the statue of Sir Rowland Hill, the creator of the Penny Post, standing proudly in front of the building. Kidderminster became famous throughout Europe for the manufacture of carpets.

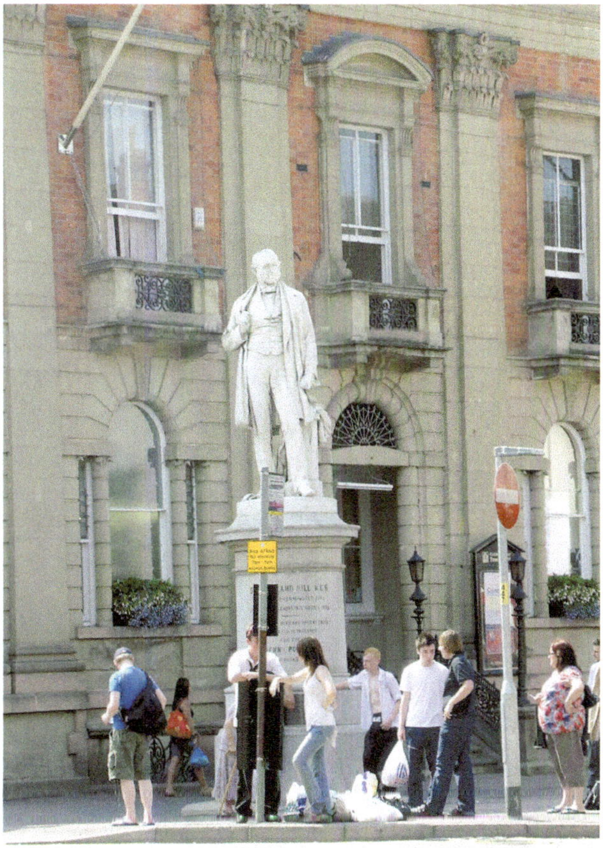

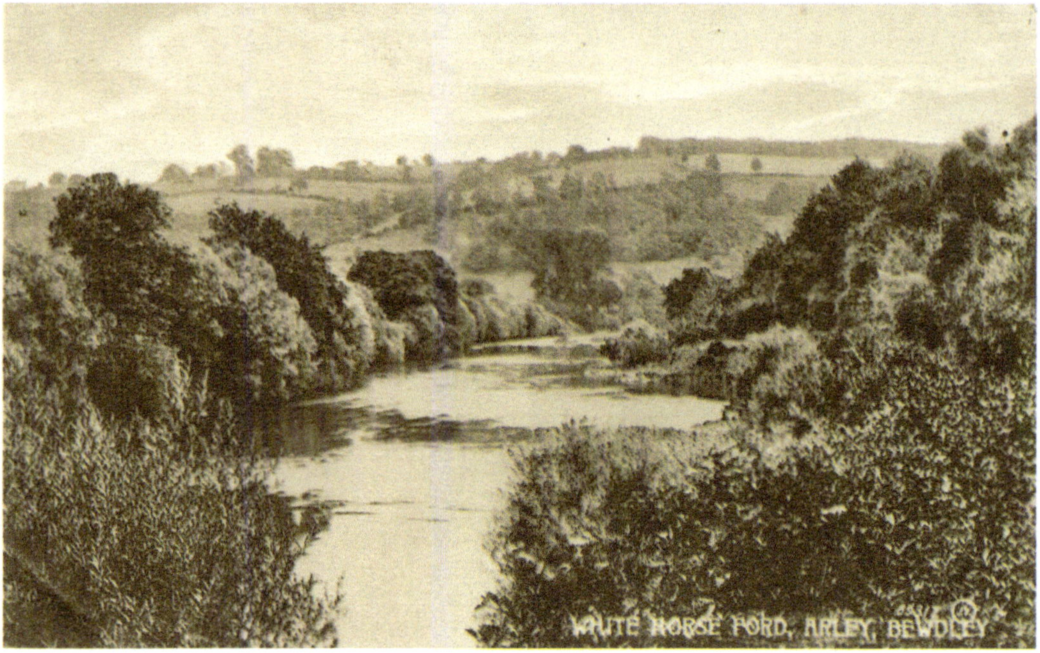

Bewdley

The White Horse Ford, Arley, Bewdley. In Saxon times, the name of Bewdley was Wribbenhall, but the Normans were so impressed with its setting that they renamed it 'Beaulieu' (beautiful place). Bewdley's main trade in Tudor times was in caps.

Below is a photograph for the train buffs among our readers. Here we see Western Courier leaving Highley Station for Bewdley on the Severn Valley Railway's 'Western Weekend'. These trains were introduced in 1961 on the western region of British Rail, but were withdrawn from service in the late 1970s.

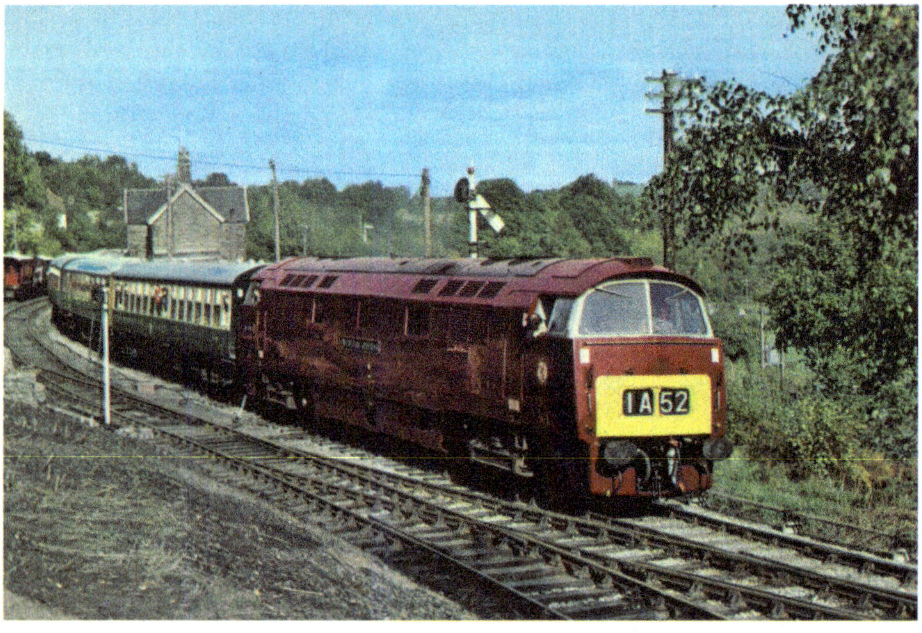

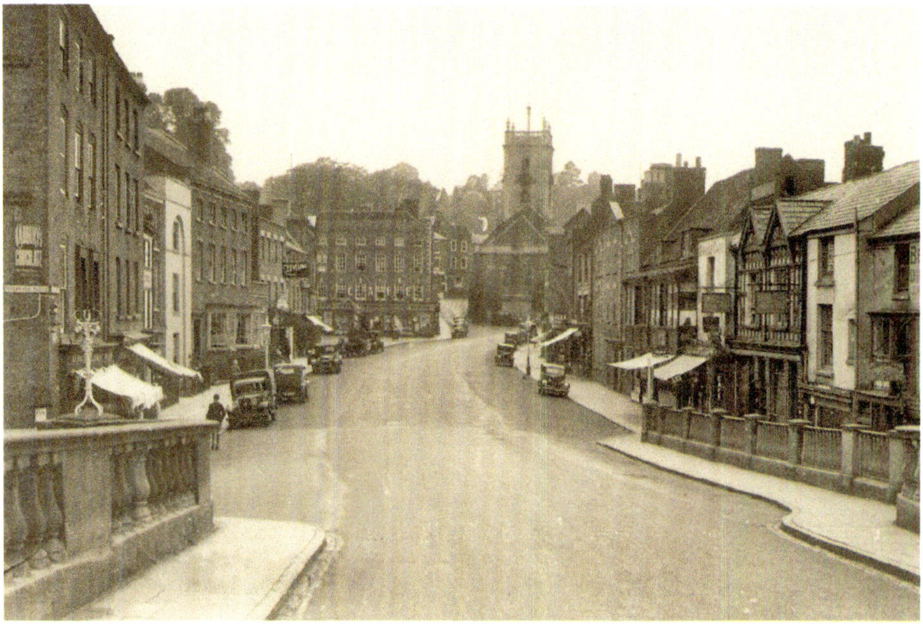

Load Street and Telford's Masterpiece, Bewdley

Taken in 1938, this lovely view of Load Street, Bewdley (*above*), is far removed from the traffic of today. The eldest son of Henry VII, Prince Arthur, married Catherine of Aragon at Tickenhill Manor in Bewdley by proxy, as she was an absent bride. Arthur died very young, leaving the throne to his younger brother Henry VIII and his wife.

Completed in 1801, Thomas Telford's impressive Bewdley Bridge over the River Severn (*below*) is a mixture of cast iron and stone. Upon his retirement, Prime Minister Stanley Baldwin represented the town as Earl Baldwin of Bewdley as its MP for many years.

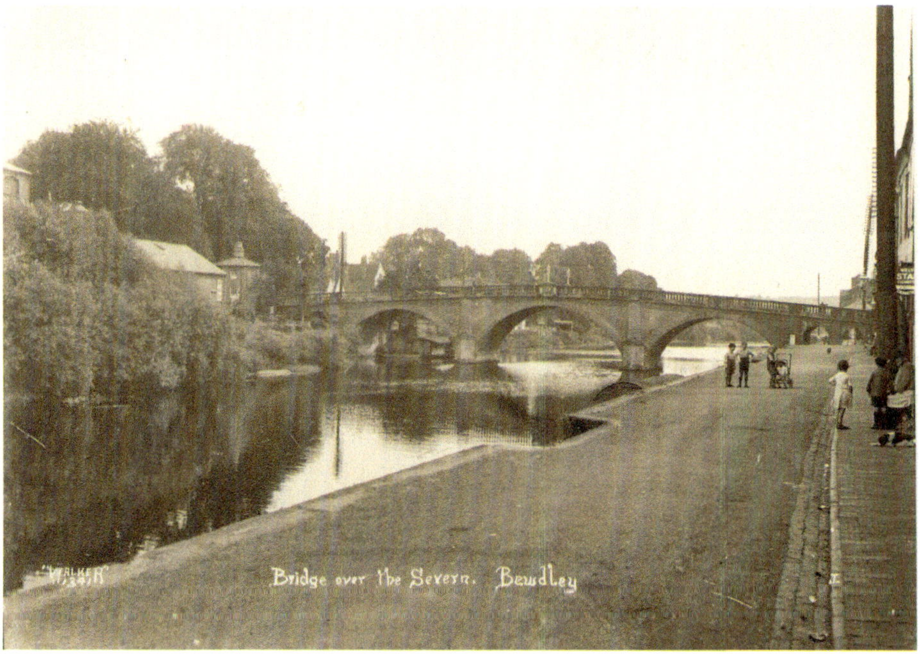

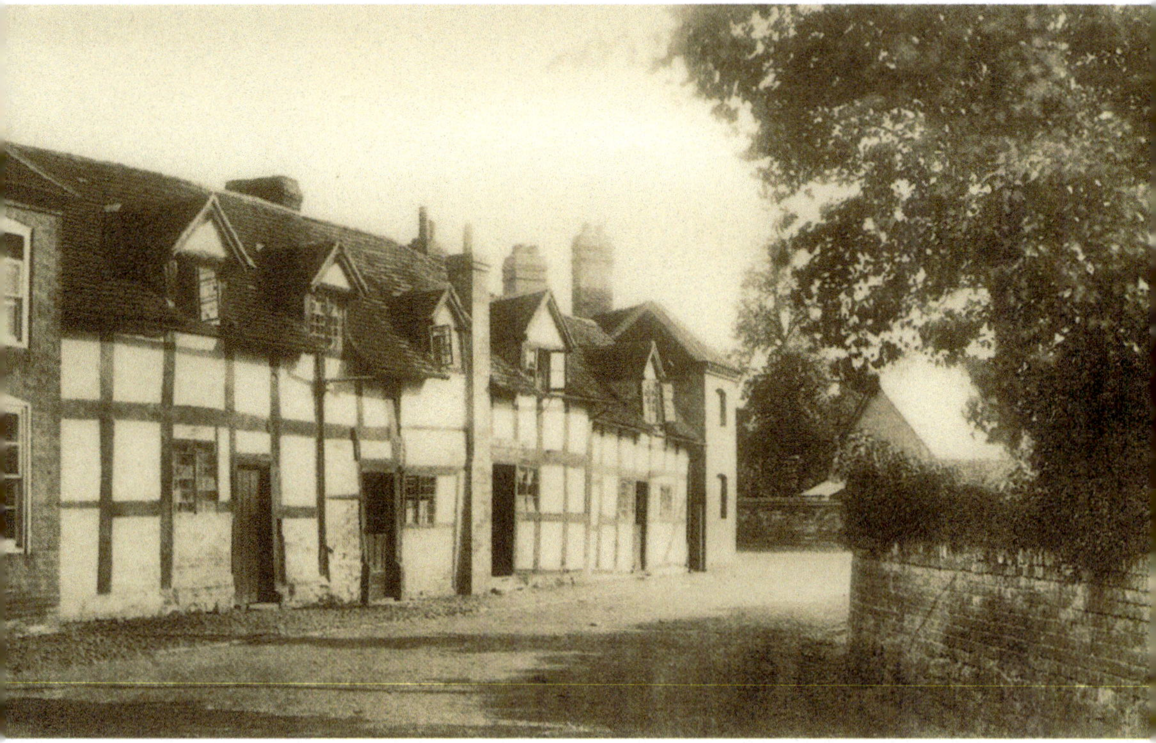

Tenbury Wells

Rich in small farms and market gardens, the market town of Tenbury Wells lies on the old coaching route between London and North Wales. Rising in Wales, the River Terne, after flowing through Shropshire, enters Worcestershire here. Taken around 1900, this photograph of a row of lovely old houses depicts the serenity of a bygone era. The picturesque postcard below shows St Michael's church and college.

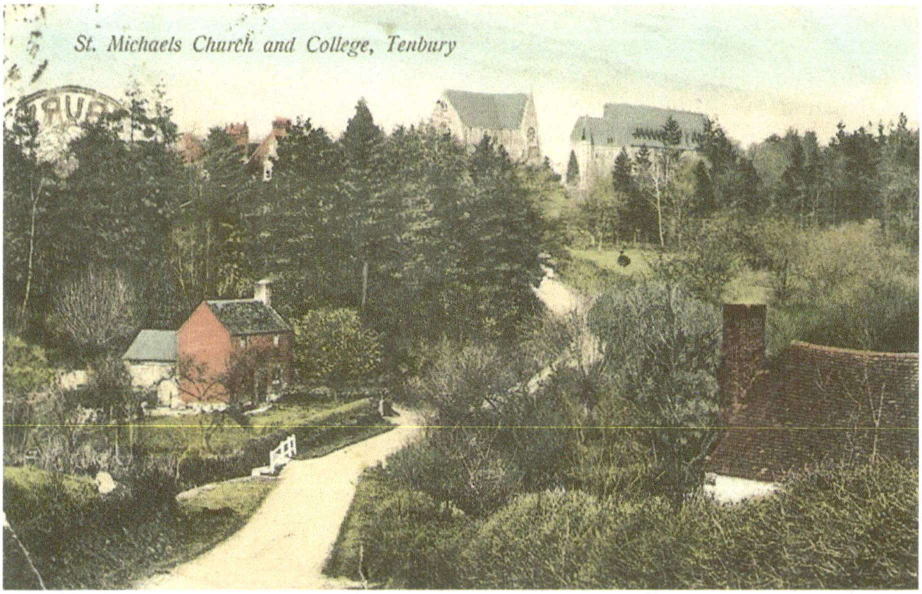

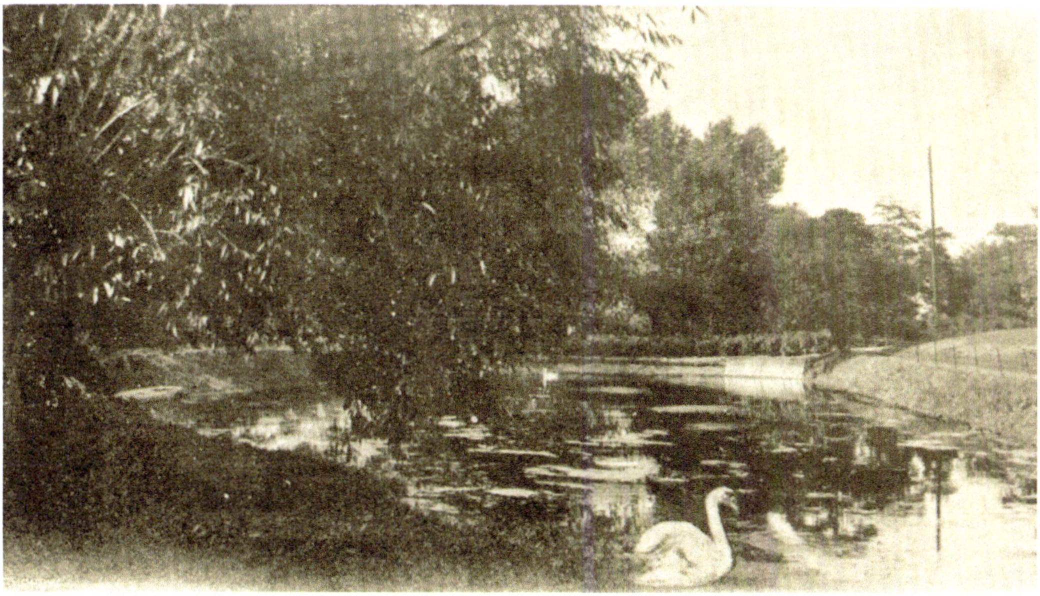

Droitwich Spa

Droitwich developed as a spa town in the early nineteenth century. Local businessman John Corbett opened the St Andrews Brine Baths for visitors in the 1830s. He also built the French-style Chateau Impney for his wife, just outside the town, although she never actually lived there. Here we see Heriot's pool from the Brine Baths Park, Droitwich. Below, a view of the canal.

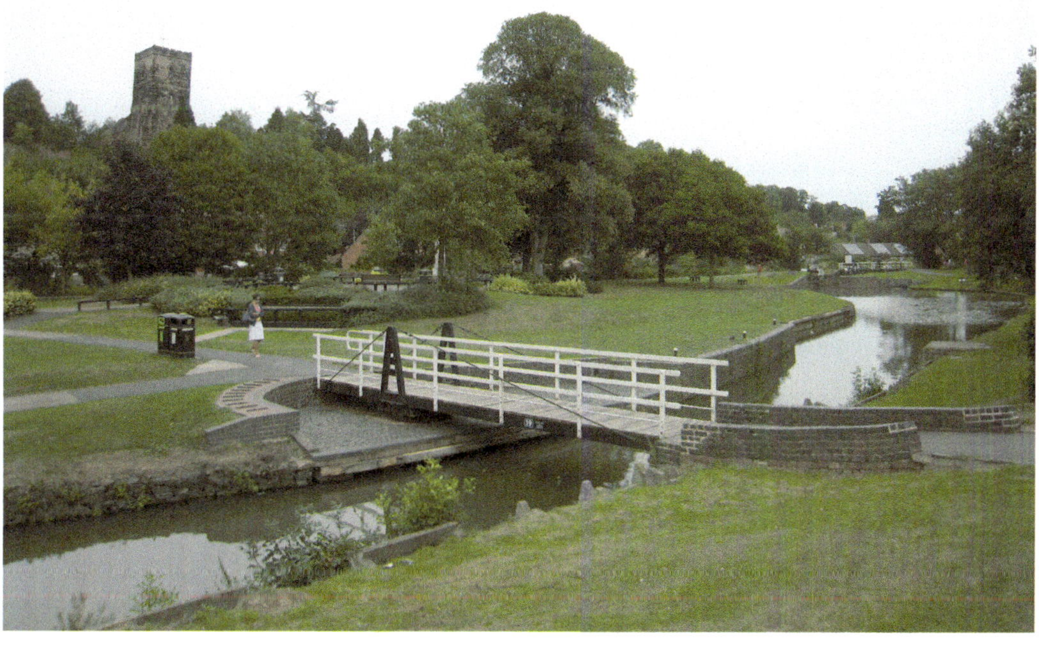

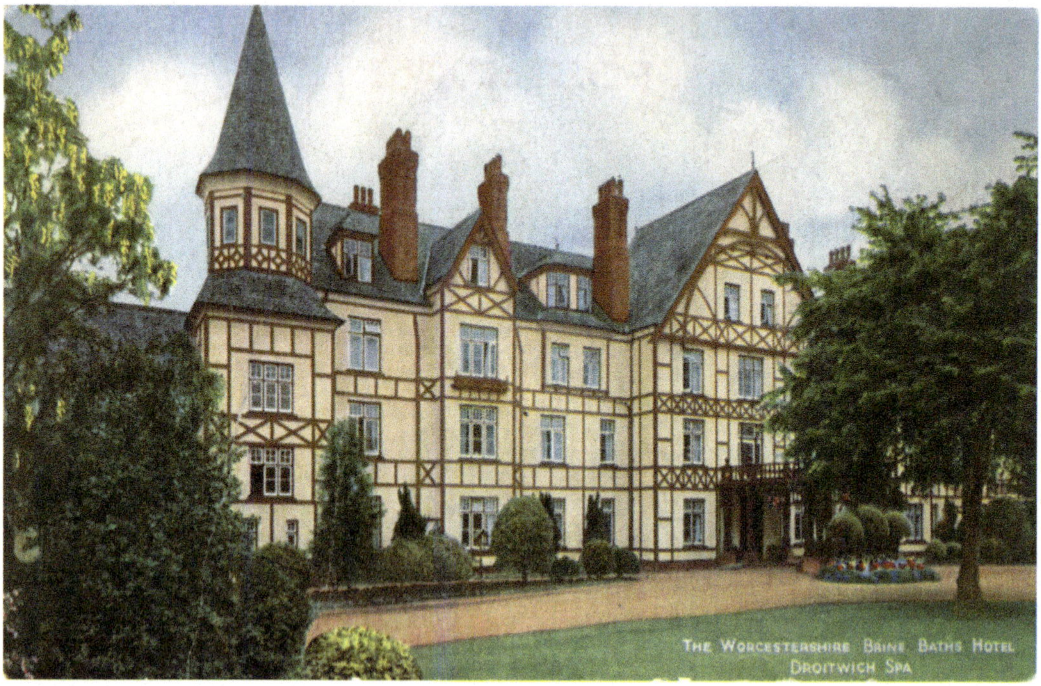

Brine Baths and Museum, Droitwich

Droitwich is renowned for its spring water, which rises from beneath Droitwich and is reputed to be ten times saltier than seawater. In the early nineteenth century, local businessman John Corbett opened the St Andrews Brine Baths in the town. Here we see the Worcestershire Brine Baths Hotel in Droitwich Spa, an obvious spin-off from the increased visitors coming to take the waters. Below, Saint Richard's House and a shot of the High Street (*inset*).

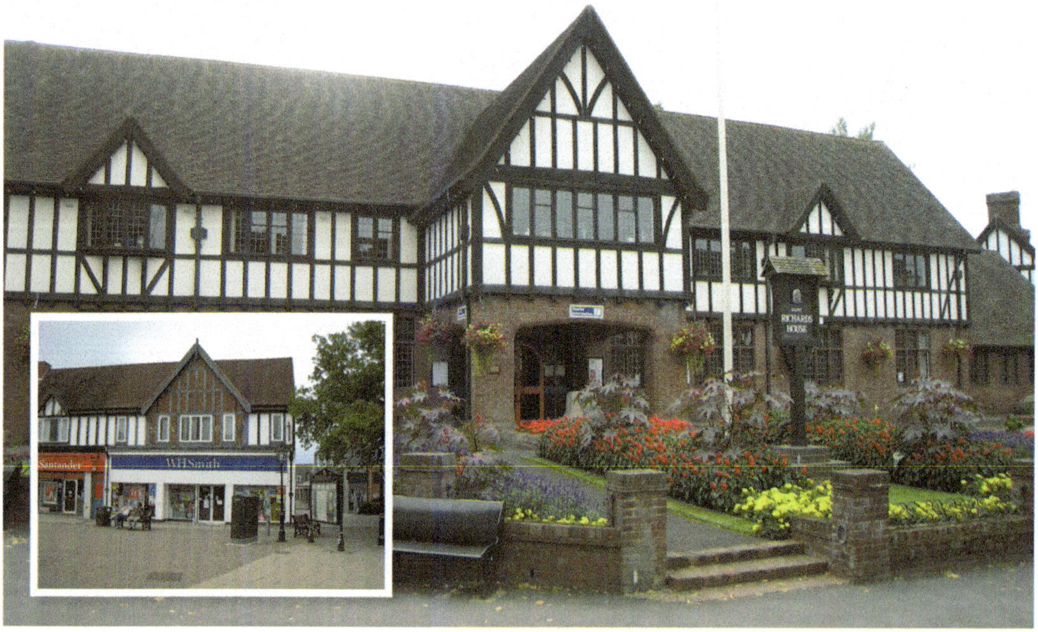

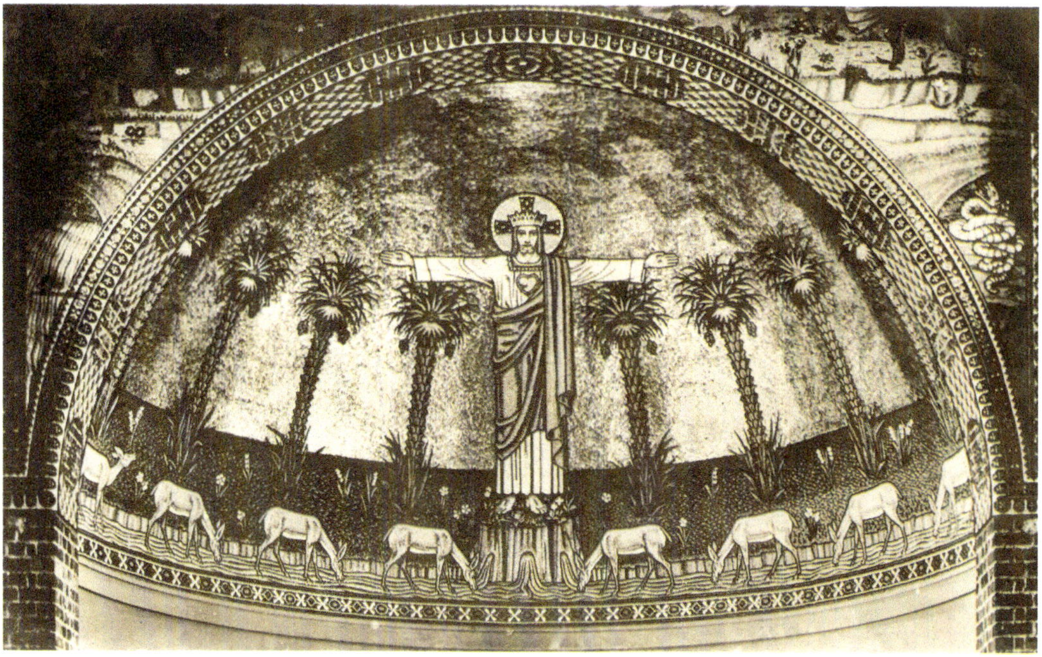

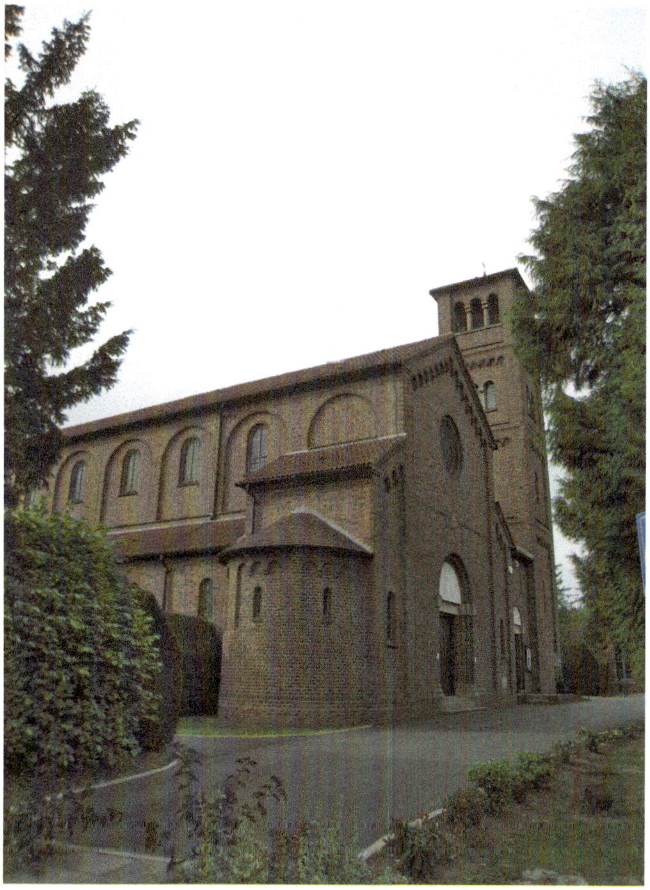

Sacred Heart and St Catherine of Alexandria, Droitwich

I love stained-glass windows and the delightful paintings to be seen inside churches. One such example of the talents of these artists is the beautiful interior of the church of the Sacred Heart and St Catherine of Alexandria, which stands in Droitwich.

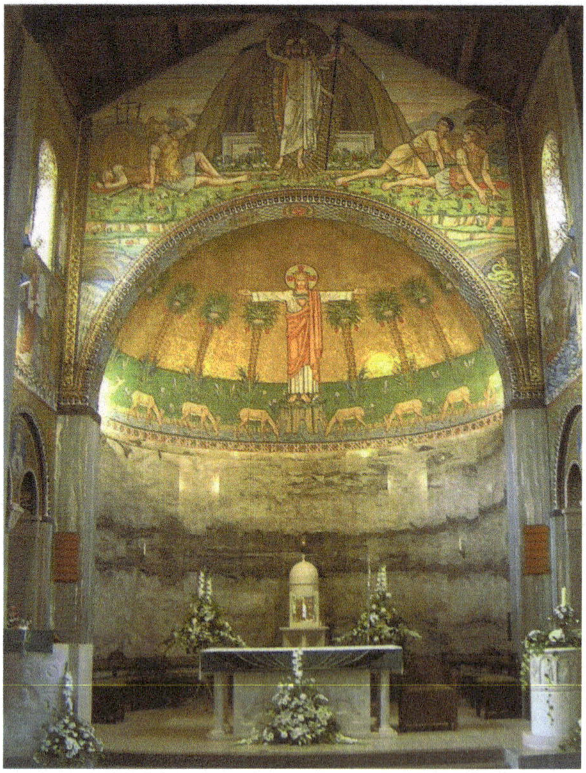

Sacred Heart and St Catherine of Alexandria, Droitwich

Droitwich was known to the Romans for its salt and brine springs, and was called *Salinae*. The medieval parish churches grace the town, one of which is the Sacred Heart and St Catherine of Alexandria.

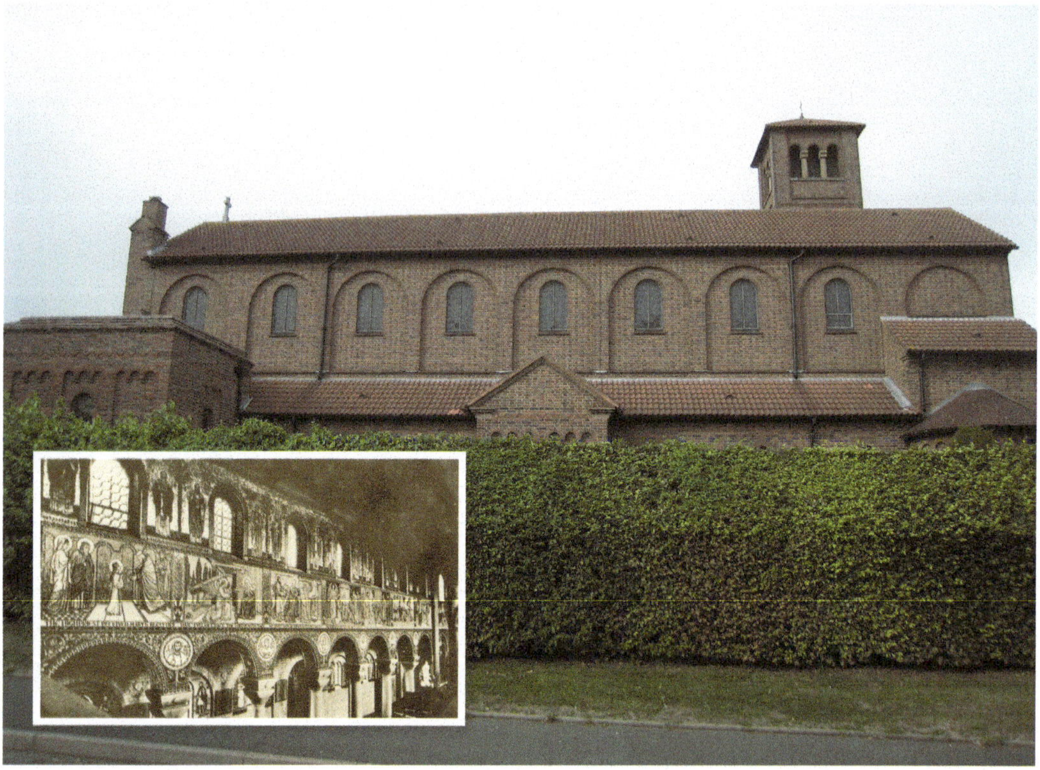

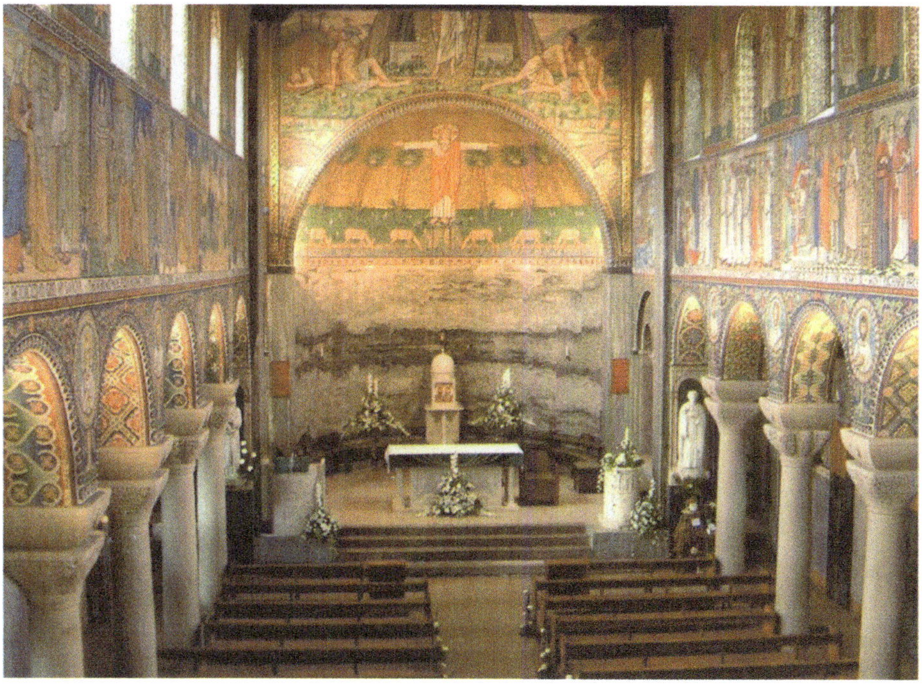

Sacred Heart and St Catherine of Alexandria, Droitwich
Another delightful glimpse of the Sacred Heart and St Catherine of Alexandria church, Droitwich. One cannot help but admire the workmanship and beauty to be found here.

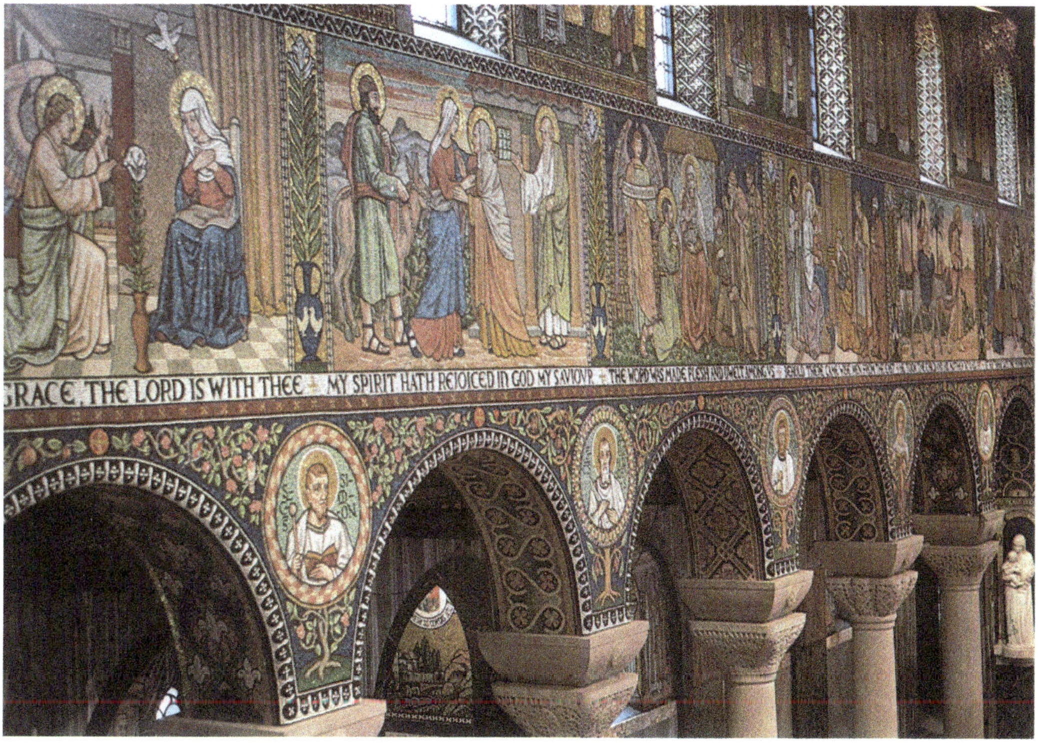

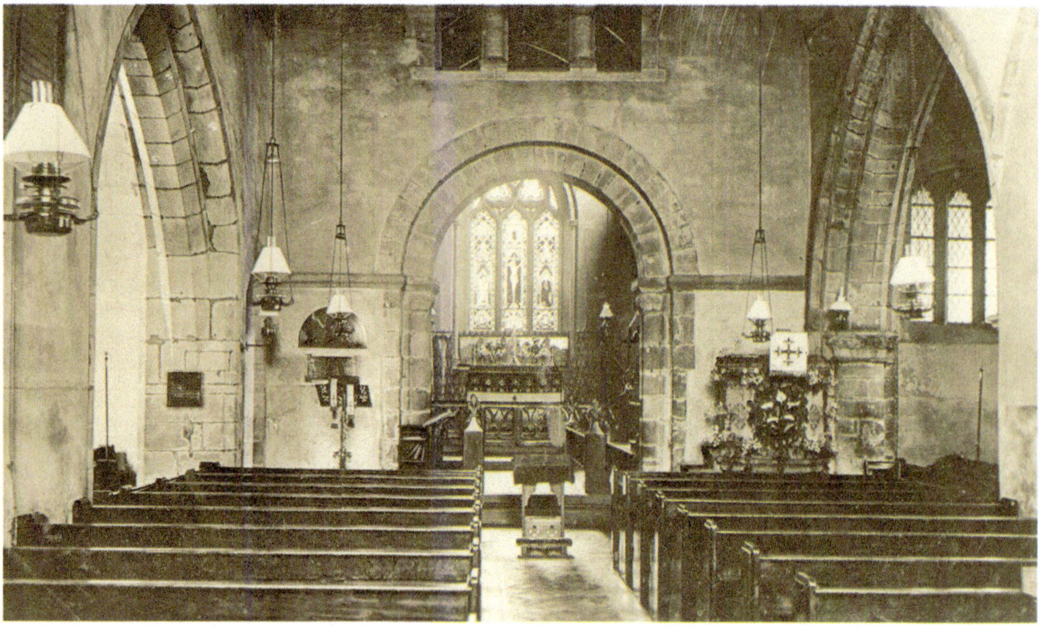

St Peter's and St Andrew's, Droitwich

I have sat many times quietly in prayer in St Peter's church, Droitwich, and have savoured the tranquillity of this delightful corner of the town where one is always welcome and the doors are always open. Below, another fine church, St Andrew's, caters for the spiritual needs of the Droitwich community.

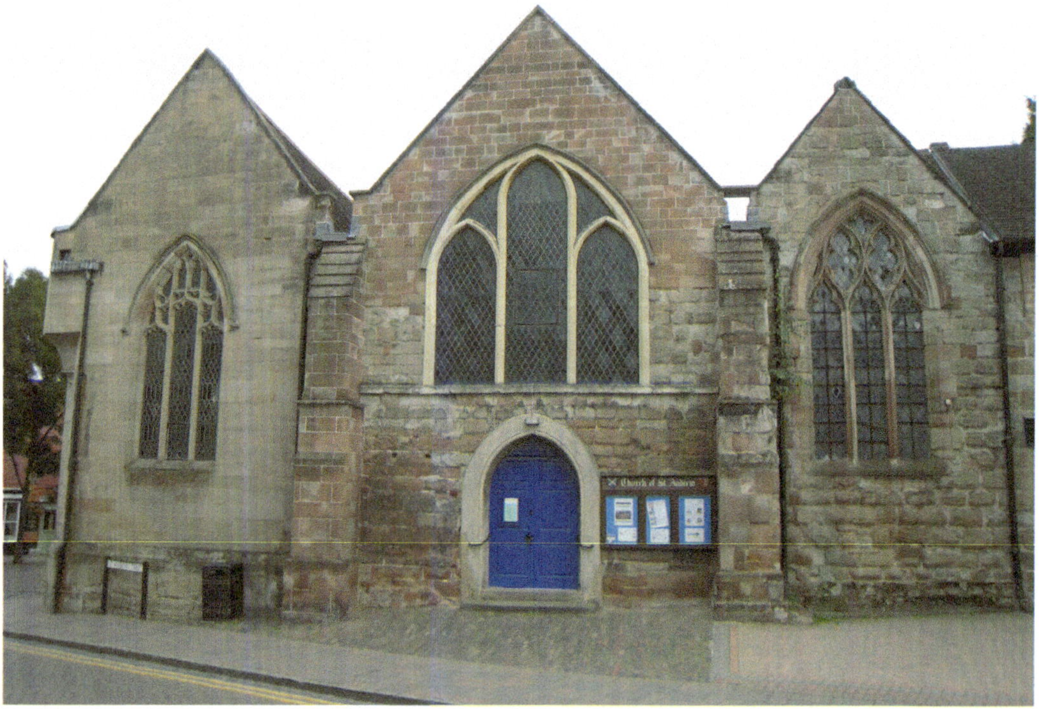

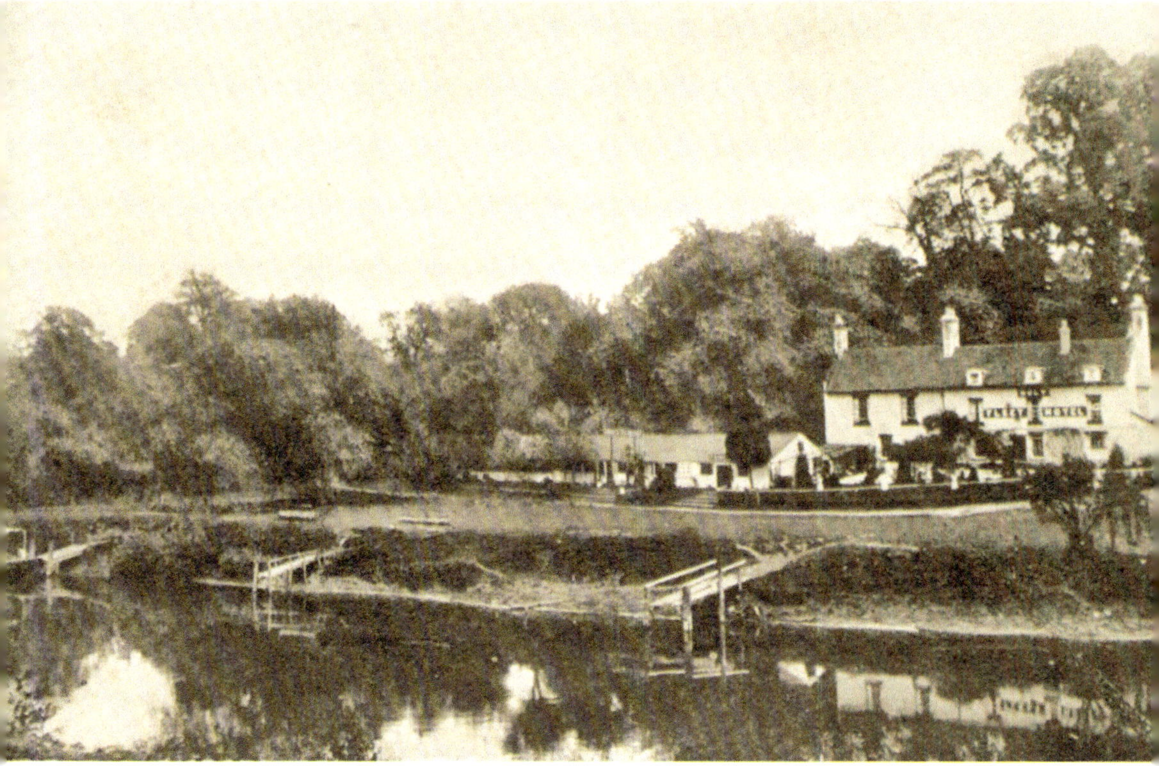

Malt Fleet Hotel

The Malt Fleet Hotel stands on the banks of the River Severn, and can be seen from the cruise boats that take tourists on a delightful trip up the river.

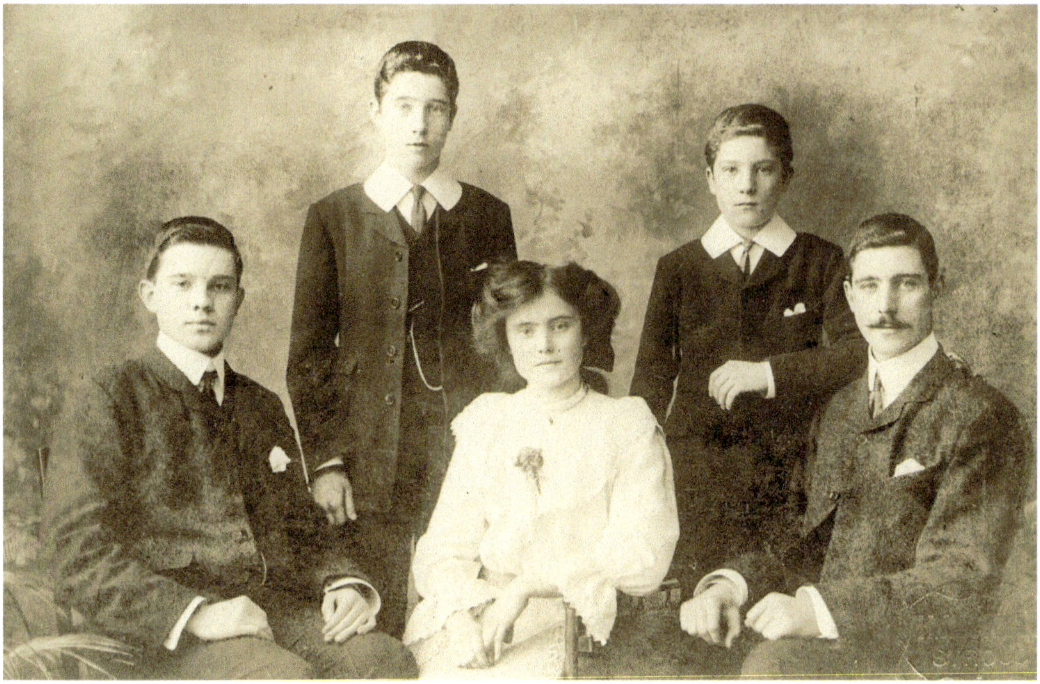

Nostalgia

This lovely family group typifies the fashion in postcards in the nineteenth century. I was given a pile of old photographs taken in Worcestershire and thought it provided an interesting example of how concepts of recording the family album have changed through time. The bottom postcard is much later in time and shows that humour crept into postcards in the twentieth century.

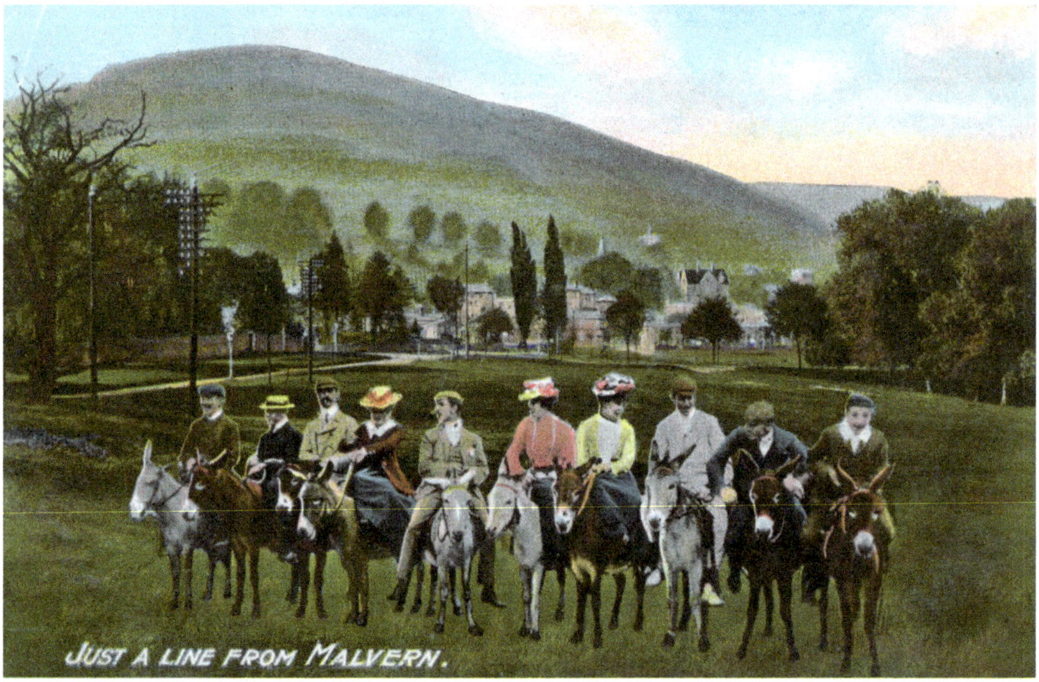

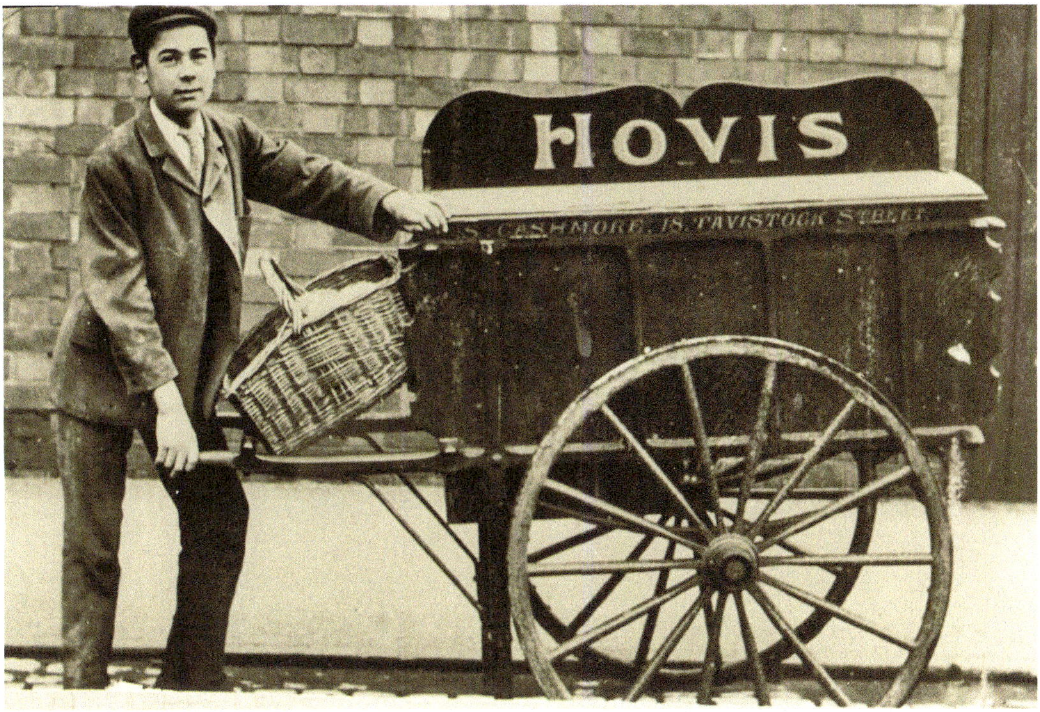

Hovis

I love this old picture of the young man and his Hovis cart. I remember seeing a similar lad and his cart when I was a little girl, long before the days of the supermarkets. I came upon this photograph in an old envelope full of photographs of Worcestershire, which I was given by a reader.

Acknowledgements

Many thanks to Ray Jones for the images on the following pages: 7, 15, 16, 17, 18, 19, 21, 74, 81. All other modern photographs were taken by Joe Pettican and Beth Cartwright.

Printed and bound by CPI Group (UK) Ltd, Croydon, CR0 4YY
17/03/2026
02073006-0002